Jerusalem

JERUSALEM
City of Longing

Simon Goldhill

The Belknap Press of Harvard University Press

Cambridge, Massachusetts ∎ London, England

2008

Library of Congress Cataloging-in-Publication Data

Goldhill, Simon.

  Jerusalem : city of longing / Simon Goldhill.

    p.   cm.

  Includes bibliographical references and index.

  ISBN-13: 978-0-674-02866-1 (alk. paper)

  ISBN-10: 0-674-02866-X (alk. paper)

1. Jerusalem—Description and travel.   2. Jerusalem—Buildings, structures, etc.

3. Jerusalem—Ethnic relations.   4. Jerusalem—Religion.   5. Christian

shrines—Jerusalem.   6. Jewish shrines—Jerusalem.   7. Islamic shrines—

Jerusalem.   8. Architecture—Jerusalem.   I. Title.

  DS109.15.G66 2008

  956.94'42—dc22   2007050309

Contents

Preface   vii

1. The Center of the Christian World   1

2. The Center of Jewish Jerusalem   45

3. The Center of Muslim Jerusalem   93

4. The Old City   131

5. The Oldest City   187

6. The Victorian City   227

7. The Modern City   278

Bibliography   335

Acknowledgments   341

Illustration Credits   343

Index   345

Preface

THERE ARE MANY books these days which sell themselves as "the idiot's guide" or as the manual "for dummies." This book is meant for the intelligent reader who wants to understand what it might mean to stand here or here in Jerusalem—to experience Jerusalem not just as a tourist site or as a day-to-day, mundane urban landscape but as a city where every space is layered with historical significance, religious intensity, and extraordinary stories about the people who have visited and lived in this city over the years. What makes Jerusalem unique is the heady mix in one place of centuries of passion and gossip, kingdom-threatening wars and petty squabbles, architectural magnificence and bizarre relics, spiritual longing and political nastiness. Of all cities, the Jerusalem of today cannot be understood without these layers of buried and exposed memories. This book undertakes that weird archaeology of human imagination, hope and disaster.

Jerusalem: City of Longing is not just another history of Jerusalem. The book certainly travels from the earliest days of the city up until today, but it does not set out to run through the narrative of Jerusalem's different conquerors. Rather, it looks at the various places that are most important for understanding Jerusalem and that every visitor or resident of Jerusalem would expect to visit. It explores how we can understand the history of Jerusalem through the buildings and understand the buildings through that history. You could call it an exercise in historical urban geography. Or a tour guide for the thinking visitor.

My intention is that this book can be read before visiting Jerusalem, while visiting Jerusalem, and after visiting Jerusalem—or even instead of visiting Jerusalem, though that is a sorry option. Jerusalem is not the sort of place you can just look at: it remains baffling, even rebarbative at first glance. It is far from clear why there is so much fuss, and why so much fuss about that rock or that stairway or that pillar. For every visitor, Jerusalem needs preparation—and reflection. It leaves a mark. Although there are no opening times, restaurant hints, or hotel recommendations in this book, my hope is that these chapters will provide a more pertinent guide to appreciating the city.

The structure is clear enough: seven chapters, each with its own map, one for each day of the week (though in Jerusalem everyone will encourage you to take the Sabbath off). It begins with the Church of the Holy Sepulchre, the center of the Christian world; Chapter 2 moves to the Temple Mount and the Western Wall, the Jewish-run plaza and tunnels below, and Chapter 3 to the Muslim-run Haram al-Sharif above, with the Dome of the Rock and the al-Aqsa Mosque. Chapter 4 explores the Old City, the walled space that once marked the limits of the city, and that now provides its much-contested historical center. Chapter 5 looks at the oldest city, the city of David, and the most ancient remains of Jerusalem. Chapter 6 takes a tour of Victorian Jerusalem, when the city first spread outside its walls. Chapter 7 looks at the modern city from the time of the British Mandate, through the era when Jerusalem was divided, to the current conflict-torn society. Most groups who visit Jerusalem do so within a particular and restricted framework: the Jews tend to visit the Jewish sites, the Muslims the Muslim sites, and the Christians the Christian sites. This book attempts to show how much of the experience of Jerusalem is missed in such blinkers. The city has to be viewed from multiple perspectives if it is to be appreciated.

I am fully aware that each of these chapters could be expanded into a book of its own, and most paragraphs to a chapter: Jerusalem is so rich in its historical texture and so full of stories as well as buildings that it would take many books to feel that one had adequately covered the city and its buried memories. I have made my selections of the buildings to talk about, the anecdotes to recount, the historical emphases. As with everything about Jerusalem, people will no doubt disagree.

I have given all dates according to the Christian calendar. This is for the ease of the reader rather than from any ideological predilection or agenda. I have not added the Jewish and Muslim dates in brackets on each occasion. Those who work professionally in this area know all the arguments about such decisions (I will not rehearse them here) and should be capable of understanding why this is an easy option for a book of this type. I should say finally, to forestall any false expectations, that I have made no attempt, let alone promise, to solve the Middle East crisis here. The history the book tells will provide some explanations of how we have reached the current wretched state of affairs. The situation changes so swiftly and often so painfully that I hesitate even to refer to the current wretched state of affairs, aware as one must be that by the time this book appears things may be even more wretched or, one can only long, touched with some greater glimmer of hope. It is impossible to write about Jerusalem in any period without becoming implicated in the politics—religious, social, military—of the city. It is all too easy for anyone talking about the Middle East to slip into the aggressive and naïve stereotypes of identity politics: he's a Jew/Arab/Muslim/fundamentalist/liberal, so of course he thinks like that. . . . This book would like to stand out against such reductive and coercive postures, not least because the individual stories I have found so engaging in my exploration of Jerusalem have always turned out to be much more complicated and much more interesting than the stereotypes. I will just say here that I have tried to be equally insulting to all parties.

Jerusalem

Map 1

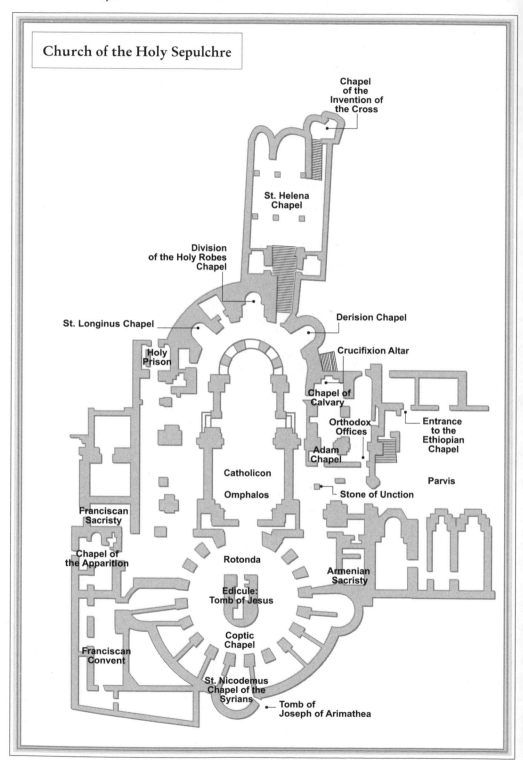

Church of the Holy Sepulchre

1 The Center of the Christian World

SAIDA EL-ALAMI IS A TALL, gaunt, and imposing Palestinian woman who teaches mathematics in one of the villages around Jerusalem. She also lives in one of the most extraordinary pieces of real estate in the world. It's a private house—and Saida is an intensely private person—that has been in her family for eight hundred years. It is a crusader building: her small sitting room is domed and the old stones are clearly visible. Near the single window is a raised dais on which stands, like a throne, her father's straight-backed chair. Her father was a distinguished judge who would conduct marriages for poor Jerusalemites from the chair. His grave, a raised tomb covered by a straggly tree, is outside in the courtyard, from which you climb toward Saida's house. What makes this simple building so remarkable is its location (as real estate agents will always tell you). For Saida's house is perched high up next to the dome of the Church of the Holy Sepulchre (Figure 1).

From her back door, you step out down some stairs onto a roof

Figure 1. The looming domes of the Church of the Holy Sepulchre above Saida el-Alami's small terrace.

space between the looming domes. Saladin, she says, slept in what is now the storeroom-cum-spare room. To reach the house, you need to climb up past the mosque attached to the minaret that Saladin built in a pointed architectural gesture up against the church, the central site of Christian worship in Jerusalem. This roof space is *waqf* property; that is, it is held in trust and administered by the Muslim religious and legal authorities. From here the views across the roofs of Jerusalem are endlessly fascinating: strange angles, new vistas.

This house epitomizes all the surprise and wonder of Jerusalem and embodies the delights and perils of writing about this city above all others. To begin with, the el-Alami house is not beautiful in the conventional way that architectural historians talk about beauty. It is a simple, crusader form, not designed by any celebrated architect or artist, but a basic artisan's dwelling, made to last, as it has, and adapted sometimes clumsily to changing modern needs. The room inside is beautifully kept with shining, polished brass tables and carved Syrian furniture. But it is not Versailles or the Pitti Palace. (There is the fridge with the large photo of Yasser Arafat stuck on it.) Apart from the Dome of the Rock, one of the genuine wonders of Arabic architecture, there is scarcely a beautiful building in Jerusalem to match the grandeurs of Rome, Florence, or Paris. This book cannot lovingly itemize the swags and pillars and statues of Renaissance palaces or even lead you to masterpieces of art on scarlet walls. Jerusalem—as generations of travelers have noted with awe, disgust, or regret—is a small, rather dirty, and unimposing city, now sprawling far beyond its historical boundaries, and today often scarred by the worst styles of utilitarian or, worse still, bombastic, modern architecture.

Yet this city can fire the imagination like no other. Its buildings evoke a powerful sense of lived history and a deeply invested longing for a better world. Saida's house is set high between buildings over which wars have been fought, a tiny private space between aggressive public architecture designed to promote a worldview. Its long history interweaves her family with those events, with that architecture—from the noble general Saladin to the memorials for her father, judge for the local Muslim community. It is this buried life of passions and violence, as much as its location, that makes this house so engaging.

There is also a more local oddity here that goes to the heart of Jerusalem's hold on the imagination. The flat roof on which we stood is *waqf* property, Muslim owned; below is the Church of the Holy Sepulchre, Christianity's holiest site. Above is God's. You cannot ask how thick the conceptual layer of roof is (and certainly should not consult a property lawyer on such a question). Jerusalem is rife with such problems of multidimensional ownership. Here is a crusader building, owned for centuries by a Muslim family, attached to a Christian holy site—all now under the Jewish authority of the Israeli state. It is a commonplace to say that Jerusalem is the city that is holy to three world religions, the three Abrahamic faiths. On the ground, this commonplace takes on bizarre physical as well as political configurations.

Jerusalem's earliest inhabitants, as far as we know, were the mysterious Jebusites, a Canaanite tribe conquered by the early Israelites (this is all before the ninth century B.C.: the Jebusites seem to have been there at least from the fourteenth century). The Israelite city was destroyed by the Babylonians in the sixth century B.C., but it was rebuilt and re-inhabited by descendants of its former Israelite population only seventy years later. The Romans first conquered the city in the first century B.C. The Jews revolted from the Roman Empire twice, both times with disastrous effects for Jerusalem: in the first century A.D. the revolt led to the sacking of the city and the destruction of the Temple; in the second century A.D., the whole city was razed, rebuilt, and renamed Aelia Capitolina. Eventually in the fourth century it became a Christian city. It was captured in turn by the Muslims in the seventh century and, apart from the century of crusader domination (1099–1187), was ruled by a series of different Muslim kingdoms until the breakup of the Ottoman Empire in the early twentieth century. At that time it came under the British Mandate and then, first partly, and since 1967 wholly, under the control of the modern State of Israel.

This bare history is physically expressed right across the Old City of Jerusalem and its immediate surroundings. It would be possible to walk from crusader building to crusader building, or to hunt down the Roman remains in a straight Roman way, or to spot the stripy Mameluk decorations in the Old City. But that would be

to miss the true thrill of Jerusalem. For it is how these different in-
heritances are interwoven with one another, or set in conflict, or
layered on top of each other, that makes Jerusalem so perplexing
and complex. Saida's house embodies more than eight hundred
years of this complexity in its simple brick structure. That is the
beauty—or perhaps better the *wonder*—of Jerusalem.

It is also telling that Saida says Saladin slept here. Jerusalem is a
city that puts a huge investment in the authentic. This is the place
where Abraham prepared to sacrifice his son, where David danced
before the Lord, where Jesus walked, spoke to his disciples, and was
crucified, where Mohammed's night journey took him to heaven
to learn the rules of proper Muslim behavior. The intensity of feeling that Jerusalem provokes is intimately tied to the claim that "this
is the very place where . . ." In Jewish writing, the Temple Mount is
often called simply *hamakom,* "the place"; in Arabic, Jerusalem is
called *el-kuds,* "the holy," as if the city were synonymous with its
holiness. To be in Jerusalem is in itself a holy and life-changing
event for all the city's pious pilgrims. Yet it is a city full of the
inauthentic. Nearly every building discussed in this book has been
rebuilt, sometimes several times and often after total destruction.
The Old City is a hive of new construction. Many of the most
iconic images of Jerusalem—the golden roof of the Dome of the
Rock, the mass of worshippers in front of the Western Wall—
looked quite different even a hundred years ago, when the dome
was a dull lead, and the Western Wall approached only by a few sad
mourners down a dank alleyway. The famous walls of the walled
city are from the sixteenth century only, the walkway around the
ramparts, so beloved of current tourists, a product of the 1920s. This
is a city that fabricates, forgets, and forges its past—in both senses
of "forge"—through misrepresentations and politically motivated
fictions. I do not know whether Saladin slept in Saida el-Alami's
storeroom or not. As a historian, I have to say I suspect that he did

not. But the story acts like so many in Jerusalem: as a foundational myth, giving weight and luster to a small gray crusader cell.

This multidimensional sedimentation of history is revealed everywhere in Jerusalem. On the one hand, the city is built on bedrock. Archaeologists and planners go down to the bedrock and no further. As with Manhattan, where the rock of the island itself is fundamental to the development of its skyline of skyscrapers, Jerusalem's geological formation is integral to the development of the city. Some of the most awe-inspiring vistas in Jerusalem are actually looking down, from the current street level, past generations of silting, to the rock on which the city has been slowly built up. Jerusalem is a city lived and explored on multiple levels, from crypts and underground cisterns, up past the noisy and crowded streets, to the life on the roofs and the soaring views from minarets and steeples and towers. Up toward heaven, as many in Jerusalem would tell you.

On the other hand, the buried life of the city is everywhere there to be discovered on a different, less physical level. Every spot is layered not just with the grand narrative of the clashes of world history but also with the long, anecdotal traditions of families like that of Saida el-Alami, of travelers' tales in this city of pilgrims, of the heartfelt and constantly retold stories of religious groups, sects, and organizations so often drawn to Jerusalem. This book will uncover the physical cityscape of Jerusalem, but it will always be setting these buildings in the web of words, the personal and local spinning of tales, that makes the buildings alive in the imagination of so many. This is the memory of Jerusalem, a history of generations of longing: longing for a touch of the divine, longing for a better world, longing for a lost home, longing to find an answer, here in this place, only here.

So let us leave Saida el-Alami's roof-top courtyard between the domes and circle back down to the Church of the Holy Sepulchre itself to start our journey through Jerusalem.

FINDING THE CHURCH OF THE HOLY SEPULCHRE

The first shock to anyone used to the great cathedrals of Europe such as Chartres or Notre Dame, or even to the vast institutional edifice of the Vatican, is just how hard it is to find the Church of the Holy Sepulchre. It is easy enough to say that from the Jaffa Gate you go down David Street, take your first left (Christian Quarter Road), and then turn into the opening (second on the right, Queen Helena Street), which becomes Souk el-Dabargha. It is actually quite straightforward and quick once you know what you are doing. Of course, the first time it can be distracting that there are no signs to the church itself, that the street names are different in Arabic, Hebrew, and English, that the stalls of the *souk* (marketplace) are usually bustling with all too mundane and garish life, and that the entrance to the church's courtyard is through a small and easily misrecognized opening. But what remains surprising, even shocking, is that the holiest site of Christianity, fought over by so many, should be so fully surrounded by a mass of undistinguished buildings. You cannot look up from the surrounding streets and navigate by the church's towering dome, as you can by the spires of Notre Dame or Chartres. You simply cannot see it until you are right upon it. And when you are there—especially in comparison with Notre Dame or Chartres—it seems as small, brown, and undistinguished as a duck.

The Church of the Holy Sepulchre is set in a mess of buildings. Many Victorian town planners, had they had the chance, would have cleared away the medieval jumble and allowed the church to stand out, like a jewel in an elegant setting. (The front of King's College Chapel in Cambridge, for example, now one of the most photographed views in England, was surrounded by low-grade medieval shops until the nineteenth century's version of conservation boldly cleared them away.) Any such treatment here would reveal the irredeemable confusion of the church itself, which in its current form was built over many years to apparently conflicting designs. But the first image of this church today comes from standing in its cramped courtyard and looking up at its two floors of Romanesque arches, doors below, windows above (Figure 2). The doorways are flanked by slim columns with foliate decorations, and one of the doors is bricked up, with a casual disregard for the evident symmetry of design. To the right, steps lead up to a small domed chapel with one very obviously restored square pillar (it is the only white marble there, quite a different color from the rest of the stone) and arches covered by grills. This is usually called the Chapel of the Franks (or the Chapel of St. Mary of Egypt). To the left, high above the court, rises a bell tower (it was once higher, but two floors have been lost to earthquakes). The courtyard itself is irregularly paved, with low steps at the rear on which the modern backpacking tourists sit and smoke. It is always called the *parvis* (a term for a church courtyard apparently corrupted from the word "paradise," which means originally "garden"), and it is small and asymmetrical, and seems scarcely capable of holding or even directing the mass of pilgrims we know to have visited Jerusalem. It does not look like much.

But first impressions should not be trusted. This is a place to stop a while and take in what there actually is to see and hear, before entering the church itself. For the façade and parvis of the Church of the Holy Sepulchre deserve to be viewed within a very particular and rather startling history of conflict and compromise. The façade was built between 1163 and 1167, and architectural historians describe it as the keystone of one of the "most magnificent pilgrimage and tomb churches in the Christian world." The design of the pillars looks back to the Roman origins of Christianity (and the crusaders as the warriors of the Latin Church), and this gives the church a feel quite different from the near-contemporary Gothic masterpieces of the cathedral tradition in Western Europe. Some of the stonework may indeed have been taken from destroyed Roman

Figure 2. The Church of the Holy Sepulchre: the parvis and the entrance viewed from the top of the buildings opposite.

buildings: the crusaders were great recyclers of material. But by 1187 Jerusalem had fallen to Saladin, and most of the Christian clergy had fled Jerusalem. It was at this time that all but one of the doors to the building were blocked off, and the great front doors took on their strange asymmetry, a permanent sign of the medieval conflict between the crusaders and the Muslim warriors over the holy places.

There is still only one door to the Church of the Holy Sepulchre. When Jerusalem was preparing for the celebrations of the millennium in 2000, and expecting thousands of pilgrims, the city authorities suggested that it would be wise to open one of the several blocked doors both to aid the circulation of visitors and as a necessary precaution in case of fire or riot. This proved impossible to negotiate. The three major religious authorities of the church, the Greek Orthodox, the Latin Franciscans, and the Armenians, could not agree which door could be opened, because to choose a particular door would be to give preferential treatment to one of the established groups over the others. As one of the tired and cynical Israeli officials involved in the negotiations commented to me, "The one good result of the Intifada was that there were far fewer tourists than expected, and the problem of the door quietly slipped away."

Different parts of the Church of the Holy Sepulchre are owned by different orders of Christians, as we will see vividly when we enter the church itself. Some areas are shared, and these cannot be altered or even restored without the agreement of all three major parties. This has affected the façade of the church in a disturbing way. Above the doors in the original crusader design were beautiful figural mosaics (now lost) and, on the lintels, a particularly fine set of sculptures of stories from the life of Jesus, as well as an intricate vine-scroll relief. These sculptures were in desperate need of repair and were taken down for restoration by the British authorities under the Mandate in 1929. They were taken to the Rockefeller

Museum, where they can still be viewed. The western lintel (the left-hand door as you look at it) shows Lazarus being raised from the grave; then Jesus and the disciples meeting Mary Magdalene and Martha. The third scene shows the preparation of the Paschal Lamb at the bottom and further preparations for the coming events above; the fourth shows the bringing of the Ass and the Colt; and the final two scenes on the right are the arrival in Jerusalem and then the Last Supper—all scenes from the Gospels. Although the sculptures are damaged by the wear of time, they are still wonderful examples of crusader art. Figure 3, a detail of the second scene, is indicative of their quality. Martha falls to kiss Jesus' feet, while Mary Magdalene raises her hands, stretching out her cloak, in a gesture of pleading. Their movement and hunched forms contrast with the still, erect body of Jesus, whose hand blesses them. The whole scene is framed by the disciples, who turn toward the central tableau in a variety of poses. On the eastern lintel from the other door, spiraling branches curl around naked boys, predatory birds, and strange hybrid creatures, such as harpies with a woman's head and the body of a bird. These two sets of sculptures are an integral part of the design and of the magnificence of the entrance to this church.

The panels have finally been restored, but they are still too delicate to be returned to their original site. So the museum has painstakingly constructed excellent replicas that could be set above the doors. They have not been put there; but this refusal is not because of any high-minded notions of authenticity. The Greek Orthodox patriarchate, under the terms of the three-way agreement, has blocked the return of the sculptures because they are *Latin* art, a glory of the Franciscan heritage. The now-blank spaces above the doors serve as a visual reminder of the vindictive turmoil in the church.

The conflict between the groups in the church, each aiming for greater control over the holy site, has been so severe and so long-lasting that in 1852 Sultan Abd al-Majid I, the Muslim ruler,

Figure 3. A detail of the Western lintel of the Church of the Holy Sepulchre.

passed a *firman* (a permission, or ruling) aimed at ending the constant brouhaha. The "status quo agreement," as it has always been known, declared that there could be no change from the current state of affairs. Before this date, as power ebbed and flowed between communities, each tried to take control over different parts of the holy site—stealing keys, blocking services, and surreptitiously or overtly making land-grabs on chapels and altars. The British Mandate authorities, with typical bureaucratic zeal, not only reaffirmed the agreement but also published in detail exactly what it meant in terms of each square of floor space, each window, each step. The Israeli authorities have followed the same blueprint. Part of the status quo agreement concerns the huge wooden door of the church. It is locked every night, fifteen minutes after sunset (except during festivals that require the church's use at night). It is opened every morning with a bizarre ceremony that could happen only in Jerusalem. From inside the church, the sacristan passes a ladder through a hatch in the door. The key holder receives it. The key has been owned since 1831 by the Joudeh family, a Muslim clan (who took it on after a sexual misdemeanor of the Nusseibeh family). Then, as now, the day-to-day opening is handled by the Nusseibeh family, also Muslim. Mr. Nusseibeh sets the ladder against the door, climbs up it to the padlock, and unlocks the gate. Clergy who have slept in the church, protecting their own enclaves, and pilgrims waiting to leave and enter the church then start the day's business. Until the nineteenth century, the Muslim authorities controlled entrance to the church; they charged not only pilgrims but also clergy entering and exiting (hence in part the church officials' habit of sleeping in the church). This history explains the possession of the key by a Muslim family at one level. But it also has come to be seen as a symbol of the interfactional struggle of the church. So conflicted are these groups—all committed to brotherly love—that the very key to the building has to be held by someone who is not Christian at all.

The status quo agreement may also explain one of the oddest features of the front of the church. If you look up to the right-hand window (Figure 2), you will see a ladder propped against the wall. This might look as though it has been left there by a handyman. But it is always there. The balcony and the window are owned by the Armenians. They use the balcony to watch events in the parvis below, and also to sun themselves. In the past, especially when many officials lived in the church to avoid the entrance tax, the Armenians used the balcony to grow vegetables. So, since the ladder was there before 1852, there a ladder will remain under the terms of the agreement! As the ladder rots, it is replaced with an exact copy—so that there is always the ladder that was always there.

The parvis is also the site of one of the more striking ceremonies of the Greek Orthodox community. On Maundy Thursday, the patriarch of Jerusalem (the head of the Greek Orthodox Church in the city) processes in the full splendor of his robes out of the church, surrounded by his congregation, and mounts a raised platform. His heavy brocade robe is lifted from him by the archimandrites of the Brotherhood of the Church of the Holy Sepulchre. Then, with water from a large, ornate silver rose bowl, which rests on a finely decorated blue carpet, the patriarch washes the feet of twelve archimandrites, also dressed in their most lavish ecclesiastical robes, representing the twelve apostles. (Each archimandrite removes one sock.) The ceremony replays the scene from the Last Supper when Jesus washes the feet of the twelve disciples. As so often in religious history, a gesture of extreme humility is remembered in a ceremony of utmost pomp. Each of the major religious groups in the church has a similar ritual. On such occasions the parvis is heaving with people, every window and balcony sways with spectators, and the colors, smells, and sounds are overwhelming. The small drab square becomes a spectacular scene.

ENTERING THE CHURCH OF THE HOLY SEPULCHRE

We can now enter the church (remembering not only the generations of pilgrims and tourists, famous and unknown, who have crossed these flagstones, but also the fact that, until 1967, no Jew was allowed even into the parvis—and that a tourist, suspected of being a Jew, was nearly lynched for stepping here as recently as 1922. He was saved only by the sudden arrival of the British police. This was not just a custom enforced by the Christians. A *firman* [edict] from the sultan on April 29, 1534, made it a rule that in every synagogue on Sabbath, an announcement had to be made from the pulpit that Jews were forbidden to cross the parvis.). So what are we entering? The Church of the Holy Sepulchre is the building— or collection of buildings—built around the site of the Passion of Jesus Christ, that is, the places where Jesus was crucified and buried. But it is one of the most confusing buildings, historically, architecturally, and even spiritually. Most of what is instantly visible was built after the great fire of 1808: it is a nineteenth-century building. The rotunda, the inside of the dome that is the most recognizable landmark of the church from the hills and towers around, was rebuilt after the earthquake of 1927, and the decorations were completed—after a massive interdenominational fight—only in 1997. But the tomb of Jesus dates back to the first century. The church contains wonderful shards of many intervening periods of building, often shoved, jaggedly, against one another. The deliberate acts of destruction that have scarred the building are still visible, as are aggressive gestures of building and counter-building between different sects. There are relics; moments of grotesque myth-making; touches that open a vista of profound religious feeling. Since the first records of pilgrims visiting this church, there have been ambivalent, passionate, and dismissive reactions to the building and its rituals.

The best way to try to bring some order to this profusion is to begin with a brief history of the building. But this is not a story that can be told with simple objectivity, because from its very inception it has been marked by the commitments of faith. The simplest facts are these:

- In 326, the Roman emperor Constantine ordered the construction of the Church of the Holy Sepulchre. It consisted of a domed rotunda, the Rotunda of the Anastasis (Resurrection), which was built around the so-called edicule, the shrine erected over the tomb itself; the parvis, the court before the cross; and the basilica of the Marturion, a church with apses and nave. Figure 4 is an artist's reconstruction of this compound, which visualizes it rather well.

- In the seventh century (617), the church was sacked by the Persians. The relic of the True Cross, which was taken then, was recovered in 630 by the Byzantine emperor Heraclius. In 638, Jerusalem was taken by Caliph Omar, but no damage was done to the church.

- In 809–829 the Rotunda of the Anastasis was rebuilt as an open cone, a form it maintained until 1809.

- In 1009, the church was destroyed by Caliph al-Hakim, the ruler of Egypt, and only the walls of the rotunda

and part of the tomb survived. Rebuilding began almost immediately, as al-Hakim repented of his destructive act, but it took many years to complete.

∎ In the twelfth century, the crusaders constructed chapels around the Rock of Golgotha, and then added a
new choir, transept, and the south façade and bell tower
(which we have just been exploring)—fundamentally
altering the shape and feel of the church. Basically, they
filled in the gap between Constantine's rotunda and
Constantine's basilica (see Figure 4).

∎ In 1555, the edicule was completely rebuilt by Boniface
of Ragusa, the leader of the Franciscans in the Holy
Land.

∎ In 1808, the whole church was badly damaged by fire. It
was rebuilt beginning in 1809 by a Greek architect,
Nikkolaus Kommenos.

∎ In 1868, the dome was reconstructed.

∎ In 1927, an earthquake resulted in the need for extensive reinforcement of the building. The edicule is still
surrounded by steel braces from this period.

∎ In 1997, the newly redecorated rotunda was inaugurated.

It should be clear already that over eighteen hundred years, Constantine's design has been covered over, reoriented, and in places
simply destroyed, so that its form is hard to perceive in the current
building. Not only has a sheer jumble of chapels, denominations,
and pathways grown all around the central shrines, but also the
compound itself is hemmed in on all sides by other constructions.
  I have tried to give the facts in as bare a way as possible in the

Figure 4. An artist's reconstruction of Constantine's compound.

bullet points above. But even here conflict and compromise push in on all sides. The very name of the church is contested: the Western Church calls it the Church of the Holy Sepulchre, the Eastern Church calls it the Church of the Resurrection. The story of the foundation of the church is typical of the difficulties that arise as soon as you scratch the surface of the building's history. Eusebius, the Church historian who was contemporary with the foundation, describes how Constantine, the Roman emperor who made Christianity the accepted religion of the empire, decided to build the church, led, as he says, by the Holy Spirit. When Hadrian had built Aelia Capitolina over the ruins of Jerusalem in 135, the current site of the Church of the Holy Sepulchre was covered by a temple, part of the official buildings of the forum of the new city. Constantine instructed Makarios, bishop of Jerusalem, to clear away the earth under which the tomb—he calls it a cave—had been hidden for so long, and to destroy the idol worship that lay like a weight on it (the Roman temple). In Eusebius' account Constantine saw Hadrian's decision to build over the tomb as a misguided attempt by the Romans to destroy Christianity (and some modern religious commentators have agreed, though it is not very likely that the Roman city planners were much concerned with what was then a very minor subcult of Judaism). Finding the tomb was apparently no problem for Constantine's workers, though it is described as a miracle beyond the comprehension of man that it should rise again, as if "in imitation of the resurrection of the Lord." The new church, declares Constantine, is to be the finest church anywhere in the world.

Cyril, writing only slightly later, gives a different version. Here Makarios is baffled as to how to find the tomb; he is led by a dream to make the miraculous discovery, "against all expectation." In a similar way, Cyril tells us that Helena, the mother of Constantine, who built a church at the place of Jesus' birth and one for the Ascension, wondrously discovers the three crosses of the Crucifixion, miraculously undamaged, still in a trench near Golgotha. The True Cross, Jesus', is identified by the miracles it can perform. It is worrying to a historian that while Cyril tells this story, Eusebius makes no reference to it. Surely if Helena had discovered the True Cross, Eusebius, historian of the Church, who had been at the dedication of the church, would have mentioned it. Could this be a fabrication, only a few years after the visit of Helena? The business in relics is big business indeed, and it has proved easy for modern critical thinkers to be suspicious of the whole story of the bishop's discovery of the tomb, let alone the cross, through miracle and divine guidance. There is a great deal at stake in the (authentic) symbols of Christianity, especially as the nascent church is coming into power.

In the nineteenth and twentieth centuries, as German Protestant theologians in particular put rationality, science, and historical investigation at the center of religious learning, this suspicion became fully articulated. First, it was pointed out that Jesus was crucified outside the walls, but that the Church of the Holy Sepulchre is in the middle of the city. Here modern archaeology has trumped modern cynicism. It is now clear that the walls of the city at the time of Jesus ran not far from the Church of the Holy Sepulchre, which was located outside them. Historians of Jerusalem are obsessed with walls: the boundaries of this city have always meant more than the mere marking of a topographical limit. Here, for once, the authenticity of the shrine for which so many crusaders and others died can rely on archaeological science.

Second, it was pointed out that the whole city of Jerusalem was destroyed by the Roman emperor Hadrian after the Bar Kochba revolt. Aelia Capitolina, a new city with a different layout, was built over it. All the Jews were banned from this city, and, as Eusebius himself notes, up until this point in 135 all the Christian bishops and their flock in Jerusalem were (converted) Jews. Although non-Jewish Christians came back to Aelia Capitolina, could there be an unbroken tradition recording the site of Jesus' burial, especially when it was underneath a temple on the new forum? (To which traditional Catholic critics replied, simply, "Yes." If any site would be remembered and memorialized it would be this.)

Third, no one even knows what happened to the tomb from the time of the Crucifixion until the construction of Aelia Capitolina. Herod Agrippa extended the city walls in 414 and brought the site of the current church inside them. Since Jews do not allow burial inside a city, this site must have been ritually purified and may have been covered over even then. Here is another difficulty for assuming an unbroken tradition of knowledge of the precise site of Jesus' tomb—to which the Catholic critics replied, "Why would anyone choose to dig in such a difficult and unpromising site, if there were no knowledge of the site of the tomb?"

Scientific history had no difficulty poking holes in the standard story—especially in the hands of historians from the Protestant countries of Germany and England, who also repeatedly and tellingly expressed their revulsion at the Catholic rites in the Church of the Holy Sepulchre. Edward Robinson, the great American archaeologist of Jerusalem (Robinson's Arch), summed up these doubts in what became a notorious sentence in his book *Biblical Researches in Palestine and the Adjacent Regions* (which won the Royal Geographical Society of London gold medal in 1842): "Jerusalem has been the abode not only of mistaken piety, but also of credulous superstition, not unmingled with pious fraud." Indeed, Robinson was so sure of his doubts that he did not deign even to visit the Church of the Holy Sepulchre. His phrase "pious fraud" became a particular bone of contention in the long-running disputes about true religious expression throughout the nineteenth century. As F. J. Bliss wrote more than sixty years later: "The phrase 'pious fraud' separates us still. Take it back, Dr. Robinson!"

Robinson was famous for his "objective scientific archaeology." To modern eyes, however, his statements of lack of prejudice reveal how deep the hostility to the Catholic Church ran in this academic debate. When he describes the Latin clergy in Jerusalem, he writes, "There was hardly a face among all those before us, that could be called intelligent . . . I make these remarks merely as relating a matter of fact, and not, I trust, out of any spirit of prejudice against the Roman Church and her clergy." Herman Melville was typically blunt and typical of the dismissive response of Protestant tourists when he wrote of the church: "All is glitter and nothing is gold. A sickening cheat." Most Protestant tourists took the same tack: "The Christianity peculiar to Jerusalem is unmittigatedly repulsive," wrote George William Curtis, one of the founders of the Republican Party in America, in 1855. The distinguished British archaeologist Sir Charles Wilson (who gave his name to Wilson's Arch), tried—and failed—to find an acceptable compromise: "There is no decisive reason for placing Golgotha and the Tomb at the places that were accepted as genuine in the fourth century, and . . . there is no distinct proof that they were not so situated." As ever, reasonable doubt satisfied no one when it came to Jerusalem.

This Protestant reaction led to one of the most extraordinary acts of religious discovery even in Jerusalem's long history of such discoveries. General Gordon, Gordon of Khartoum, a military celebrity of the British Empire, was relaxing in Jerusalem, on the roof of the house of Mrs. Spafford, founder of the American Colony (the American and Swedish cult, which we will trace in Chapter 6). As usual, he was reading the Bible and reflecting on the Gospels. From his deckchair he looked over the walls by the Damascus Gate and saw a rock formation that looked to him like a skull. Golgotha, the site of the Crucifixion, means "skull place." He decided to investigate further. As he tramped over the scrubby hill, he found a tomb. He put the two together and decided that this must be the tomb of Jesus. Being a "can–do" sort of fellow, he immediately began to write articles in support of his theory and to gather support from archaeologists and the great and good of English theological circles. Eventually a fund was set up to buy the site for posterity.

Gordon's arguments were bizarre in the extreme. He consulted the relief map of Jerusalem at the time of Jesus that was drawn up by Captain Warren (the explorer, archaeologist, and adventurer who will reappear in several guises in this book). He decided that Jerusalem itself looked like a body, a skeleton, and that when this skeleton was superimposed back onto the map, lo and behold, his new site for Golgotha was exactly where the skull was (and the Dome of the Rock is in the skeleton's arse!) (Figure 5). He took no notice of archaeologists (unless they happened to agree with him) and proceeded to champion this new site for the Passion against all comers. What is perhaps most remarkable is that many people in the Victorian period and later believed this farrago. It certainly answered a need among Protestant pilgrims that was differently answered, as we will see, with a string of Victorian churches and institutions intended to bypass the pull of the Church of the Holy Sepulchre. The Garden Tomb, as it is known, is now a beautiful, calm garden behind the bus station outside the Damascus Gate. It is run largely by volunteers, who give a rather apologetic tour, complete with explanations of how this could perhaps be the tomb of

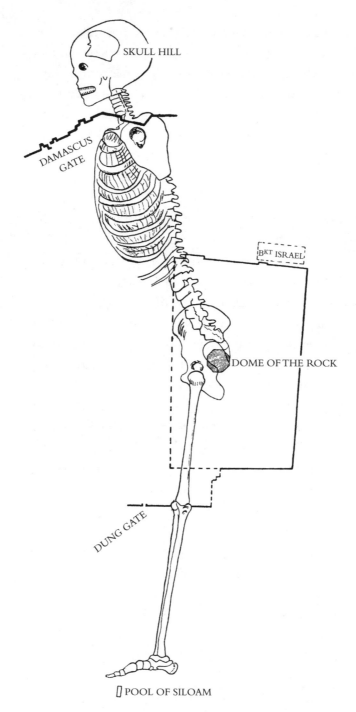

Figure 5. General Gordon's image of Jerusalem as a skeleton, "proving" the site of Golgotha.

Jesus. But Jerusalem, for all its hopefulness, is a city particularly cruel to "perhaps."

Each moment of the bullet-point history of the building of the Church of the Holy Sepulchre is surrounded by such stories of ideology and contention, fantasy and willfulness. This is one reason that the church is so fascinating to visit. So, with a glance at the high bench just inside the doors on the left, where the Muslim gatekeepers sit, let us now finally enter the doors.

INSIDE THE CHURCH OF THE HOLY SEPULCHRE

Immediately opposite the entrance from the parvis is a low, intensely smooth, red marble slab, set in a stone surround (Map 1). Dedicatory lamps hang above it, four candlesticks stand one at each corner. This is the Stone of Unction, on which, as tradition holds, Jesus' body was laid out and anointed after the Crucifixion. Pilgrims fall to their knees and kiss the stone, while tourists gawk. The marble covers the original stone, which was being chipped away by zealous relic hunters. It is necessary to say "as tradition holds," because it would take a great deal of faith for a historian to recognize a first-century artifact here, or even to imagine how such a temporary location could have been memorialized through the vicissitudes of the site's history. At Easter, the Latin patriarch processes to the stone, kneels on a cushion before it, and sprinkles it with holy water and incense. The Stone of Unction is an arresting first sight as you enter the church.

The Stone of Unction is the thirteenth Station of the Cross. The fourteen Stations of the Cross mark the major scenes in the story of the Passion. They are stimuli to prayer and reflection on the life and death of Jesus. Many churches have their own representations of the fourteen stations; Pope John Paul II used to celebrate the Stations of the Cross on Good Friday in the Coliseum in Rome, carrying a cross himself from station to station, until he became too frail for the task. Many different sets of prayers and reflections have been written over the years for each station. The Via Dolorosa in Jerusalem is the model on which all these stations are based, and the final five Stations of the Cross are in the Church of the Holy Sepulchre: the stripping of Jesus' clothes; nailing to the cross; death on the cross; taking down from the cross; burial in the tomb. We can turn left toward the tomb from the Stone of Unction, or right toward Golgotha. We will turn left, but first a brief word on the Stations of the Cross, because in many ways the problem of this route is a problem we will face again and again in Jerusalem.

Of the fourteen stations, only nine appear as events in the Gospels. The other five—the three falls of Jesus, Jesus meeting his mother, and Veronica wiping his face with a cloth—are products of the medieval imagination (and four stations were given their current location only in the nineteenth century). We do not know where the first station should be, where, that is, Pilate judged Jesus, because we do not know exactly where he set up his court or palace, but it was most likely in the citadel on the other side of town. We can be sure that the so-called Ecce Homo arch, where Jesus was shown to the populace, is not a structure Jesus saw: it was built many years later. As for the falls to the pavement, the street level then was many feet below the level today (and the whole city relaid by the Romans). So a straightforward archaeological account would have to sniff at the Via Dolorosa as a misleading fabrication. But I don't think that such an easy dismissal will do. The route has become hallowed over time, by generations of intensely moved and devout pilgrims, and its function as a stimulus to reflection and worship is not dependent on its historical authenticity. Christians, Jews, and Muslims over the years have all created sites in Jerusalem like this: sites where historical truth stands at odds with religious fervor, or, rather, where the passage of time has invested a place with a sanctity, setting aside all archaeological nicety. We will see the same effect at the Western Wall plaza and at al-Aqsa—two of the most holy sites for Jews and Muslims. For some, no doubt, this will confirm a necessary rejection of all religion in the name of science or rationality. For others, it will strengthen a recognition of people's need to worship something greater than themselves or their own wisdom. But this process of sanctification is an absolutely integral factor in the life of Jerusalem.

As we turn left from the Stone of Unction, past the Armenian sacristy, we enter the rotunda through large, yellowing pillars. Some of these pillars have their collars at the top, others at the bottom. As ever, any detail tells a story. After the church was destroyed by Hakim, the mad caliph from Egypt, there were few funds for its reconstruction and many restrictions on the rebuilding; consequently, old Roman pillars were cut in half and reused. Hence the mishmash. In 1809, when the church was restored after the great fire, the pillars were replaced exactly as before, fresh stone, old troubles. The edicule itself is a four-square dusky construction with a small turret on the top and a quotation from the Gospels in Greek inscribed around the top of the walls. It is shored up by English steel, after the earthquake of 1927, with huge braces, which give a very strange impression of industrialization. The inner rim of one of the girders reads "Bombay Metal Company India," which is a neat reminder of the empire at work here—and of the strategic importance of the Middle East as the route to British imperial holdings in Asia. It is not an aesthetic triumph. (In one of his wonderful novels starring the character Henry Bech, the American novelist John Updike has his [Jewish] hero comment to his Christian wife, with Updike's customary cynical and leery gaze: "You should have let the Arabs design it for you.")

The low, narrow entrance is surrounded by a forest of large candles, each dedicated by different sects in the church, and glittering with crosses and lamps. You enter first the Chapel of the Angel and then the tomb itself. The tomb is overhung with dedicatory lamps, and the air is heavy. The forty-two candles are each placed by different communities, and the thin grooves on the sepulchre itself are not the scratches of time but marks to indicate where different priests can stand for their rituals. Even—or especially—here the divisions among the sects need the control of ritualization. It is a tight space, as one might expect. There is usually an immediate pressure to move on, as people outside are waiting to follow you in. A heavily bearded monk may sit and direct traffic, imperiously. The smallness of the tomb and the importance it has played for men of peace and war are strikingly evident. The clash of West and East still focuses on the Crusades as a metaphor and historical model. Godfrey of Bouillon, the crusader conqueror of Jerusalem, may not have used the title himself, but from those days he has been known as *advocatus sepulchri sancti,* the protector of the Holy Sepulchre. This empty space is what he fought for. As with the Holy of Holies in the Temple in Jerusalem, emptiness can be a more potent sign than splendor.

As you go around the edicule toward the rear, do not miss a hole in the side of the wall, about five feet from the ground. This hole (there is one on each side) is part of one of the most bizarre rituals of the church, and one that has particularly vexed European Protestants over the years: the ceremony of Holy Fire. This occasion is the climax of the Orthodox Holy Week, and it results in scenes of devotional hysteria unparalleled in the church calendar. Abbot Daniel, writing at the beginning of the twelfth century, said: "He who has not taken part in the glory of that day will not believe the record of all I have seen." Nineteenth-century European visitors were more shocked, or revolted, than the awe-struck Daniel.

On Good Friday the lamp in the Holy Sepulchre has been extinguished. The purpose of the ceremony of Holy Fire is to rekindle this lamp, which also symbolizes the resurrection of Jesus. The door of the church is opened ceremoniously at 8:00 in the morning under the guidance of the Armenian dragoman, and the crowds that have been waiting pour into the church. Each congregation has its own place in the church, and rivalry is intense. (In 2003 a Syrian stabbed an Armenian in the bottom . . .) Everyone holds a candle, and the congregations try to outshout one another with religious chants, while the black-robed pilgrims cross themselves intently. The Armenian patriarch enters and takes his throne in the gallery, some two and a half hours after the doors have been opened. Then the edicule is searched for any signs of matches, and the tomb is sealed with wax by a group of different Christian clergy (and the Muslim doorkeeper, no doubt to ensure fair play). Then younger men enter, carried on shoulders, yelling and encouraging their congregations. Finally, the Greek patriarch himself enters the church and takes up his throne. After further ceremonial greetings between the patriarchs, a procession of priests parades around the edicule three times. The seal is broken and the patriarch escorted into the tomb. The doors are shut. The crowd becomes silent. Bells ring out. A flash of flame is seen from inside the tomb. Immediately, a cluster of candles is passed through the hole in the south side of the edicule, and an Armenian layman runs helter-skelter to the gallery to present them to the Armenian patriarch. From the hole on the north side, candles are rushed to the catholicon, the Greek chapel at the center of the church. Amid scenes of fervid excitement, the patriarch emerges with candles, and the light is spread throughout the church.

The Greek Orthodox clergy explain quietly that this is not a miracle. But it has been treated as such over the centuries, and the reaction of the community is startling, even frightening. The ritual is not merely a picturesque show, however. One of the chants regularly heard in the nineteenth century was, "Your feast is the feast of devils, our feast is the feast of Christ, Christ who has redeemed us, and with His blood has bought us. We today are happy, and you are sorrowful. Oh the Jews! The Jews! Oh, the infidels! Your feast is the feast of devils and our feast is the feast of Christ." There have been regular scenes of disorder, verging on violent clashes, and on one occasion in the late nineteenth century a riot left nearly thirty dead. The British consul James Finn described the chaos: "The pavement all around the Sepulchre Chapel . . . was strewn with broken lamps, fragments of glass and pictures, and oil swimming over the floor. Many valuable pictures had been torn; vases, lamps, candlesticks and church ornaments thrown down and destroyed. In the gallery of the Syrians there were women dancing, clapping hands and shrieking the *tehihleel* of joy." Harriet Martineau, the English feminist and novelist whose travel writings on the East were a Victorian best seller, hated "mummeries done in the name of Christianity," and she described the ceremony of the fire memorably as "like a holiday in Hell." But A. W. Kinglake, old Etonian traveler and historian of the Crimea, was far more sanguine. He found pretty well everything in Jerusalem grist for his ironic gaze, and he was amused after one of the bigger fights to hear of an Englishman who

> had taken his station in a convenient part of the church, and was no doubt displaying that peculiar air of serenity and gratification with which an Englishman usually looks on at a row, when one of the Franciscans came by, all reeking from the fight, and was so disgusted at the coolness and placid contentment of the Englishman, that he forgot his monkish humility, as well as the duties of hospitality (the Englishman was a guest at the convent), and plainly said, "You sleep under our roof—you eat our bread—you drink our wine—and then, when Easter Sunday comes, you don't fight for us!"

But not even Kinglake could have ironized the shocking events of 1834, which were witnessed by Robert Curzon, the English diplomat, manuscript collector, and travel writer. He describes the riotous behavior of the worshippers ("some, almost in a state of nudity, danced about with frantic gestures, yelling and screaming as if possessed"), the increasing heat, airlessness, and hysteria. As he tried to walk out, he realized that he was walking over bodies, "many of them were quite black with suffocation, and further on were others all bloody and covered with the brains and entrails of those who had been trodden to pieces by the crowd." The Ottoman guards, panicked by the crowd's reaction, thought the Christians wanted to attack them, and rushed them with bayonets. "So desperate and savage did the fight become," Curzon recalled, "that even panic-struck and frightened pilgrims appeared at last to have been more intent upon the destruction of each other than desirous to save themselves." Curzon, "tearing and wrestling with a thin half-naked man whose legs were smeared with blood," barely escaped. More than three hundred were killed. Some were found still upright, the life crushed out of them by the press of bodies. Curzon was amazed to discover the next day that people were going about their business as usual in the parvis, as if nothing had occurred; only the occasional distant cry of mourning hinted at the awful events.

The politics of race and religion loves to use the spectacle of processions and ceremony as gestures of solidarity and displays of bragging rights. It is depressingly predictable that the church in Jerusalem should be fully part of this politics of the street.

The decorations on the inside of the dome of the rotunda were only recently completed. The dome has a fiberglass casing (the modern materials here are less jarring than the steel casing of the edicule), and already the bright white finish is stained with candle smoke. The committee to decide on the design was set up in 1927 and consisted of representatives of the major groups in the church. The standard Greek image of Christ Pantakrator was not acceptable to the Latins or the Armenians, of course, but after seventy years a potential standoff has finally been averted in what seems to me a wonderfully ironic way. The heads of the four Gospel writers decorate the pillars (as in so many churches of varying denominations), but the huge central tondo represents the sun with twelve rays emerging from it. The design was created by a suitably multicultural figure, an Anglican from Armenia living in California. The official story is that the twelve rays represent the twelve apostles. But to any historian of iconography this looks like nothing so much as the familiar late Roman image of Sol/Helios, the Sun God, whose presence in Jewish synagogue mosaics has so upset the Orthodox (who always wish the past were as pure as their fantasies for the future). In order to escape the interchurch conflicts, the authorities seem to have agreed on a pagan symbol.

At the rear of the edicule is a little chapel that is the small, lovingly tended, and garish space allotted to the Coptic monks, the Christians from Egypt. This chapel is rarely empty because, it is said, even this little spot might be taken from the monks by their more powerful neighbors, should they ever leave their post. Usually a single, sadly dignified Copt tends this shrine night and day. When it is left, it is bolted, padlocked, and covered with more security than any celebrated artwork. Directly behind this shrine is a more rough-hewn chapel in the wall. It is dark—lit by a single light bulb—with a mud floor and a collapsing altar. This is the Chapel of Nicodemus. To the rear of the chapel is a first-century tomb, identified as the tomb of Joseph of Arithamaea by those who wish to tie every element in the region to an element of the Gospel story or its medieval expansions. The chapel is so run down because it is owned by the Armenians but leased to the Syrians (that is, Syrian Christians, one of the oldest sects of Eastern Christians), and neither side can agree who has the responsibility for any repairs; nor is either group willing to cede such responsibility to the other. When the light bulb blew, a crisis loomed. Both the Syrian and the Armenian patriarchs phoned the Israeli state Office of Religious Affairs to claim the right to change the bulb, each saying they would fix it in the morning. The official went down to the church at dawn, and "did what I had to do. Do not ask me what I did . . ." He then returned to his office and phoned the Armenian patriarch and complained, "Why did you make me waste my time and come down to the church? The bulb is fine!" He then phoned the Syrian authorities and said, "Why did you make me waste my time and come down to the church? The bulb is fine!" Thus the crisis was averted. How many religious officials does it take to change a light bulb. . . ?

The Armenians were also involved in what must be the most ridiculous dispute between the groups. At Easter 2006, the toilets in the Holy Sepulchre became blocked. The toilets had been built in the nineteenth century for the monks who live in the Sepulchre all year round, but with the increase in tourism, they had become increasingly stretched. The blockage started to release sewage into the church. The Armenians refused to allow the plumbers to get to work until an outstanding disagreement with the Greeks about the Holy Fire ceremony was resolved. Holy Week proceeded in the most unsanitary of conditions. Even the public health officials wouldn't intervene in the politics of The Agreement. The Greeks huffed, the Armenians were almost apologetic—but the foul-smelling standoff continued.

From the Chapel of Nicodemus, you can walk back past the edicule into the catholicon. The catholicon is the center of the Greek Orthodox community's religious space, where the regular services take place as well as many of the most important ceremonies (Figure 6). At the far end of the mosaic floor, up the shallow steps, is the ornate *iconostasis,* a screen of icons that is a typical feature of a Byzantine church: it separates the nave, where the worshippers are, from the sanctuary with the altar, where the priests' most sacred rites take place. The *iconostasis* is especially splendid here. To the left is the Jerusalem throne, to the right the Antioch throne, for the relevant church leaders. But the most surprising object in the catholicon is the small marble dais in the middle of the floor, often covered with a little forest of candles. This is the *compas* or *omphalos,* the stone that marks the center of the earth.

Figure 6. The catholicon, the central chapel of the Greek Orthodox Church in the Church of the Holy Sepulchre. In the foreground is the *compas* or *omphalos*, the traditional center of the world.

The *compas* is one of the images highlighted again and again in representations of the church in the medieval period, but it is hardly even noticed by tourists today. On medieval maps, the church where Christ was crucified and buried was the literal and metaphorical center of the world, and this small stone plinth was the visual, physical demonstration of that centrality. Once the world is seen as a globe, this idea of a midpoint becomes conceptually rather difficult. Any classicist, however, will immediately hear a disconcerting echo of ancient Greek religion here. Delphi, in Greece, was always said to be the center of the world, discovered when Zeus let two eagles loose from opposite ends of the world, and they met just where Apollo's temple stood. A stone marked that spot and was called the *omphalos*. Perhaps we see here the Byzantine Christians' appropriating a celebrated pagan religious symbol into their own cartography. Medieval Christianity is for most modern Christians a very strange beast indeed—not least because the Reformation and the Counter-Reformation, as well as the Renaissance, spent a good deal of intellectual and emotional effort separating modernity from its medieval shadows and superstitions (as the standard story has it). The sheer misery of the Black Death (which killed a quarter of the population of Europe), the sheer brutality of the Crusades, the sheer difficulty of enjoying scholastic argumentation, do result in a modern thankfulness just not to be there. But the inheritance is deep in Jerusalem's physical fabric and is regularly lurking in the stories that explain the where and why of the Christian buildings. The *compas* is a good spot to reflect on how religions change as the world changes, and how old physical objects consequently come to tell sad tales of passing and loss as well as of permanence.

As we continue out of the catholicon and back past the edicule, we enter the territory of the Franciscans, also called the Latins, or the Roman Catholics. The spatial divide is instantly visible. The stone flagging becomes black and white marble paving: there is a hard edge between the communities. (The floor is fifteenth-century Venetian marble but was only uncovered in the 1970s. Concealment and revelation are as much a part of the architecture in Jerusalem as they are of the religion.) In this chapel alone we can see an organ. The shaven monks in their brown habits contrast immediately with the Greek priests in black with their long beards. It is as if we are in a European church. The Latin community in the Church of the Holy Sepulchre arrived later than the Greeks and the Armenians—its presence was established only after the crusader capture of the city in 1099. But especially in the nineteenth century, the European powers of France and Italy in particular engaged in heavy political lobbying to increase the power of the Catholic Church in Jerusalem, and the Franciscans were at the forefront of this power play. The consular files of this period are full of reports of shenanigans between the representatives of the European countries, all tied up intricately with elaborate diplomatic protocols. This is now one of the quietest parts of the church. It even contains a strange recollection of the Latins' close connections with the marauding crusaders. In a dingy cupboard of the sacristy the Franciscans keep the sword and spur of Godfrey de Bouillon, leader of the first Crusade. It is a relic carefully unpublicized by the monks these days.

From here we will walk around the north end of the church toward Golgotha. This part of the building is gray and underused, though since almost all the ceremonies of the different groups involve elaborate, ground-staking processions, we are following the route of many a glorious parade. The area is murkier than it should be because of yet another mind-boggling piece of aggressive modern building. In the 1970s, the Greeks decided to erect two huge concrete walls on either side of the catholicon. One forms the backdrop to the Stone of Unction and is decorated with a modern mosaic mural of undistinguished quality. The other is grimly visible here. It is a bare, concrete lump that blocks what used to be

the views right through the church. Since these walls were built by
the Greeks on Greek-owned religious ground, neither the other
sects nor the Israeli government had any recourse. It is an aesthetic
disaster.

Even in the half-light, this is one of the most interesting places to
see the effect of the crusader redesign of Constantine's compound.
If you stand under the pillars and look up, you can see exactly how
their new walls were just jammed up against the old columns of the
Constantinian cloister. The back stones are the Constantinian cloister, the front, the new wall of the crusader apse. Both now are inside the walls of the current church. This church displays its opportunistic reconstructions, ancient and modern, like the unconcerned
nakedness of a child. To the modern eye, with the contemporary
ideology of conservation and authenticity, this will seem either a
wonderful, almost post-modern collage, or a further sign of the
confusion of this building and the people who look after it.

BELOW AND ABOVE

As we come to the east end of the church, past the Chapel of St.
Longinus, named for the soldier who pierced Jesus' side with a
spear, broad stone steps descend to the right of the little Armenian
Chapel of the Division of the Holy Robes, sometimes called the
Parting of the Raiments, to memorialize the moment recorded in
the Gospels when the Roman soldiers divided up Jesus' clothes as
booty. These steps lead down to the Chapel of St. Helena, and as we
reach the bottom of the steps we are in Armenian-owned space. On
the walls of the stairway down, medieval pilgrims have carved crosses
to record their safe arrival: the Armenians are especially keen on
marking their walls in this way, as we will see when we get to their
cathedral of St. James (Chapter 4). The Chapel of St. Helena takes us
below ground level, but there is a small dome in its center that opens
out to the roof above. The chapel is dominated by the large mosaic

on the floor, which looks at first sight as if it might be antique, but which was actually constructed in the twentieth century by a female Israeli artist, Hava Yofe (when you look, the animals are most obviously modern in their representation). As she finished the work and was doing her final clean and polish of the stones, a guide came in and told his troop of tourists to look at the fifth-century mosaic. History is quickly fabricated . . . The mosaic depicts a politically charged vision of the destroyed towns and churches of the Armenian homeland, assaulted by the Turks. The image of Noah's Ark is prominent because it came to rest on Mount Ararat, which is in Armenia (as the Armenians love to say). Politics and religion are intertwined everywhere in the Church of the Holy Sepulchre, but here, more obviously than elsewhere, twentieth-century national politics dominate the ecclesiastical imagery.

There is a small grill on the left-hand wall of the Chapel of St. Helena as you enter. It is usually locked, but an Armenian religious official in the Armenian sacristy, back by the door from the parvis, may open it if asked. (Sometimes the key "cannot be found." If the grill is opened, it is customary to make a financial donation to the church by leaving a few coins on the bench inside the sacristy.) A staircase behind the grill leads down to the Chapel of Varda, an Armenian military hero and saint from the fifth century, which contains the most fascinating inscription in the whole church. Drawn on the wall is a rough representation of a boat, under which is written in clear Latin "Domine ivimus," "O Lord, we have gone." Psalm 122 begins, "I rejoiced when they said unto me, 'we will go to the house of the Lord'": "in domum domini ibimus" (in Latin). The graffito seems to answer the psalm: here in the house of the Lord we can say, "Lord, we have made the journey." The inscription may be as early as the second century but is no later than the fourth. That is, it is either from the earliest days of Christianity, before even Constantine's building, indicating that this was already perhaps a site of Christian worship. Or it may be from the church as built up by Helena and Constantine—and one of the earliest relics of the church on this site. Does it record pilgrims taking their farewell or marking their arrival? Christians going into exile? Or does it have some symbolic meaning? Is the mast broken or furled? It has even been suggested (inevitably) that it is not a Christian memento at all, and that "domine," "master," refers to the owner of the boat, addressed by his sailors (a rather relentlessly nonreligious reading that perhaps does not pay due attention to the location of the object or the echo of the psalm). The image remains poignantly mute, despite its words. But, as so often with graffiti, it is easy to feel a closeness to the ancient Christians who memorialized their passing here with a simple picture and haunting phrase.

From the Chapel of St. Helena you can descend further, to bedrock, into the Chapel of the Invention of the Cross. This roughhewn area is actually a second-century quarry (the stonemasons' marks are still visible on the walls), where Helena is said to have found the cross—hence "the Invention" ("inventio" means "discovery" in Latin). A life-size statue of Helena holding a cross is placed by the altar on the left as a simple reminder of all this. A builders' workplace, sanctified retrospectively by a dubiously attested religious history, for the political purposes of the nascent Christian Empire . . . But that is Jerusalem.

Back up the steps, we can now finally proceed, past the Chapel of the Derision (an altar to memorialize the deriding of Jesus by the mob), up the stairway by the south wall, to Golgotha itself, or Calvary (to give it its usual English name; Golgotha is the original Hebrew name for the place, as the Gospels indicate). The rock itself is under glass (beneath the altar there is a hole through which you can touch it), and the small chapel is owned and decorated by the Greeks with glittering lamps and icons and an image of the Crucifixion. Next to it is the Latin Chapel of the Nailing of Jesus to the Cross, with a restrained twelfth-century mosaic of the nailing on the ceiling (the one behind the altar is modern), and a sixteenth-century silvered bronze altar from Florence, donated by Ferdinand I de' Medici. The juxtaposition of these two chapels, so different in style, crammed onto the small outcrop, vividly captures the underlying tensions of ownership and religious authority evident everywhere in the church. The pope visited Jerusalem in 1964. He wished to pray in the Greek chapel by the foot of the cross. The Franciscans asked the Greek authorities for permission. They asked for the request in writing. And then turned it down. The written application was demanded, explained the Greeks gleefully, so that they could have in writing the pope's recognition of their prior right to this chapel. Even more pointedly, the Greeks asked for an apology from the pope for the crusaders' violence. The crusaders, Northern Christians, did not recognize the Eastern Greeks as Christian brothers and slaughtered them, along with the Jews and Muslims, as just some other infidels.

Beneath these chapels, also under glass, is a split rock said to be the tomb of Adam, the first man. According to an ancient tradition attested as early as Origen in the third century, Jesus was crucified over the spot where the first man had been buried. Whatever associations this story was meant to evoke in Origen's symbolic universe, in the hands of the medieval churchmen it took a rather blunt physical shape. "How touching it was," wrote Mark Twain, adding his own sense of humor to Protestant cynicism in his travel book *The Innocents Abroad,* "here in a land of strangers, far away from home, and friends, and all who care for me, thus to discover the grave of a blood relation."

Nonetheless, for all the aesthetic limitations and mythical nonsenses of this place, it is impressive to see the pious passion of the Ethiopian monks and nuns, in their startling white robes, rolling on the ground in humble devotion before the site of Jesus' Crucifixion, or the Russian pilgrims in black, kneeling tearfully. Part of the continuing difficulty of the Church of the Holy Sepulchre for a historian, tourist, or pilgrim is the clash between tawdriness and transcendence that each visitor has to negotiate. Mark Twain in general saw "clap-trap sideshows and unseemly humbuggery of every kind" in the Church of the Holy Sepulchre, but even he wrote with a nice mixture of yearning and irony, "Oh for the ignorance & the confidingness of ignorance that could enable man to kneel at the Sepulchre & look at the rift in the rock, & the socket of the cross & the tomb of Adam & feel & know & never question that they were genuine."

Before we leave the church and go out into the parvis again, we should glance at two more memorials, both of which tellingly speak to us about our changing relation to this church and its history. The first is another emptiness. Once, by the wall on the left as we prepare to leave the door into the parvis, stood the tombs of Godfrey of Bouillon, Baldwin I, and Baldwin V, three of the leading kings of the crusader forces, buried by the foot of Calvary, as rich a symbolic site as could be imagined for warriors who fought in the name of the cross to preserve this church from the infidel. The tombs have now disappeared, probably destroyed in the fire of 1808. There is no sign of them (no doubt the Greek authorities would not care to memorialize their Latin saviors). I do not know quite how I feel about this absent presence. The crusaders were violent and bloodthirsty murderers who casually and cruelly slaughtered Jews on the way to the Holy Land, and treacherously murdered thousands of Muslims when they took Jerusalem (as we will see in Chapter 2). Godfrey himself led the assault on Jerusalem. They have also been romanticized for many years, most notably perhaps by the English tradition epitomized by Walter Scott, who set chivalry, the yearning of pure love, and heroic derring-do at the heart of his image of the Middle Ages, and thereby influenced a generation of Pre-Raphaelite artists. Modern popular fiction is no less fixated on the Knights Templar and their myths. At the same time, modern Muslim rhetoric revels in hating the crusaders as the sign of all that is detested about Western power and its incursions into the Muslim world. So what would it mean to reinstate a memorial to Godfrey now? What form could it take? Perhaps the empty spot by the wall is the best solution after all, for the figure who lives so much in the myths of later imagination.

The final room is easily missed. It looks from the entrance like a set of offices of the Greek patriarchate (and that is what it is), but the rear-most room is the treasury of relics. You need to ask to go through to it, but it is worth it. The most important relic is a fragment of the True Cross. Heraclius, the Byzantine emperor, went to war with the Persians in 630 to recover this relic after it had been sacked from Jerusalem in 614. The earliest pilgrims, kissing the cross, used to bite off splinters to take home as relics; pieces were sent abroad as part of diplomatic deals; eventually—in the face of so much demand—it was declared that one of the miracles of the True Cross was its ability to regenerate itself. But you can also see the right hand of Mary Magdalene, the former prostitute; a piece of the head of the Good Samaritan; the left hand of Basil; and many other bones and relics. These were once the holiest possessions of the church, capable of miracles, and producing awe and reverence in pilgrims. Relics started to become important in the sixth century, when each major church needed its saint's body, or at least part of a body. They were transported around Europe with great pomp, not just as part of the spread of institutionalized Christianity, but as a new and significant way of expressing the relationship between man and God through the intermediary force of the saints. At that time, and throughout the medieval kingdoms, miracles attached to such relics were a fundamental aspect of the awesomeness of religious experience. We have the record of a late sixth-century pilgrim to the Church of the Holy Sepulchre from Piacenza in Italy. He records the thrill of seeing amid the treasures donated by emperors "the altar of Abraham, the wood of the Cross, the sponge and reed mentioned in the Gospel, the onyx cup which He blessed

at the Supper, Mary's girdle, and the band from her head." The Enlightenment has helped push such relics into the backroom. Miracles, which were once the bedrock of the proof of Christianity's
certain divine nature, require great care from embarrassed theologians (and have proved a fascinating topic in the history of science).
Relics even more so. When we see displayed a piece of the head of
the Good Samaritan—since when did characters in a parable, a
fiction, have a real physical existence?—we are brought face to face
with how different medieval Christianity can seem from today's religious expectations.

Yet before we feel too comfortable in our sense of the modern, it
is important to go back into the parvis and through the door of the
chapel in the corner of the left (eastern) wall—or on the right as
you face the façade of the church. Here a narrow stairway climbs
through the Coptic Chapel of St. Michael to the strange Ethiopian
chapel on the first floor, with its slim wooden pews and wonderful
African mural. The picture shows the Queen of Sheba meeting
Solomon, a story told in the Bible but much extended by later tales.
This meeting is the foundation of the Ethiopians' links with Jerusalem. Most characters in the picture are wearing sandals, but the
queen and the king sport hiking boots that stick out from under
their robes (and nicely show the value of good strong footwear in a
country where shoes are rare). The most surprising feature is the
presence of two Belzer Chasidim in the corner of the picture complete with flowing *peyes* (sidelocks) and black homburgs, nicely
emphasizing the unity of the nations at this momentous meeting.
This chapel is called the Chapel of St. Abraham because the Ethiopians believe it is the true top of Mount Moriah, where Abraham
took Isaac for sacrifice. The monks here are especially craggy and
impressive, dressed all in black, with black beards and black hats,
leaning on black staves for their mass, which seems, with its intent
African rhythms and intonations, very far from the European An-

Figure 7. The convent of Deir es-Sultan, on the roof of the Church of the Holy Sepulchre.

glican rite. But walk through this chapel out onto the roof. Here is the little Coptic church, with its Egyptian harmonies, and, when I last visited, just two monks, in silver-embroidered and cowled black robes, leading a service for no congregants but me. Here too is a tiny, walled Ethiopian convent, with small lean-tos, the occasional goat, and a straggly tree or two. There is a more open courtyard centered around the cupola of the Armenian Chapel of St. Helena. The underground chapel opens up here into another world on the roof—as the church takes us from the crypt to the open sky (Figure 7).

This Ethiopian convent is called Deir es-Sultan, and, with its little church on the stairway, it is the only part of the compound allowed to the Ethiopian community, the latest and most impoverished community to attach itself to this Christian center. If the relic of the Good Samaritan's skull offers modern Christians a difficult version of medieval Christianity, the desperately simple, poor dwellings of these pious Africans, excluded from the inside of the church, offer an equally perplexing image of modernity. There are many mirrors in which you might catch a view of yourself at the Church of the Holy Sepulchre.

Map 2

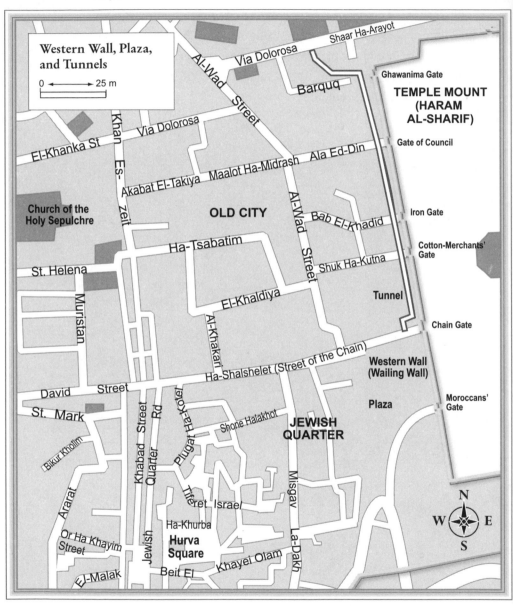

Western Wall, Plaza,
and Tunnels

0 ⟵⟶ 25 m

Shaar Ha-Arayot

Via Dolorosa

Al-Wad

Barquq

Ghawanima Gate

TEMPLE MOUNT
(HARAM
AL-SHARIF)

Khan

Via Dolorosa

Street

El-Khanka St

Es-

Gate of Council

Zeit

Akabat El-Takiya   Maalot Ha-Midrash   Ala Ed-Din

OLD CITY

Al-Wad

Bab El-Khadid

Iron Gate

Church of the
Holy Sepulchre

Ha-Tsabatim

Shuk Ha-Kutna

Cotton-Merchants'
Gate

St. Helena

Street

Muristan

El-Khaldiya

Tunnel

Al-Khakari

Chain Gate

Ha-Shalshelet (Street of the Chain)

Western Wall
(Wailing Wall)

David   Street

Plaza

Moroccans'
Gate

St. Mark

Khabad   Street

Bikur Kholim

Quarter   Rd

Plugat Ha-Kotel

Shone Halakhot

JEWISH
QUARTER

Ararat

Misgav

Jewish

Tiferet Israel

La-Dakh

Or Ha Khayim
Street

Ha-Khurba

Hurva
Square

El-Malak

Beit El

Khayei Olam

N

W ✦ E

S

2 | The Center of Jewish Jerusalem

IN 1909, SELMA LAGERLÖF WAS the first woman to win the Nobel Prize for Literature. She is hardly read these days, except in her native Sweden, and one of her great masterpieces, the two-volume novel *Jerusalem,* has the strange fate of being well known only in German and Swedish evangelical circles. For some strange reason, the second volume has not been available in English translation for fifty years. It is a pity, because this volume brilliantly traces the history of the American Colony in Jerusalem under the inspired leadership of Mrs. Spafford, from whose roof by the Damascus Gate General Gordon thought he saw Golgotha. You would have thought that everyone who stayed at what is now the rather grand American Colony Hotel would have wanted to read it.

Lagerlöf paints a deeply evocative picture of Victorian Jerusalem, and much of what she says has long resonance today. "In truth," she writes, bitterly pinpointing the intense strain of daily life in this city, "everyone is not strong enough to live in Jerusalem." And she depicts as well as anyone the internecine rivalries of the religious city from her insider's perspective: "This is the Jerusalem of soul-hunting, this is the Jerusalem of evil-speaking, this is the Jerusalem of lies, of slander, of jeers. Here one persecutes untiringly; here one murders without weapons. It is this Jerusalem which kills men."

The first chapter of volume 2 is called "The Holy Rock and the Holy Sepulchre." Mrs. Gordon (the name of the Mrs. Spafford character) on a particularly hot night climbs a hill and looks down over the city. In a mysterious scene that stands apart from the realism of the rest of the novel, she hears a long, cantankerous conversation between the Church of the Holy Sepulchre and the Dome of the Rock. The Rock begins, "None is like unto me in might and holiness," and slowly records how he remembers the whole history of the religious life of Jerusalem from the time when it was but a wild and inaccessible ridge that Abraham climbed to sacrifice his son: "I am the first and the only one: I am the one whom men shall never cease to adore." But the Rock is also magisterially dismissive of the sepulchre, in words that recall all too precisely the Victorian theological and archaeological disputes invigorated by General Gordon: "I am the great Rock, the everlasting; but what is Golgotha? I am what I am—no one can be in doubt where to find me; but where is Golgotha? Where is the mountain where the cross was lowered into the rocky ground? No one knows it. Where is the grave where the body of Christ was laid? No one with certainty can point out the spot."

The Church is somewhat petulant in her reply (which falls into Bible-translation English): "Thou oughtst to know better. Thou art so old that thou shouldst know where Golgotha lies." The Rock's reply is not wholly convincing: "Yes, assuredly, I am old, exceedingly old. But the old cannot always remember. There were many barren hills outside Jerusalem, and there were endless number of graves cut in the rock. How can I know which is the right one?" Eventually, after some twenty pages of this academic wrangling between monuments, Mrs. Gordon has had enough: "What kind of holy temples are you? You strive and contend and because of your dissensions the world is filled with unrest, and hatred, and persecution." This opening chapter's dialogue of buildings acts as a broad historical canvas against which to view the colony's own petty troubles in the religious communities of Jerusalem.

Lagerlöf strikingly dramatizes one of the defining tensions of the topography of Jerusalem: the contrast between the Dome of the Rock and the dome of the Church of the Holy Sepulchre. From many different angles, these two domes are set against each other in the skyline of Jerusalem. They are the same size—as big as could be built with the technology of the time. The Dome of the Rock was designed not just to soar over Jerusalem but to dominate the church of the Christians below.

The contrast is not merely architectural, of course. The tensions between the three Abrahamic religions are intently aimed at the holy places, their possession, their guardianship, their symbolic value. And no single place has been as important in the imagination of Jerusalem as the Temple Mount, as it is called in English, or the Haram al-Sharif, as it is called in Arabic, or the *har habayit,* in Hebrew, the "mount of the House [of the Lord]." Even to choose a name is immediately to be lined up by zealots on both sides in the current political situation. I will refer to the Temple Mount when speaking of the Jewish and Christian Temple, the Haram al-Sharif when referring to the Muslim shrines. Even this ecumenical stance will no doubt offend those who violently assert that there is only one proper name for the place. But before going any further we should note that Lagerlöf in 1906 sees the Rock as a combined Jewish and Muslim tradition, together in opposition to the institutional Christianity of the Church of the Holy Sepulchre. This shows how quickly political alignments can change. It would be hard today to construct such a religio-political team sheet. These days, Jewish and Muslim traditions would have to be set in opposition to each other. Mrs. Gordon's final hope—"God's last word to mankind is Unity"—remains as far off as ever, but the battle lines have changed.

It is typical of a Protestant evangelical like Mrs. Spafford to distance herself from the rivalries and rituals of the Church of the Holy Sepulchre. But Lagerlöf's Mrs. Gordon is no less ambivalent about the Rock—the Muslim and Jewish traditions. Her particular style of generous, hard-working, and non-preachy evangelical Christianity is repelled by the sheer cantankerousness of the religious conflict of Jerusalem and its lasting and damaging consequences. But this little dialogue also reveals how deeply conflicted Christian attitudes to the Temple Mount have been over the last two millennia. It is hard to understand the topography of Jerusalem without understanding this changing religious map.

Jesus visited the Temple—Herod's great building, which we will look at shortly. He went there to worship, to teach, and, in a memorable scene, to throw out the dealers in doves and to overthrow the money-changers' tables, a highly politicized gesture acted out in the name of asceticism and purity: prayer not ritual. As he left the Temple, his disciples tried to show him the magnificence of the stones of the buildings, and he responded: "There shall not be left here one stone upon another, that shall not be thrown down." This prophecy of the destruction of the Temple may have been written after the Temple had indeed been destroyed by Titus and the Roman legions in 70 A.D.: the argument still simmers over the dates of the Gospels, with conservative scholars in general keen to promote an early date, closer to the time of Jesus himself, and with more liberal scholars suggesting a later date; and 70 is right in the middle of the most hotly contested range. But the issue is not really whether Jesus foretold the physical destruction of Herod's building. The prophecy is actually making a more general claim that the Temple is the wrong frame for the religious spirituality Jesus is promoting.

"Think not that I have come to abolish the law and the proph-

ets," Jesus says in the Gospel of Matthew. "I have come not to abolish them but to fulfill them." Although the first Christians do seem
to have taken part in the full panoply of Jewish ritual, as did Jesus,
this idea of fulfillment came to be understood as a rejection of
Temple ritual and above all the rejection of animal sacrifice, the
central ritual of Jewish Temple religion, just as it was the central religious ritual of Greek, Roman, and other dominant cultures of the
Mediterranean. Many a Christian martyr was killed for refusing to
take part in a Roman sacrificial ritual, and some went out of their
way to make sure they could publicly refuse to participate in order
to display their belief as aggressively as possible and win the crown
of martyrdom. The Gospel of the Ebionites is not a Gospel that
made the canon, but it makes the point as bluntly as possible: there
Jesus says, "I have come to destroy sacrifice." Refusing sacrifice separated and distinguished the Christians from all the surrounding
cultures. It became a key act of Christian self-definition.

Jesus sees himself as in some way replacing the Temple. In the
Gospel of John he not only criticizes the legal restrictions of the religious exegetes of Temple law but also promises his disciples that
his resurrection after three days will inaugurate a new Temple:
"Destroy this Temple and in three days I will raise it up again." This
prophecy sees the architectural Temple as now in Jesus himself. It is
through Jesus that man will now experience the presence of God—
and not through the Temple. In the same way, Jesus takes onto himself the positive evaluations of sacrifice. The law of sacrifice is
"fulfilled" because the death of Jesus is represented as a willed loss
for a greater good, a sacrifice in the modern sense—indeed the
one primal sacrifice whereby one death brings eternal life for the
whole world. The Lamb of God is not just an image of gentleness;
it also recalls that after Jesus' sacrifice, Christians will no longer require the sacrificial lamb of the Passover ritual, which was the occasion of the Crucifixion.

The Gospels were a spur to a negative view of the Temple and its cultic activity. But it is St. Paul who made this new sense of the Temple integral to his theology as well as to Christian theology. First of all, he claimed that the Christian community itself is the Temple: "For we are the Temple of the living God." There is no need for any special building: wherever men gather together in the name of the Lord, there, now, is the Temple. The rejected building is replaced by a spiritual community. But it is not just any community. Paul seems to have been deeply influenced by the extremist ascetic sects typified by the Essenes of Qumran, whose scripture was preserved in the Dead Sea Scrolls (see Chapter 6). The Christian community, like the Essenes, should be completely pure and chaste. So Paul begins by demanding that men should not sleep with prostitutes (an easy enough moral stance, you might think): "Shun sexual immorality!" he thunders. But this leads to a more extraordinary conclusion: "Every other sin that a man commits is outside the body. But the sexually immoral man sins against his own body. Or do you not know that your body is a Temple of the Holy Spirit inside you, which you have from God? You are not your own. You were bought with a price. So glorify God with your body."

From rejecting sex with prostitutes, Paul has moved to lauding a spiritual union with God (a far harder idea to promote). It would seem—and this is the hardest idea of all—that the physical union of bodies in sex prevents a spiritual union with the Lord. For this reason the next chapter of the Letter to the Corinthians, from which I have been quoting, praises virginity as an ideal for Christians. But the image on which this whole passage relies is the Temple. Now each person's body is a Temple. You must glorify God with your body. Sex is like defiling the Temple. The Temple has become the key metaphor for Christian obsession with purity of the body. What has today become a trite catchphrase of the modern gym ("My body is a temple") in Paul's text is the most radical, world-changing theology of the flesh.

I have begun with this little theological excursus because with-

out it, we simply cannot understand the history of the Temple
Mount, or the ambivalence of Christian attitudes to it. When the
Christians took over in Jerusalem in the fourth century, they cleared
the Temple Mount of the exiguous signs of old Roman religion—
no more than a couple of statues of the emperor—and then left
the whole site as a rubbish dump. It stayed like that for more than
three hundred years. Helena and her son Constantine inaugurated a
building program to memorialize the sites of Jesus' ministry, of
which the grandest project was the Church of the Holy Sepulchre.
But they deliberately left the Temple Mount empty (even though
Jesus had taught there). The Temple Mount had to stand as a monument to the failed religion of the Jews who had rejected Jesus. Its
emptiness and desolation were a visible sign that the Jews had been
superseded by the triumphant new religion.

St. Jerome, writing in the fourth century, sums up the Christian
attitude well, though not in terms we would normally associate
with saintliness. He describes how a few Jews would struggle back
from exile to lament the destruction of the Temple: "You see a sad
people coming, decrepit little women and old men encumbered
with rags and years, exhibiting in their bodies and their dress the
wrath of the Lord . . . they are not worthy of pity." The Jews had
been punished by God—they embody in their decrepitude his
wrath—because they rejected the Messiah. Hence to the Christian
saint they are not worthy of pity, the prime Christian emotion.
Origen, the third-century theologian, so keen on chastity that he
castrated himself, had already happily declared: "What nation but
the Jews alone has been banished from its own capital city?" The
empty site where the Temple had stood proclaimed the transcendence of Christianity to the world.

This negative attitude to the physical Temple is seen throughout
the Christian tradition and spreads to the whole city of Jerusalem.
For Augustine at the turn of the fourth century, Jerusalem was only
to be the heavenly city, the perfect city of God, and any human ver-

sion was bound to be flawed, an object of false desire. Many have followed Augustine in rejecting the mundane world in the search for a heavenly Jerusalem. According to the Montanists—a Christian group of the second century, eventually stigmatized as heretics, though the passionate African rhetorician and Church Father Tertullian joined their sect—Heavenly Jerusalem would descend to earth. They even suggested that this had already happened, bizarrely enough in Pepuza and Tymion, two tiny towns in Phrygia that have played no further role in the imagination of world history. But even with such apocalyptic visions, there was no place for the physical Temple. Typically—if anything in this odd text can be said to be typical—the first-century Apocalypse of John, when it imagines a New Jerusalem descended to earth, declares: "And I saw no Temple in it." (In striking contrast, medieval Jewish apocalyptic literature, such as *Sefer Zerubbavel* or *Nistarot Rabbi Shimon ben Yochai,* does imagine the Temple descending with the city from heaven to earth. The return of the Temple is central to Jewish Messianic longing.) This language of a New Jerusalem was easily politicized. First Rome, then Constantinople, and finally Moscow were proclaimed to be the New Jerusalem, and each one of these claims to earthly authority worked against the status of the actual Jerusalem, which remained a small backwater town of the empires that came and went.

As late as the nineteenth century, books were still being written with titles like this mouthful from one George Holford: *The Destruction of Jerusalem: an absolute and irrefutable proof of the divine origin of Christianity including a narrative of the calamities that befell the Jews so far as they tend to verify our Lord's prediction relative to that event, with a brief description of the city and the Temple.* It should be no surprise that the destruction of the Temple is seen by this preacher as "the condign and predicted punishment" of "the exasperated bigotry of the Jews." In 1897, with slightly more political bite than the always obscure Holford, the Vatican declared: "One thousand eight hundred and twenty seven years have passed since the prediction of Jesus of Nazareth was fulfilled, namely, that Jerusalem would be destroyed. A rebuilt Jerusalem which would become the centre of a reconstituted state of Israel . . . is contrary to the prediction of Christ himself." It would take a great deal of work to disentangle the politics and the theology in such a statement at such a time.

This may be the dominant attitude of Christians toward Jerusalem, but it is not the only strand of Christian thinking on the Temple Mount. The great church of St. Polyeuctos in Constantinople was built around 525, and its patron, the fabulously rich noblewoman Anicia Juliana, put up an inscription that proclaimed, without any apparent humility, that she had "surpassed the wisdom of Solomon, raising a Temple to God." In the same vein, when Justinian finished Hagia Sofia he is said to have declared: "Solomon, I have surpassed you." The medieval text the *Scroll of Achima'az* tells of a disputation—a formally staged pseudo-trial, a "show debate"—between the Byzantine emperor Basil I (867–887) and Shefatiah ben Amittai, a Jew who lived in southern Italy, on the subject of whether Hagia Sofia was better than Solomon's Temple. "In which structure had greater wealth been used?" asked Basil crushingly, perhaps not thinking of Jesus' words on riches, though certainly recalling his own love of ceremony and magnificence: he was the emperor who restored images to Hagia Sofia after the iconoclasm disputes. Christian builders, it seems, could compete with the vanished Temple in their pursuit of monumental glory, for all that the theologians took a quite different tack.

But it was the crusaders' aggressively physical pursuit of an earthly Jerusalem that fundamentally changed Christian attitudes to Jerusalem and its buildings.

The first Crusade was sent by Pope Urban II in 1096, and his and other preachers' rhetorical call to arms stressed repeatedly the need to regain the actual, material city of Jerusalem and free it from the stain of the infidel's sacrilege. Baldric, bishop of Dol-de-Bretagne, wrote of the crusaders: "The children of Israel took the land by force of arms, under the leadership of Joshua: they prefigure you. They expelled the Jebusites and other peoples and settled the heavenly Jerusalem in the form of the earthly Jerusalem." The old rhetoric of Christianity is here turned inside out. Earthly Jerusalem has become the form of the heavenly ideal. In the same tone, Arnulf, chaplain to Robert, Duke of Normandy, spoke to the troops on the eve of the final assault: "This Jerusalem you see, which you face, prefigures and represents the heavenly city." He even claimed— most bizarrely of all—that "we must certainly be filled with anxiety, lest the heavenly city be locked and taken away from us if, owing to our own weakness, malevolent foreigners keep us from our house." If the crusaders do not take the all too earthly Jerusalem by force of arms, then the heavenly city will somehow be denied them. Successful war has become a religious imperative, and capturing the earthly city is now the key to the heavenly. To the earlier Christians this would have sounded like the most shocking heresy.

The Christian army did conquer the earthly Jerusalem in 1099. Their sacking of the city was horrendous. Although they had promised free passage to the Muslim residents, they slaughtered everyone indiscriminately. They set fire to buildings full of people, including the synagogue. When Raymond of Aguilers, one of the least attractive of the leaders, visited the Temple area, he is said to have walked over so many corpses that he was knee-deep in blood. Nor was this a solitary act of grotesque bloodthirstiness. Most horrifically of all, Radulph of Caen tells us how his troops "boiled pagan adults in cooking pots" and "impaled children on spits and consumed them grilled." This, remember, is a Christian describing his own troops on campaign.

Bernard of Clairvaux (who disarmingly had written of Clairvaux, "Hic est Ierusalem," "Jerusalem is here") described the crusaders as "unbelieving scoundrels, sacrilegious plunderers, homicides, perjurers, adulterers, whose departure from Europe is a double benefit, seeing that people in Europe are glad to see the back of them, and the people to whose assistance they are going in the Holy Land are delighted to see them." Bernard is one of the more worldly saints, as his cool calculation here indicates. But with the full weight of his religious authority he also gave these morally dubious crusaders carte blanche to kill (a shocking license to the modern mindset). Because they fight for Christ, he said, they kill without sin and for a glorious reward: "The soldier of Christ kills safely; he dies the more safely." This sounds all too much like the religious distortions of current terrorist rhetoric from the Middle East, where slaughter is justified in the name of a higher religious calling by clerics far from the frontline. It is perhaps hardly surprising that the medieval Arabic sources express such horror at the cruelty and violence of the crusaders. But the crusaders changed the image of Jerusalem for the West forever.

When the crusaders captured Jerusalem, they took the crescent from the roof of the Dome of the Rock, replaced it with a cross, and called it the Templum Domini, the Temple of the Lord. Although for so many years and for so many theologians of the early church, the Temple Mount had symbolically been left empty, now it had become another, quite different sign of Christian triumphalism. The crusaders regarded the al-Aqsa mosque as the Palace or Temple of Solomon (though that had been destroyed by Nebuchadnezzar, king of Babylon, in 587 B.C.). They had—they declared—recaptured for Christendom God's House. They set up shop in the Dome of the Rock; they kept their horses in what they called "Solomon's Stables"—a name that has stuck till today in most guides to the spot—they turned the area into a Christian holy site with a minimum of architectural fuss. Jerusalem's history is full of forgetting as much as memorializing. The crusaders had no memory of early Christian attitudes and no sense of architectural history. They were happy to regard the seventh-century building as coming from the far distant past. But ever since the twelfth century, it has become impossible to escape their legacy. Since then, any conflict over Jerusalem can tip into the old rhetorical oppositions. It's either Western assault and Saladin-like resistance to the attack on Islamic values; or it's the defense of Western culture against the barbarian and infidel.

The shift is made fascinatingly visible in the Christian pictures of Jerusalem. The earliest map of Jerusalem we have is the famous sixth-century mosaic found in a church in Madaba in Jordan, a copy of which is displayed prominently in the cardo in Jerusalem's Old City (Figure 8). (There are many triumphant stories of archaeology in the Holy Land; here is one of the also-rans: Bliss, the archaeologist we met briefly in Chapter 1 when he disagreed with Robinson on the issue of "pious fraud," had taken detailed measurements of the church of Madaba for the Palestine Exploration Fund, but he did not explore enough to realize what a treasure lay beneath the few inches of rubble he was standing on. (When he heard of its discovery, he immediately wrote for permission to examine and publish it, but he was refused, and sulkily left it to other, more favored scholars.) The map was made before the city fell to the Muslims. It shows clearly in white across the center the colonnaded street of the cardo, the main thoroughfare of the Roman city. The columns are spread open like teeth. The largest building, upside down on the middle of the cardo, is the Constantinian Church of the Holy Sepulchre. You can see the Dome of the Rotunda, above, as it were, the triangular roof of the basilica, with it rising steps in front. But there is no sign of the Temple or the Temple Mount.

The Uppsala manuscript map (Figure 9) is a crusader map. The city is depicted as a circle surrounded by a wall. The two Roman streets, the cardo and the decumanus, form a cross (making the whole city look like a blazon or emblem). At the bottom of the cross to the left is the Church of the Holy Sepulchre (with the citadel on the right). But at the top of the cross is the Dome of the

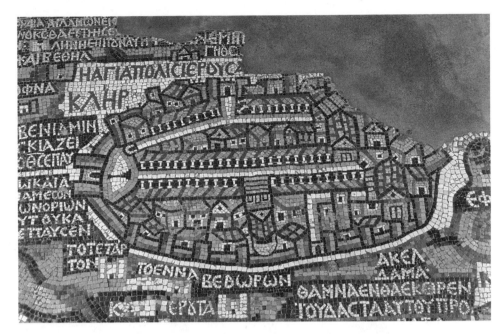

Figure 8. A detail of the Madaba map, which may have been made as early as the sixth century, discovered in the church of Madaba, Jordan, in 1881.

Rock, firmly topped with a large cross. Now the city has a new symbolic geography. The Hague manuscript map (Figure 10) is also twelfth century and depicts the city in a similar, highly formalistic way. Again, the Church of the Holy Sepulchre, now drawn in the most schematic way, is at the base of the less clearly defined cross of streets. The citadel is more clearly identified with three spears rising from among the crenellated ramparts. Above, identified by its title, as well as its domed roof, is the Templum Domini (the Latin is abbreviated to *têplum dni*); and, to the right, the Temple of Solomon, the al-Aqsa *(templû Salomonis)*. At the base of the manuscript a pair of crusaders, with their characteristic armor, flowing robes, and shields marked with a cross, put some Saracens to flight. The castle, the crenellated walls of the city, and these charging knights give this map a markedly military feel—and make the point vividly of how strong the connections are between map-making and imperialism, interwoven technologies of domination over a new world.

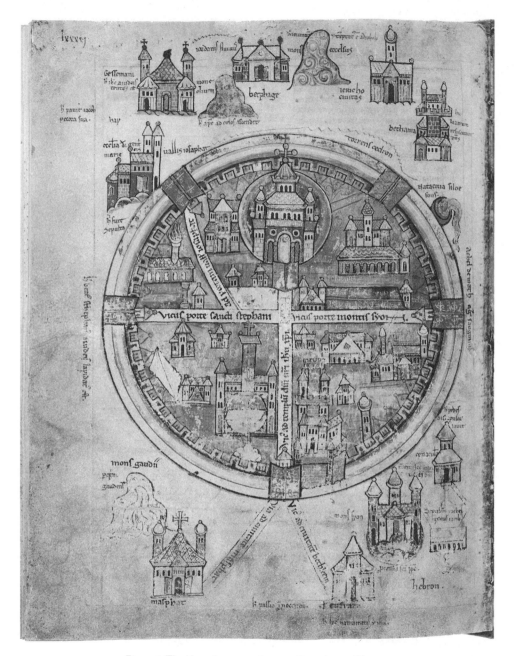

Figure 9. The Uppsala manuscript map, from the twelfth century.

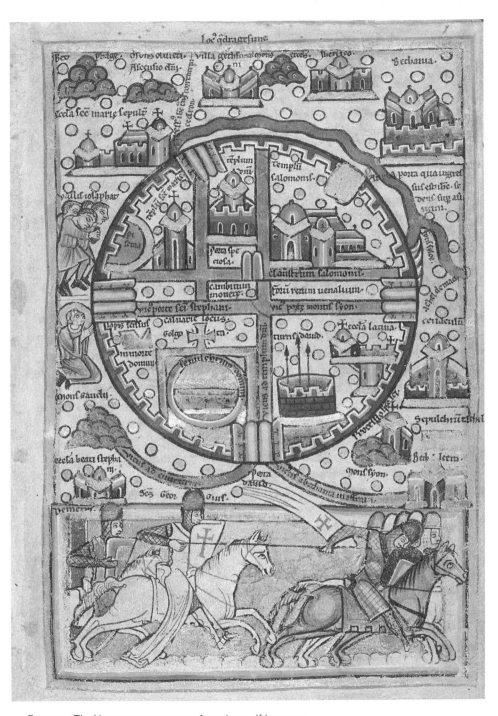

Figure 10. The Hague manuscript map, from the twelfth century.

By the sixteenth century, the crusader symbolic world had given way to a different style of map-making, but these new maps still give a fascinating sense of the artists' worldview. Zuallardo's map of Jerusalem (Figure 11) now gives us a ground plan that corresponds in shape to the city as we know it. Now there are buildings with a mathematical key (this habit of numbering items in a picture will be one of the signs of the Enlightenment's scientific organization of knowledge). But the city is schematized into a set of churches, monasteries, religious memorials, and gates. The one item—the last, number 36—to fall outside this pious topography is the bazaar, and the market is set in the top right-hand corner well outside the city walls anyway. But perhaps the most fascinating detail is the black line drawn across the top third of the city. This is marked *Linea della mura di Gerus. Antica,* that is, "the line of the walls of ancient Jerusalem." The Church of the Holy Sepulchre is placed just beyond this line. The map is also engaging in apologetic argument, explaining how the tomb of Christ could now be within the city walls, but was once outside, and is therefore the authentic site of the Crucifixion and Jesus' tomb. Maps make statements about the physical world—political, religious statements to direct the user's view of the world.

Shortly before Zuallardo's map was published, Raphael painted his beautiful *Betrothal of the Virgin.* Raphael had never been to Jerusalem, and for the impressive backdrop of his painting he drew on the representations of the Dome of the Rock as the Temple of the Jews, which the already long post-crusader tradition had made familiar in the West. It is one of the typical ironies of the history of Jerusalem that when a Christian artist wanted to paint the Jewish Temple, he modeled it on a Muslim shrine.

For many centuries, then, Christian soldiers, artists, and theologians were deeply involved with the place of the Temple in Jerusalem, and with the role of the Temple Mount in their religious and political thinking; and there are few moments in this story when

Figure 11. Zuallardo's map of Jerusalem, 1587.

conflict is not at its center. Lagerlöf's Mrs. Gordon expresses her ambivalence in the harsh light of this history, recognizing the antiquity and powerful lure of the site for her imagination, even though the old and grumpy Rock fails to acknowledge the Christianity she aspires to cherish in Jerusalem. My sense is that in contemporary Christianity there has been a turning away from the Temple Mount as a holy site to excite the imagination—except in certain

extreme evangelical sects that wish to see the Temple rebuilt to hasten the end of days. (The literature of Armageddon associated with
these groups is as difficult to read with pleasure as any genre I have
encountered.) Christians today have no shrines here or even direct involvement with the Temple Mount. Many Anglicans appear to have no burning wish even to go to Jerusalem, and the
Catholic Church has shied away from engaging openly in what has
again become the most reliably inflammable spot in the world
for East-West, Muslim-Jewish tension. But like an underground
stream, Christian engagement with the Temple, so long an unre-
solved passion, will resurface in time.

FACING THE WALL

But it is time to leave Lagerlöf's Mrs. Gordon, contemplating history from the hills outside the city, and make our visit through the
Old City to the one place that for Jews and Muslims makes Jerusalem so holy and so worth fighting over, the Temple Mount or
Haram al-Sharif.

Many routes lead down through the Old City to the Temple
Mount. For a Muslim, there are many gates into the Haram al-
Sharif from the Muslim quarter. But for a non-Muslim traveler or
worshipper, who may not enter those guarded doors, there is only
one route—to the plaza in front of the Western Wall (see Map 2).
After the tight streets of the Old City, the expanse of the plaza immediately demands a change of perspective (but whichever way
you approach, you will need to go through an armed security
checkpoint, which also affects your attitude to the spot. The informal insolence of the necessary soldiers and guards is scarcely uplift-
ing). So what is in front of us on this square? Why does it matter so?

The plaza, with its circle of buildings—*yeshivot* (religious schools),
charitable foundations, platforms where rabbis light *menorot*, eight-
branched candelabra, on the festival of *Chanukah*—is an amphithe-

ater designed to frame a wall. This is the Western Wall, sometimes called the Wailing Wall, normally termed *ha Kotel* in Hebrew or *el-Mabka* in Arabic. For Jews, it has become the single most holy and evocative space in Jerusalem. At any time of the day or night, there are Jews praying here, or just looking. (It is a great place for people watching.) For the major festivals, the plaza is filled with thousands and thousands of people, swaying, calling on God: at Shavuot (Pentecost), after studying all night, thirty thousand gather at dawn to pray, jam-packed and multinational. On weekdays and especially on the Sabbath strings of different services take place, each with its own rhythm and its own little community. People wander in and out. Rabbinical students rush past, eyes lowered. Beggars, who should not be there, try to panhandle a shekel or two. Groups sing and dance for a wedding or other celebration. So many worshippers write prayers on scraps of paper and put them in the crevices of the wall that a special bunch of cleaners come to collect them every few days and piously bury them to make room for more. It has become a central arena for the Old City.

For generations, Jews have prayed "Next Year in Jerusalem!" They have also prayed for the restoration of the Temple. These prayers, and, since the nineteenth century, a sense of national identity, have been directed toward this wall as the icon of such hopes and longings. For some Jews, the first sight of the wall is overwhelming—it is large, ancient, and invested with so much emotion. For others, the sheer press of people and the blankness of the stones give rise to feelings of confusion and doubt about one's relation to the history of a people and to the religion of the Temple. After all, many Jews live and have lived for centuries in the diaspora, would not want a return to the sacrificial cults of the Temple, and find modern alienation an easier emotion than religious intensity. One reason so many people are standing and looking and milling around this plaza is that between the fervent praying men, faces to the wall, and the tourists, uncertainly photographing the fervor, there are many people negotiating, alone or together, their own feelings about religion, politics, and history. It is a heady mix.

All too few people who go to the *Kotel* actually know what they are looking at. It is easy enough to see that the wall is an impressive edifice. The stones are huge, fitted together without mortar or ties, and the wall rises twenty-eight courses high (only the bottom seven layers are from the ancient Jewish construction; the remainder are from later Muslim repairs). The original would have been higher still and topped with a columned portico: Josephus, the ancient historian who saw the compound's construction, describes how dizzying it was to look down from its immense height. Even more remarkable is the thought that there are actually another seventeen courses below ground still covered, down to bedrock. The wall also stretches for hundreds of meters to the north, though here, too, it is buried under the housing and detritus of centuries. Since the walls are so impressive, and since there is always a tendency to associate size with significance, many visitors are all too happy to think that the *Kotel* is the wall of the Temple, and major foundations like the Western Wall Heritage Foundation proudly declare that this is indeed the last remnant of the Temple. But this claim is simply not true, and it is an ideologically motivated fib, which is all the more regrettable because it is so unnecessary. The story here is riveting enough, without reaching for false religiosity.

THE TEMPLE

Once again, we need a basic history to appreciate what we are looking at—though as with the Church of the Holy Sepulchre, we will find that bitter disputes have a way of overtaking the story. We will then need to look at what is one of the great archaeological adventure stories of the nineteenth century (and beyond).

The First Temple, according to the religious tradition inscribed in the Books of Kings and Chronicles, was built by King Solomon.

King David, the father of Solomon, united the two kingdoms of Judah and Israel and made Jerusalem, captured from the Jebusites, the capital of the new state (the date for all this is standardly given to be around 1000 B.C., but it is, of course, much argued about). King David's life is told in remarkable depth in the Bible, from his youthful killing of Goliath, through his passionate relationship with Jonathan, his violent desire for Bathsheba, to his killing of his own son, Absalom, and his turbulent rule over the united kingdom. (The combination of beautiful songs, political shenanigans, a wild sex life, and family tragedy make him a natural hero for modernity, and David attracts more novels and poems than any other biblical figure.) The Psalms transmitted in his name remain the basis of Christian and Jewish liturgy, and in religious tradition, despite the excitement of his life story, he embodies the power of pious prayer as well as the achievements of the greatest of kings. *David melech, melech Yisroel,* "King David, King of Israel," is the most familiar of party songs at Bar Mitzvahs and weddings, though no one dancing and clapping thinks about the full life story of David. David brought the Ark of the Covenant, the most sacred object of Israelite religion, to Jerusalem. It had been temporarily housed in a shrine some eight miles from Jerusalem, after it had been regained from the Philistines who had captured it in war. David led the procession that escorted the ark to his new capital, "leaping and dancing before the Lord," much to the shame of his wife, watching from a window, who didn't like the idea of the king kicking up his skirts in public, and who was cursed with barrenness for her snootiness, as the rabbinical stories have it.

The politics of this move seem clear enough. Jerusalem, poised between Judah in the south and Israel in the north, was to be the new administrative and religious capital of the kingdom. As the Book of Samuel tells it, David intended to build the Temple as the culminating act of his program of centralization: "Here am I dwelling in a house of cedar, while the Ark of the Lord dwells in a tent!"

But Nathan the prophet prevents his plan: the Lord does not need a house *(bayit)*, he announces, but will form a dynasty *(bayit)* from David, the dynasty from which the Messiah will come. The Book of Chronicles, written much later than the Book of Kings and Samuel, gives a more sharply moralizing account. David collects the money and draws up the plan for the building. But he is not allowed to build the Temple, because he is a "warrior and a man of blood." His checkered military past and his violence prevent David from building so holy a sanctuary.

So his son, Solomon, wisest of men, gets to build the Temple. It is to be a "House for the Name of God." This is a phrase worth pausing on. In the ancient Mediterranean, temples were a normal part of the landscape, and, as far as we can see, the design of the First Temple followed in its ground plan what was a standard form for temples in Syria and Canaan. These temples usually had a cult statue of the god at their center and an altar for sacrifice outside. But Solomon's Temple, though it was a monumental building for a national religion (as many other temples also were), was a very weird building indeed. It was a Temple for the *Name* of God— which explains how you could have a temple for a God who is without bodily form and everywhere. It also explains how you can have a temple and still maintain the law in Exodus which demands that you do not make any graven image. In the central room of this building, at least when it was first built, there were two statues of cherubim (though it is unclear what these looked like, a fact that has fueled many fantasies since), and the ark was placed between them. The ark had already disappeared by the sixth century B.C., and it is not certain that there were any statues of cherubim in later constructions of the Temple. But there was no statue of God, and no ritual objects, and no special construction for ritual activity, an altar or table, say. At the center of this temple, the Holy of Holies, was an empty space.

There is a pleasingly knowing story about Pompey, the Roman

general, who marched into Jerusalem in 63 B.C. after a three-month siege. With the bluff disregard of local sympathies that made the Romans what they were (and has all too often characterized the rulers of Jerusalem), he walked straight into the Holy of Holies. This sacred space could not be entered except by the High Priest, with many ritual precautions, on one day of the year, the holiest of days, Yom Kippur, the Day of Atonement. But Pompey walked straight in, we are told, to see what he no doubt expected to be a glorious statue to match the significance of the Temple for the Jewish people. Romans regularly took cult statues of other cultures and transported them back to Rome in triumphant appropriation. He was amazed to find nothing there and remained baffled by the whole experience. This story is told by Tacitus, the Roman historian, but it is retold by the Jews. History is not always controlled by the victors. The contrast of the emptiness of the shrine and the practical man of war's confusion is eloquent—and for once allows the non-material its moment of assertion over the powerful realities of war and conquest.

As Jews continued to lament the loss of the Temple over the centuries, the Holy of Holies, as the place where the spirit of God is made manifest, became the object of intense longing. The Zohar, a mystical text of Kabbalah written down in thirteenth-century Spain, imagines how the Shehinah, the divine spirit in its female aspect, laments the destruction. It depicts the Shehinah returning by night to the Holy of Holies, where she remembers her unity with the Godhead in terms that disturbingly echo the erotic poetry of the Song of Songs:

> At midnight, the shehinah enters the Holy of Holies
> and sees it destroyed and the place of her dwelling and
> her couch defiled . . . She cries bitterly, raises her voice
> and says, "My couch, my couch, the place where I used
> to dwell . . . My husband would come to me and lie in

my arms and all that I asked him, and all my requests he would fulfill, and when he came and made his house with me, and took delight between my breasts . . . Do you not remember the days of our love, when I would lie in your arms?"

The empty center of the Temple becomes here a place filled by the kabbalists with an eroticized image of the yearning for the presence of God. This mysticism is not mainstream Judaism, but it does capture something of the emotional investment and sense of loss that runs throughout Judaism's recollection of the Temple.

But it is not only its empty center that makes this temple a surprising building. Even more surprising is that this was also the only temple in the kingdom—the one and only place where the major cultic rituals of the religion could take place. Every citizen was required to come up to Jerusalem three times a year for the major pilgrim festivals; every citizen had to pay the Temple tax. The most pious kings of Israel, Hezekiah and Josiah in particular, even tried to stamp out *all* other signs of religious worship outside Jerusalem. This is an absolutely staggering gesture of religious centralization, quite unparalleled in the ancient or modern world. It helps explain why the Temple is often called *hamakom,* "the place": it is indeed the one and only place invested with the power to mediate between man and God, the one and only place where man can through religious ritual experience the presence of God. It also helps explain why Jews have so much invested in this place. It is, in religious terms, *the* place.

We have a description of the construction of the Temple from the Book of Kings, which paints a portrait of a glorious building, glittering with gold and resplendent with cedars from Lebanon, a monument to the royal status of Solomon, as well as a glorification of the God of the Israelites. We are given figures for thousands of workers and an immense expense. But the building itself was not huge: sixty cubits long, twenty cubits wide, and thirty cubits high. It might seem unhelpful to give the figures in cubits, but one of the great arguments in biblical archaeology is just how big a cubit is. The exact position of the Holy of Holies, as well as the size of the whole building, turns on such measurements, and for many archaeologists it has become an obsessive bone of contention—as it was for Isaac Newton, who spent years calculating the dimensions of the Temple, as his papers in Trinity College, Cambridge, reveal, a task he undertook more successfully than most contemporary theologians. (This obsession is catching, too: the first time I saw the model of the Temple in the Western Wall tunnel complex, which we will come to shortly, my immediate reaction, rather sadly, was, "They have the wrong cubit for their scale!") But if we were to say that the First Temple was about thirty meters long, ten meters wide, and fifteen meters high, it would not be too misleading. If you include the walls, porches, and porticoes, then the whole structure is about fifty meters long and twenty-five meters wide—the size of an Olympic swimming pool or, to give a more pertinent parallel, two-thirds the size of the Parthenon.

Figure 12 is a scholarly attempt to present a ground plan of the Temple. It is a simple rectangular structure. The front was flanked by two pillars, Jachin and Boaz (names that play a great role in Freemasonry), and steps led up to the porch and further steps from the *hechal* (sanctuary) to the *dvir* (inner sanctum). Around the Temple was a courtyard, with the altar and other monumental and costly ritual paraphernalia. This First Temple, Solomon's Temple, is the model for all other temples, spiritual and physical, built over the centuries, and is foundational for all the emotional and political investment that this site invokes. It is Solomon's Temple that appears on the crusader maps, as we have seen, though it had disappeared seventeen hundred years before.

Solomon's Temple was destroyed by Nebuchadnezzar in 587 B.C., when Israel was conquered by the Babylonians, as we are also

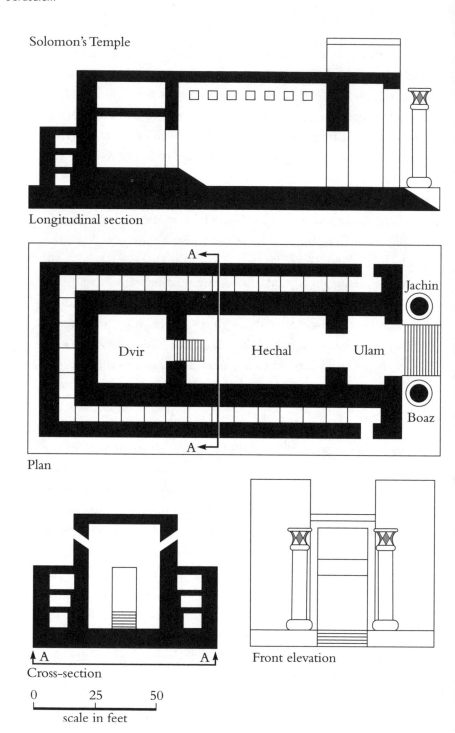

Figure 12. Historical reconstruction of the ground plan of Solomon's Temple.

told in the Book of Kings. The Israelites went into exile, where, as the psalmist puts it, "by the Rivers of Babylon, I lay down and wept, as I remembered thee, O Zion." There is no material evidence surviving today for the First Temple or for its destruction. Even the Book of Kings, which describes the Temple's construction, was completed after the destruction and is tinged with nostalgia for a lost period of Israel's greatness. Again, as we found with the authenticity of the site of the Church of the Holy Sepulchre, from the nineteenth century onward skeptical historians have not found it hard to question whether the image of a building covered with gold is just the dream of a glorious past for a downtrodden people. Some recent Muslim writers have taken this a step further, denying that there ever was such a Temple at all, despite the role of Solomon in their own religious roster of prophets, and the evident recognition of the Temple at this spot in early Muslim writing. Their claims are so obviously motivated by a desperate contemporary ideological need to disprove any connection between the Jews and the land of Israel and the Temple Mount in particular that it would be unnecessary to take them seriously, if such myth writing did not add to the entrenchment of violent extremism in the region. (There has been talk of a crisis of faith or a crisis of belief from the middle of the nineteenth century in particular. Jerusalem's problem is rather a crisis of doubt: far too much misplaced certainty.) But such wild mythic invention should not detract from the fact that Solomon's Temple has been the object of imaginative reconstruction for many centuries, and from our earliest sources.

The Jews returned to Jerusalem thanks to King Cyrus (though plenty stayed in Babylon, where they had made homes). The Persians conquered the Babylonians, and part of their imperial policy was to publicize widely their generosity to the communities uprooted by the former rulers. Hence we have the Cyrus cylinder, a cylindrical, clay cuneiform record, now in the British Museum, which proclaims how Cyrus returned the gods stolen by the Babylonians to their proper temples. The resettlement of the Israelites was part of this policy, though Jerusalem is not mentioned as such on the Cyrus cylinder. (Harry S Truman, the American president in 1948 when the State of Israel was founded, was introduced to a delegation as the man who helped create the State of Israel. "What do you mean 'helped create,'" he snapped. "I am Cyrus, I am Cyrus!") The return picked up steam under the rule of King Darius, and the Israelites, led by a shadowy figure called Zerubbabel, began to rebuild the Temple, a project finished in 515 B.C. This Second Temple was not as grand a prospect as the first. The biblical Book of Hagai, like all prophetic texts, has great hopes for future glory, but it remains unimpressed with the Second Temple: "Who is there left among you who saw this House in its former splendor? How does it look to you now? It must seem like nothing to you." This building, however, stood five hundred years and was the central site for worship in Israel in this great era of the formation of the Jewish people. One Torah, one Temple—a single Holy Law and a single center of religion—were the defining elements of Jewish national culture and identity. This process of national formation also bolsters the Jewish attachment to the site of the Temple.

This brings us to Herod. Herod is a character to conjure with. He was an Idumenean who married into the ruling Hasmonean elite and, through the backing of his Roman patron, Marc Antony, and later of Augustus, became ruler of the province of Judaea, which he governed for thirty-four years until his death in 4 B.C. His life is as lurid as that of any royal figure in this turbulent period. He had eight wives and many children, several of whom he executed for plotting against him. He was particularly obsessed with his second wife, Mariamne, whose grandfather and brother he had also killed in pursuit of the throne. (His first wife, Doris, has not really provoked gossip or historians, then or now.) Mariamne so excited his sexual passions that he allowed her free rein, and she regularly insulted him, bullied him, and even refused to sleep with him, as

Josephus, the contemporary historian, fascinated and repelled by Herod in equal measure, tells us with salacious horror. Herod had to visit Rome, and he left a trusted guard the instruction that if he should die in Rome, Mariamne should be put to death. The guard told the tempestuous queen of the king's order to prove to her how much the king really loved her: he could not bear to be separated even in death. When Herod returned, Mariamne attacked him for having given such a cruel order. He was convinced that the guard would have revealed this instruction only if he had slept with Mariamne. The guard was put to death immediately and the queen was put on trial for adultery. She was convicted by the additional malicious evidence of her own mother and Herod's sister, who hated her airs and graces. Once she was put to death, however, Herod mourned her all his days—and later stories have her body embalmed in honey, and the king weeping constantly over her remains.

Sensational novelistic stories like this abound in Herod's biography, and it is typical that the massacre of the innocents, as told in the Gospel of Matthew, is blamed on Herod. (This tale of mass infanticide does not occur in any other source, however, even those that excoriate Herod.) But Herod was a monumental builder. He built the fortress of Masada, whose myth has proved so important for the formation of military idealism and the macho psyche in Israel. He built Caesarea, the new capital named after his patron, the Caesar in Rome. And, above all, he built the Temple Mount and a new Temple for the Jews. This was a building project, as Josephus astutely remarks, "great enough to assure his eternal remembrance." Herod's explicit reasoning was that Zerubbabel's Temple fell short of the dimensions and grandeur of Solomon's Temple. The people were aghast at the thought that he might destroy the Second Temple and not finish the new project; so he collected all the materials before starting work and trained priests to do the building in order to satisfy every religious qualm. But it is indeed a project "great enough to assure his eternal remembrance." Herod is known as Herod the Great because of his Temple.

It is an outstanding engineering feat. The Second Temple had been built on a small platform. To build his Temple, Herod redesigned the geography of Jerusalem. He built a massive platform—the size of twelve soccer fields, 144,000 square meters. He had to cut away the side of a hill to make space for the platform. The platform was supported by four huge retaining walls, each built of Jerusalem limestone blocks. Each stone block is faced on the outside and has a chiseled border between 5 and 12 centimeters broad, and about a centimeter deep. The blocks vary in size. The majority are between 2 and 5 tons, but the largest is more than 400 tons in weight, and is over 12 meters long, 3 meters high, and 4 meters wide, which would strain even the biggest modern crane. These walls are more than 30 meters high, and the foundations at all points are dug down to the bedrock. It is these stone blocks that Jesus' disciple wondered at, and which Jesus predicted to fall. Josephus, writing for the Romans, fine engineers, called them simply "the greatest walls ever heard of by man."

On top of this platform was the Temple, its courtyards and porticoes, where now stand the Dome of the Rock, the al-Aqsa mosque, and the *madrassas* (religious schools), shrines, and fountains of the Haram al-Sharif. So the Western Wall is one of these great retaining walls. When it was built it had no religious significance at all. It was a wall, which was a marvel, but its sole function was to hold up the platform on which the Temple stood. It was a totally mundane place: a street with shops ran along it, and it was one of the thoroughfares leading around to the main entrance of the Temple Mount itself.

Perhaps the earliest evidence for the Western Wall being used for prayer is found in the *Itinerary* of Benjamin of Tudela, who visited Jerusalem at some point between 1169 and 1171 on his long trip around the east from Spain, when the city was ruled by the crusaders. Most of the Jews had been expelled, but some 200 apparently stayed behind, living by the Tower of David, to work in the dye trade, over which they had a monopoly: "In front of the Dome of the Rock is the western wall," he wrote, "which is one of the walls of the Holy of Holies. This is called the gate of Mercy, and thither come all the Jews to pray before the wall of the court of the Temple." This is a confused account: the Gate of Mercy is in the Eastern Wall. But it may imply that the Western Wall was also used for prayer. When Nachmanides, the Jewish scholar known as the Ramban, visited Jerusalem in the thirteenth century and tried to reorganize Jewish life in the city, even this had disappeared. He found only two Jews, both still working as dyers, when he arrived. For the earlier Muslim period, before the crusaders expelled the Jews once more, we get a marvelous picture of Jewish prayer in Jerusalem from letters found in the Cairo Genizah (the storeroom of used and damaged documents from the great synagogue in Cairo, which gives us such insight into all aspects of medieval Jewish life). In 1026 Solomon ha-Kohen ben Yehosef explained that Jews paid a tax so that Muslims would not hassle worshippers, who prayed on the Mount of Olives and in a procession around the gates of the Temple Mount: the Gate of Mercy in the *Eastern* Wall was the most revered. Several other documents agree: the Mount of Olives and the Temple Mount gates formed the focus of public prayer. Medieval religious texts give a reason for this: the Shehinah, the (female) Spirit of God, retreated to the Mount of Olives after the destruction of the Temple. (This idea is based on a passage in Ezekiel [11.22–3] and was already familiar to Eusebius, the fourth-century church historian.) So the Jews prayed there and also lamented for the Temple around its gates. We also hear of a synagogue called "The Cave" *(al kenêsia),* which may have been in or by one of the gates, though it is unclear where or how big this synagogue was. The Western Wall is not mentioned at all.

One fascinating text suggests that immediately after the Muslim conquest of Jerusalem in the seventh century, the Jews actually tried to rebuild the Temple on the Mount. This history was written by the Armenian historian Sebeos, bishop of Bagratunik in the seventh century, and has only recently been translated into English: "The Jewish rebels . . . planned to [re]build the temple of Solomon. Locating the place called the Holy of Holies, they constructed [the Temple] without a pedestal, to serve as their place of prayer. But the Ishmaelites envied [the Jews], expelled them from the place, and named the same building their own place of prayer. [The Jews] built a temple for their worship elsewhere." This is a difficult text, but it does seem to suggest both that the Jews were still trying to rebuild the Temple in the seventh century, and that they had no interest in the Western Wall as a special place of prayer.

The *Kotel* became increasingly important, increasingly sanctified, through repeated use by the small groups of Jews who lived in Jerusalem through the centuries after the Muslim recapture of the city. The *Kotel* became then a place to pray because it was as close to the forbidden Temple Mount as possible, and conveniently close to where the small rabbinical Jewish community lived. But not because of any special sanctity *per se*. In the nineteenth century, especially after the invention of the steamboat made travel to Palestine so much easier, there was an explosion of travel literature about the Holy Land throughout Western Europe. Every book contained its vignette of Jews "wailing" at the wall: it was a prime tourist site. Some Jews would wail on demand for a few coins. The poor houses of the Moroccan quarter stretched to within a few meters of the wall, and there was only a bare alleyway where the Jews could stand and pray. This area was also used as a thoroughfare, and on occasion with conscious provocation Muslims would drive flocks of animals down the alleyway during Jewish prayer services. The population of Jerusalem in the mid-nineteenth century was small—around 10,000 in 1850, the biggest group of which by now was already the Jews—and from the 1870s at least, an absolute majority of inhabitants were Jewish. But only a few people could pray at the wall. Photographs from the period show poor Eastern Jews mainly, men and women together, praying hard up against the wall. These images, as they circulated in the diaspora, also increased the symbolic attachment of the Jews to this site. It is telling that the first modern Jew to visit the Temple Mount itself, Moses Montefiore in 1855, was unmoved by the site of the Temple and bored by the official pomp of his state visit there. But, as his diary reveals, he was profoundly affected by the Western Wall. By the middle of the nineteenth century, the Western Wall was the dominant icon of Jerusalem for the Jewish imagination. The signs around the plaza today, put up by the religious authorities, declare that the Western Wall has been the site of prayer for centuries. This is technically true, but it should be remembered that only in the eighteenth century did it actually become a generally significant place of worship.

The more interest the Jews took in the wall, the more the Muslims responded. A myth started circulating that Mohammed, when he rose to the heavens from Jerusalem, tethered his magic steed al-Burâq by the Western Wall (which is to be known thus by the Muslim community as al-Burâq wall: the Jordanians put up a sign to this effect). This story only comes into being in the late nineteenth century, and has become popular only much more recently still: older sources give a quite different spot for this brief moment in the story of the Night Journey. The myth attempts to locate the wall as a significant site for Muslim religious narrative, a claim that leads inevitably to the assertion of property rights. (This did not stop the Muslims from smearing excrement on the wall where the Jews prayed, however, or attacking the site in the latter years of the Mandate.) It is a good example of the competitive myth-making that is such a feature of the Jerusalem landscape.

Jewish myth-makers are busy today, too. It has become a commonplace among the tour guides and the official literature to encourage tourists to see in the wall the essence of Jewish identity, and to feel the history of the Jewish people in the stones. What was once a site for lamenting the loss of the Temple has become a site for the celebration of continuity. Many families from abroad and from Israel organize Bar Mitzvahs at the wall. The tunnels are sold as a journey through history back to Temple days themselves, a place where you should feel yourself "in an unbroken chain with the past" or, worse still, "as close to God as possible," which is an extremely dodgy theological assertion.

In this light, it is fascinating that Jews always speak of the First and the Second Temples, despite the fact that there are three quite separate building projects, three separate Temples—Solomon's, Zerubbabel's, and Herod's. The "Third Temple" is a term reserved for the future restoration of God's kingdom in the time of the Messiah. The Second Temple era, as it is called, runs therefore from Zerubbabel's foundation in 515 B.C. to the destruction of Herod's Temple in 70 A.D. But Herod completely destroyed Zerubbabel's building—he rebuilt the foundations and the whole building with new stones, as Josephus explicitly records, and changed the whole city with the Temple Mount. Yet it is treated as if it were a mere restoration. In part, the history seems to be told this way because the Temple of Solomon and the Temple of Herod were both destroyed by foreign enemies, with the aim of crushing the central icon of Jewish cultural and religious identity, whereas Zerubbabel's Temple was flattened by a Jewish ruler, with the aim of rebuilding the Temple in an even more glorious way. In part, however, this strange accounting seems to stem from a deep desire for continuity, or, more precisely, from a desire not to see the breaks and discontinuities in religious history. The wall is what the French call a *lieu de mémoire,* a place of memorial where a cultural identity is formed, where a national memory is invented, displayed, and propagated. So continuity is a privileged value.

Matters reached a head in the 1920s under the British Mandate. Jewish worshippers wanted to take some chairs for the elderly to sit on during the long Yom Kippur services. They also wanted to use a small barrier, a *mechitzah,* to separate male and female worshippers (as the services at the wall were becoming more strict in their formal aspect). The Muslims objected, on the grounds that the terms of agreement by which the Jews prayed there forbade them to set up such potentially permanent signs of religious activity. In 1928 Edward Keith-Roach, the British governor of Jerusalem who replaced Ronald Storrs, a committed imperial official who had little empathy with Jews or Arabs, arrived on the eve of Yom Kippur and saw the *mechitzah* in place: he demanded to know if the Arab guards had not observed what had happened. According to Duff, a British policeman who was accompanying Keith-Roach, "The cunning old men put on a show of insulted insolence and began to interpret the Jews' action as an open attempt to turn this Moslem holy place into a Jewish synagogue." The next day, Keith-Roach sent Duff with a band of policemen to remove the partition by force if necessary, even though it was the holiest day of the year for the Jewish worshippers. This led to fighting—a rabbi was carried out on the *mechitzah*—and to extraordinary outrage in the Jewish community both in Jerusalem and around the world, carefully manipulated for political rather than religious motives, Keith-Roach suspected. (Ten thousand New Yorkers passed a motion that Keith-Roach must go—though he actually did not leave his post until 1943, when asthma brought on by the stress of Jerusalem forced him to retire. His reputation in New York continued to fall. The journalist Pierre van Paassen, in what proved to be one of the best-selling books in New York in 1939, wrote damningly about Keith-Roach's response to the massacre of Jews in Hebron by Arabs, and the sight of the dreadfully mutilated bodies: "They took a hasty look around that awful room, and Mr. Roach remarked to his companion, 'Shall we lunch now or drive to Jerusalem first?'" "Stiff upper lip" was not how van Paassen judged his response.) Immediately after these scenes at the Western Wall, the Mufti, the Arab religious leader of Jerusalem, who became a close ally and supporter of Hitler, and who remains one of the most contested and indeed despised figures in recent Middle East history, ordered repairs to the Western Wall that involved driving donkeys with building materials through the services of the Jews—a calculated insult. In 1929, with equal calculation, Jews marched to the wall and waved Jewish national flags and made nationalistic speeches; Arabs, fired up by a blood-thirsty speech from the Mufti, responded with a counter-demonstration on the Haram al-Sharif that led to riots in Jerusalem and in nearby towns. One hundred and thirty-five Jews were murdered, and more than 300 injured. One hundred and sixteen Arabs died, mainly from the rifles of the British soldiers attempting to control the rioting. A full-scale inquiry was launched by the League of Nations. They published a lengthy report in 1931 which concluded that the alleyway was *waqf* property (owned, that is, by Muslim religious authorities); that Jews should have the right to pray there without let or hindrance, but that they should not blow the *shofar,* the ram's horn; that the Arabs should not disrupt services, and certainly should not drive animals through the street for such purposes. Keith-Roach felt vindicated but aggrieved. The uneasy status quo was thus maintained and uneasily marshaled by the British authorities.

When Israeli forces took Jerusalem in 1967, the exhausted soldiers ran down from the Temple Mount to pray at the wall—from which Jews had been banned by the Jordanian authorities in the divided city since 1948, though the armistice agreement of 1948 had guaranteed access to the holy sites on both sides. They said *kaddish,* the mourners' prayer, for their dead colleagues, and they wept. The *shofar* was blown. A tape of the whole occasion exists, and it is extremely moving still, forty years on—and perhaps the most celebrated scene of the Six Day War.

One of the first acts of the new government of Jerusalem was to clear away the old Moroccan buildings of the Mughrabi quarter, in order to open the plaza in front of the wall for the thousands of new visitors. Some two hundred very poor dwellings were taken over and flattened, and the inhabitants moved out. In the immedi-

ate shock of defeat, this destruction of one of the older communities in Jerusalem did not result in a heated response from the Arabs,
even from those immediately dispossessed. Yasser Arafat's family
had a house there, and even he rarely made much of this particular
loss. More recently—with the typical squabbling over the past that
makes up Jerusalem politics—it has become a bitter bone of contention: the Israeli authorities retrospectively see it as a responsible
slum clearance and a necessary part of civic planning (though the
exact chain of command for the clearance turns out to be hard to
determine), while the Arabs have made the Mughrabi quarter an
icon of colonialist destruction and cultural disrespect. But in the
first months after the capture of Jerusalem, Israelis and Jews from
around the world wandered in dazed admiration in front of the
wall, which was revealed in fresh splendor by the new prospect
from the now open space—and which seemed miraculously delivered by the sudden victory against such odds.

This long history of the Western Wall explains the passion that it
evokes in many visitors—and recent politics explain the more
cynical attempts to harness such feelings. That a wall of a platform
built by a self-aggrandizing tyrant could come to be seen as one of
the holiest places of Judaism is a fine demonstration of how Jerusalem works. Centuries of prayer and longing do invest a place with
sanctity, and understanding the history of the site does not undermine that sanctity, nor does it challenge the power and significance
of the feelings it excites. The *Kotel* is not a fragment of the Temple,
and it does not need such false hype to inspire awe or to seem important. Its own history, and its evocative place in the imagination of a scattered and oppressed and threatened people, is stirring
enough.

UNDERGROUND AT THE PLAZA

The plaza itself is still changing as archaeologists explore it. Opposite the *Kotel* at the far end of the plaza the municipality wished to

erect a new building both to help enclose the square and to provide much-needed facilities for the public space. This will not happen now. The salvage archaeology team has just made extraordinary discoveries, including a stretch of the cardo, the Byzantine Roman road, with its columns and shops, some dug into the bedrock itself. The pavement is superbly preserved. There is also a tannery—which means that this area must have been a poor district in Roman times, as the smell of urine associated with the industrial process of treating animal hides meant no rich person would live anywhere near it. There are also Mameluk and Ottoman arches. This site is still being excavated, and I cannot show photographs until it has all been published by the archaeologists, but it should be open to visitors in the not-too-distant future.

The Western Wall tunnels are the most recently opened addition to the experience of the plaza, and they are also an impressive work still being developed: new steps were uncovered by archaeologists as I was finishing this book, a discovery that will require significant re-dating of some of the elements of the constructions there. The officially published material and the official tours are less satisfactory, not least for their rather naïve demands for a rather naïve piety. The tunnels, which run alongside the Western Wall, are made up of archways, store-rooms, and other structures that were put together mainly in the period immediately after the recapture of Jerusalem by the Muslims in the twelfth century (as so often, the Jewish and Muslim levels are completely intertwined, to the dismay of those on either side who wish they were separate). It now appears that the complex includes elements from the Byzantine period also, which adds a surprising and early Christian element. These new structures had the effect of burying what was left of the Second Temple—era streetscape, and of raising the street level in the city to make access to the Haram al-Sharif easier. The tunnels were rediscovered in the nineteenth century by Captain Wilson and then explored by Captain Warren, on behalf of the Palestine Exploration

Fund. Captain Warren will reappear in Chapter 6 as one of the great Victorian heroes of Jerusalem, and the description of how these tunnels were explored is one of the adventures that won him the nickname "Jerusalem Warren" in the British newspapers.

Warren describes how he entered a passageway carved in the rock. It was full of sewage. He and his faithful assistant Corporal Birtles brought three doors with them to spread their weight. With nervous balance, they each stood on one door and passed the third ahead down the tunnel, as they made slow progress for several hundred feet: "Everything had now become so slippery with sewage that we had to exercise the greatest caution in lowering the doors and ourselves down, lest an unlucky false step might cause a header into the murky liquid—a fall which must have been fatal—and what honour would there have been in dying like a rat in a pool of sewage?" Warren's explorations put "the whole subject of the topography [of Jerusalem] on a new footing," as he himself declared with no false modesty. The Temple tunnels, now cleared out over seventeen years of painstaking work, primarily by the religious authorities rather than by Israeli archaeologists, are one of the best ways of exploring the edge of the Temple Mount in its city context.

The tunnel runs along the wall to the north (Figure 13). It passes through some cisterns (water supply is a perennial problem in Jerusalem) and some damp and musty passageways, but it also brings us to three of the most important archaeological discoveries of the Temple complex. The first is Wilson's Arch, named for Captain Wilson. The high platform of the Temple Mount, we now know, was connected to the upper city by a bridge. A road ran underneath it (Figure 14). Wilson's Arch is the remains of the support for this bridge (as Robinson's Arch at the southwestern corner is the last remains of the massive stairway that led up to the Royal Portico on the southern edge of the Temple Mount, where the money-changers and dove dealers sat). The foundations of Wilson's Arch are still in place, but the arched vault that is now visible is a much later rebuilding, as the entrance bridge was probably destroyed by the Jews during the siege of Jerusalem in 70 to prevent it from being used to attack the Temple itself. It is now used as a prayer hall. The boldness of these entrance paths is a very powerful part of the monumental design of Herod's Temple, and they add immense grandeur even to the approach to the Temple Mount.

Close to Wilson's Arch is a room that probably dates back to the Herodean period. Warren, revealing one of the motivations behind his expedition to Jerusalem, called it "The Hall of the Freemasons." (There is no evidence for the institutions of the Freemasons before the seventeenth century; but their myths insist that it all started in the porch of Solomon's Temple. And Warren, a notable Freemason, was keen to add his archaeological authority to such myths.) The room has decorative molding around the walls and a central pillar, which was actually brought in much later to hold up a shaky ceiling. No one knows what the room was used for, but it most likely had some public purpose, built as it was with such decorations so close to the Temple. Nearby, and a level down, is a superb *miqva,* or ritual bath, many of which surrounded the Temple in Herodean times, as the worshippers needed to be ritually pure before going up to make their sacrifices. This has only recently been uncovered, and it lets us see how the surrounding city was focused on the ritual life of the Temple, which loomed over its streets.

The second important archaeological discovery is Warren's Gate,

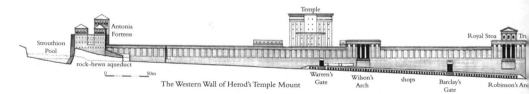

Figure 13. An artist's reconstruction of the full length of the Western Wall in Herodian times. The tunnel starts around the shops and finishes through the rock-hewn aqueduct on the Via Dolorosa, near the site of the Strouthion pool.

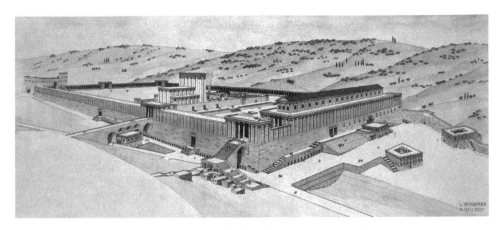

Figure 14. Leen Ritmeyer's reconstruction of the Temple Mount during Herod's time. Wilson's Arch supports the roadway in the middle of the Western Wall; Robinson's Arch supports the steep stairway in the southwest corner.

so called because it was uncovered by Captain Warren. This gate opened into a long underground tunnel, now closed, through which one climbed up to the Temple Mount from the lower street level. The same design of entrance is also evident with the double and triple gates on the South Wall. A worshipper entered from the busy street into the dark passageway, and through a set of stairs gradually rose to emerge into the bright sunlight, reflected off the polished stone columns, to be faced by the brilliant glittering white and gold of the Temple. Herod's building had its own architectural drama, which led the pilgrim from the street, to the sacred courts of the Temple precinct, and toward the Holy of Holies, the empty and forbidden center. The covered staircase behind Warren's Gate— rather than the Western Wall—may well have been "The Cave," where groups of Jews gathered to pray when Caliph Omar allowed Jews back into Jerusalem in the seventh century, and it may have been used for this purpose until the crusaders arrived and blocked the space off. This would make this entrance hall the earliest post-destruction site of communal prayer in the Old City.

Warren's Gate is the fourth gate on the Western Wall (the two walkways, named for Robinson and Wilson, and Barclay's Gate are

the others). The tractate of the Talmud called *Middoth,* "Measurements," which gives the most detailed description of the Temple
compound from rabbinical sources, says there were five gates to the
Temple Mount, and lists only one for the Western Wall. This has
produced much angst among religious archaeologists, and some
rather mealy-mouthed attempts to define the gates as some other
form of entrance, or to re-date them to a much later period. *Middoth* was written down probably in the sixth or seventh century, at
least five hundred years after the Temple was destroyed. There may
be some obscure religious thinking behind the discrepancy; it may
be a simple error or ignorance. (Certainly the descriptions of Roman religious festivals given in the tractate *Avodah Zarah* bear little
relation to any known Roman practices.) The problem of the
number of the gates is not one the tour guides to this site discuss.
It is the sort of archaeological difficulty faced only in Jerusalem,
where religious authority stands out against facts on the ground
with remarkable tenacity.

The third fascinating archaeological discovery was the Herodian
road. A broad paved thoroughfare ran alongside the Western Wall,
though it seems not to have been completed at its northernmost
boundary. Paving stones have their own romance: everyone likes to
stand where the great figures of the past once stood. More importantly for archaeologists, the discovery of this road revealed a good
deal about the circulation of the worshippers at the holy site. The
gates, the road, and the stairways on the southern side that may have
had a plaza before them are all testimony to the way in which the
compound organized the huge number of pilgrim worshippers to
the Temple Mount in the Second Temple period.

The Western Wall tunnels also go past less archaeologically exciting spots: a quarry that was used until the Herodian period; some
other passages. There is a Hasmonean aqueduct that was part of
the water-supply system to the Temple which also included the
Strouthion pool, the end of the tunnel trip. The official tour also
tries to convince visitors that the place which is "nearest to the

Holy of Holies" has some special religious or cultural significance. Not only is there a continuing dispute about where exactly the Holy of Holies was, but also this spot is some hundred meters from the Dome of the Rock, the likeliest site. It is an Umayyad—Muslim—portion of restoration, anyway. There is absolutely no evidence that it had any significance for anyone before the last few years. Nor is it easy to know whether any visitor takes such claims seriously (though you do see some people praying there). This is one of the stranger, apparently opportunistic attempts to invest a wholly unimportant section of the wall with special sanctity and religious power.

As ever, the Israeli investment in the site has produced a counter-reaction from the Muslim Jerusalemites. In 1996, the Israeli government under Netanyahu tried to open an exit to the tunnel system, near the Strouthion pool, onto the Via Dolorosa. This exit would greatly increase the tourist capacity of the site, as visitors would no longer have to double back through the narrow tunnels to find a way out. The rumor started in the Arab quarter that the Israelis were trying to dig under the Haram al-Sharif to make it collapse. In the resulting riot, seventy Arabs and sixteen Israeli soldiers were killed. After the event, the politicians and archaeologists wisely noted the lack of wisdom in the decision to try to open the tunnel into the middle of the Arab quarter of the Old City. After some quieter negotiations, this is now where the tunnels duly do provide an exit for the tourists.

It would be an obviously comfortable response to say that such rioting is merely the product of ignorance, coupled with the religious and political passions of the defeated and downtrodden, fanned by cynically manipulative politicians. And there was indeed no sign that the government had anything but the most ordinary mercantile interest in opening the new entrance. But unfortunately some Jewish extremists have indeed tried to dig eastward under the Temple Mount. Nor are they merely fringe groups. Yehuda Meir Getz, one of the rabbis responsible for the tunnel area on behalf of the Ministry of Religious Affairs, together with Shlomo Goren, the former chief rabbi of Israel, who was the rabbi who blew the *shofar* when the Western Wall was taken in 1967, and Rafi Eitan, an adviser on terrorism to three Israeli prime ministers, were all passionate in their search for the Ark of the Covenant. They believed it had been buried directly under the rock of the Dome of the Rock, and in his capacity as rabbi of the Western Wall tunnels, Getz started a dig through the Warren Gate into a cistern, with the aim of excavating under the Temple Mount. (According to one story, Goren and Getz claimed to have seen the ark, but I have not been able to trace the anecdote beyond the level of urban myth.) The dig, as soon as it was discovered, led to yet another fight between Arabs and the Israeli workers, and the operation was stopped as soon as the higher echelons of government learned about it. Getz, who prayed in the tunnels every day with his pistol on his hip, was bitter and unrepentant: "I have never felt the humiliation of Judaism that I felt today in our sovereign country," he wrote in his diary.

Incidents like this justifiably fanned the suspicions of Arabs who were already aware of the aggressive acts of Goren, who forcibly entered the Haram al-Sharif to hold a prayer service. Lunatics like Yoel Lerner and Alan Harry Goodman, who shot at Muslim guards and worshippers, were imprisoned; but the fringe groups who wish to blow up the mosques have indicated that violence is how they wish to hasten the arrival of the Messiah (and they continue to honor the lunatics' assaults). Perhaps most shockingly, the particular individuals arrested in 1985 for attempting to blow up the mosques on the Temple Mount received very light prison sentences and, in what was a highly publicized trial, even a measure of public sympathy. These groups are distinctly marginal, and very small, and carefully monitored and suppressed by the government, which has no need of such incitements. (Amos Elon, the Israeli journalist and writer, calls these yeshiva students with their machine guns and obsessive personalities "cowboys of the Apocalypse," and Thomas Friedman, the *New York Times* journalist who covered the trial, noted how their swaggering arrogance and misplaced certainties were identical to those of their terrorist counterparts in Lebanon.) But their raucous and unpleasant publicity finds supporters among extremist Orthodox religious circles, too. The Temple has excited some very noble and beautiful poetry, art, and spiritual reflections. It also attracts violence, malignant self-assertion, and a political extremism baffling and painful to liberals and outsiders. Archaeology here is constantly sucked into the storm. The archaeological exploration of Jerusalem's underground past has repeatedly ground to a halt in the face of the bitter *Realpolitik* of the street.

The archaeological garden that curls around the south end of the Temple Mount is an altogether more peaceful place, beautifully designed, and rarely full of people and passions. Yet it has some of the most important archaeological finds around the Temple Mount, and the dig itself is a story that captures the craziness and excitement of archaeology in this city. The first and perhaps most important sight to see is the monumental staircases discovered by the dig of 1967. These steps led up to the double gate and the triple gate (the Hulda Gate), which were the main entrances to the Temple Mount from the south, and which led up into the Royal Portico, the huge stoa constructed at the south end of the Temple Mount (Figure 14), which made one boundary of the Court of the Gentiles. Nearby the archaeologists discovered perhaps the most evocative new inscription to be found in Jerusalem, and a replica is now in place in the archaeological garden. It is fragmentary but reads: "To the trumpet-call building to pr . . ." Josephus explains that at the beginning and end of each Sabbath, a priest blew a trumpet to announce the arrival and the close of the sacred day from the Temple. The stone probably stood at the corner of the tower above the priests' house and marked the spot from where the trumpet's clarion was sounded. It takes us back to the ritual of the Temple as a regular part of the city of Jerusalem, and to the way sacred time was signaled in the holy city. And today, today in Jerusalem, sirens ring out on Friday afternoon announcing the imminent arrival of the

Sabbath, an echo of the ancient trumpet, sounding against the call of the muezzin and the church bells, as Jerusalem's air clamors with the noise of religion.

The remaining foundations down below the steps, marked out by the archaeologists, are largely a palace of the Umayyad period—the earliest period of the Muslim rule of Jerusalem. Although the function of the building is quite unknown, we call it a "palace" just because it was large and wealthy in its decorations. The discovery of this complex is in itself an engrossing tale of the politics of archaeology. The archaeological excavations around the walls of the Temple Mount began in 1967 under the directorship of one of Israel's most distinguished archaeologists, Benjamin Mazar, and the story of the dig has been told most amusingly by Meir Ben-Dov, one of its leading figures. He is not an impartial narrator, and his boundless self-confidence and sense of humor will annoy his opponents, but the story he tells is eye-opening. The dig was opposed by the two chief rabbis of Israel, the Sephardic Rabbi Nissim, because he was afraid that the dig might challenge the authenticity of the Temple Mount, and any threat to the faith of the faithful was dangerous. (Muslim leaders argued the same case.) The Ashkenazi Rabbi Unterman was more afraid that the ark might be discovered but that no one would be pure enough to touch it, since the Temple, necessary for the rites of purification, no longer functioned. These objections blocked the dig for a season.

Ben-Dov then hit on a plan. The Jordanians had built a girls' school over the site, though it was on some of the most fascinating remains of early Islamic Jerusalem. The school was slated for destruction, but the municipality had allowed the office of the Chief Rabbinate to use half of the rooms on a temporary basis. Ben-Dov sneakily secured permission from the mayor to move himself and his equipment into the remaining rooms (from where he started to stake out the dig and begin work). When Rabbi Nissim saw that some of the rooms of his building had been taken over for such a menial group, he was outraged. He demanded that the Minister of Religious Affairs remove Ben-Dov from the space. A screaming match broke out between government offices, officials, and Ben-Dov, who held his ground for a few days while the dig got under way. By the time the burning issue of rabbinical honor and the use of the rooms was settled, eighty archaeologists were at work.

The first major discovery was the Muslim palace whose foundations can now be seen in the archaeological garden. It was a discovery that revolutionized understanding of the earliest days of Muslim rule, as there had been no knowledge of this large building at all from written sources. Rafiq Dajani, the deputy director of the Jordanian Department of Antiquities, visited the site. "If we could leave politics to the politicians," he said, "I would heartily congratulate you on your work. The finds from the early Muslim period are thrilling, and frankly I am surprised that Israeli scholars have made them public." His remarks—as telling of the expectations of Jordanian scholarship as they are of the decency of Dajani—were overheard by a reporter, who promptly published them. Dajani was fired within a few days—another victim of the invasion of archaeology by the crassest of nationalist politics.

I said before that many people do not know what they are looking at when they see the Western Wall, and assume it to be the wall of the Temple itself rather than the retaining wall of the Temple Mount. But in a more general sense it *is* extremely hard to know what you are seeing here. Do you see a spiritual center, filled with the ingathering of a formerly dispersed people, reaching out to worship? Do you recognize a nationalist monument? How do you put together the different expressions of religiosity—and its connections with nationalism? Do you see the results of invasion and dispossession? Or return? On the plaza in front of the Western Wall is the place where the interwoven and competing claims of myth and history are most intensely felt—the constant struggle of Jerusalem, city of longing.

Map 3

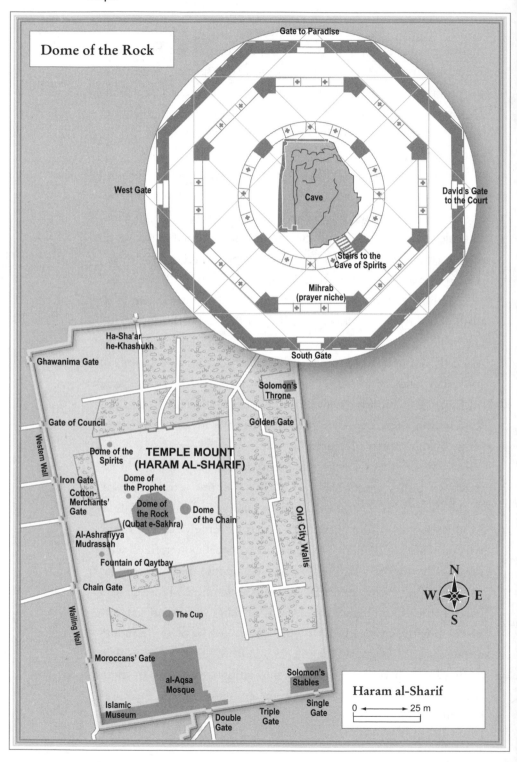

Dome of the Rock

Gate to Paradise

West Gate

David's Gate to the Court

Cave

Stairs to the Cave of Spirits

Mihrab (prayer niche)

South Gate

Ha-Sha'ar he-Khashukh

Ghawanima Gate

Solomon's Throne

Gate of Council

Golden Gate

Western Wall

Dome of the Spirits

TEMPLE MOUNT (HARAM AL-SHARIF)

Iron Gate

Dome of the Prophet

Cotton-Merchants' Gate

Dome of the Rock (Qubat e-Sakhra)

Dome of the Chain

Al-Ashrafiyya Mudrassah

Old City Walls

Fountain of Qaytbay

Chain Gate

Wailing Wall

The Cup

N
W   E
S

Moroccans' Gate

Solomon's Stables

al-Aqsa Mosque

Islamic Museum

Double Gate

Triple Gate

Single Gate

Haram al-Sharif

0 ———► 25 m

3 The Center of Muslim Jerusalem

WE HAVE TARRIED AROUND the foot of the walls of the Temple Mount for long enough. It is high time that we go up to the Haram al-Sharif. Non-Muslim visitors enter, when entry is possible, up a ramp-way from the Western Wall plaza, through another security check. There is a sign on the wall authorized by the Chief Rabbinate strictly forbidding Jews to enter. This injunction was put in place in 1968, after politically motivated attempts to lead Jewish prayer services on the Haram al-Sharif. The express reason for the ban is that a Jew might inadvertently step onto the ground of the Holy of Holies, something only the high priest is allowed to do. But a sensible degree of political expediency is no doubt part of the ruling. For many hundreds of years, entrance to the Haram was forbidden to all non-Muslims, and only a scant handful of intrepid Westerners dressed in Muslim costume dared to sneak in—or attempted, like Warren, to bribe their way in. Where Warren saw himself as an agent of civilization—that is, as we would say, he was hugely self-confident in his assertive imperialist outlook—those who attempted to gain entrance before did so more out of artistic curiosity or a sense of adventure (though an Italian who traveled and wrote under the pseudonym of Ali Bey al-Abassi was suspected of being a spy for Napoleon). The gates were patrolled by fearsome guards, black Mauritanians armed with scimitars and clubs, and tales of violent protection of the privacy of the Haram al-Sharif run through nineteenth-century travelers' tales. When a European clockmaker was required on the Haram, he was first exorcised of his Christianity and his humanity, declared a beast, and finally carried over the sacred area. Who steps on this ground has become historically a matter of intense contention, and when Ariel Sharon visited in 2000 with his entourage, an event that started the second Intifada, it was a symbolic act that was easily recognized by all the participants.

It is a remarkable space to come into. After the crowds and tight streets of the Old City, and the constant hustle and bustle of the Western Wall plaza, there is a spaciousness, calm, and brightness here, at least when the area is not filled with worshippers on their way to the mosques and shrines, at which time non-Muslim visitors are not welcome. It is a space dominated by beautiful buildings whose monumentality is elegant and sense of scale is hugely attractive. There are squares with trees, fountains, and a profusion of small domed shrines that reflect the Haram's architectural development over the centuries and give the whole compound the feeling of a spacious and wonderful garden.

The Haram slopes down from north to south, so that the Dome of the Rock is set on a platform on a higher level above the al-Aqsa mosque. The north, south, and west edges are flanked by schools and other buildings, which creates a feeling of being in a walled garden, while from the east, the view—one of the finest, with constantly shifting light and a variety of colors—stretches across the Kidron Valley toward Gethsemane and the Mount of Olives. This is one of the truly beautiful spots in the Middle East.

We come in through the Moroccans' Gate *(Maghâriba),* so called because it led to the Moroccan district, which, as we saw, was destroyed to make the Temple Mount plaza in 1967. In 2004, the wooden ramp-way leading up to this gate was damaged by a heavy snowstorm and earthquake tremors, and continued to deteriorate. In 2007, the necessary repair work was started by the Israelis. The wooden ramp was moved to the left and strengthened. The ramp had covered a small section of steep, old road, probably a fourteenth-century construction originally, part of which had also collapsed. The Israelis began the usual salvage archaeology of this last surviving bit of the Mughrabi quarter. Immediately, pictures of a bulldozer near the Haram were beamed around the world by the Arab media; Palestinian protests started; Jews were stoned in Hebron; and overheated accusations that Israel was trying to destroy the Haram started again, coupled with claims that such unilateral actions were designed to undermine the fragile peace process. It was announced that a *mihrab,* a prayer niche, had been found and thus the Jews were destroying a Muslim holy site. The Israeli archaeologists who pointed out that the work was fifty meters from the Haram, and was designed primarily to make the site safe, made little headway against the storm. For a few days, the Arabic and Western press wrote predictable columns, adding to the general air of hysteria. A webcam was installed so that everyone could see what the work was and how it was progressing. Then the archaeological work ground to a halt, as the politicians weighed in, while the archaeologists continued to labor to make the site safe.

I had been shown the damage to the ramp-way and been told about the necessary work some months before. The archaeologists who guided me had predicted the whole brouhaha, displaying the resignation tinged with anger that is such a typical sign of life in Jerusalem. But the process of protest and explanation and counter-protest had to go on like some grimly scripted dance. The site has already revealed some interesting layers of history, with remains of walls of the early Muslim period, more evidence of the Umayyad palaces that seem to have nestled below the walls here in the seventh century. The *mihrab*, however, turns out to have been built on concrete—in other words, it is a twentieth-century construction, not a medieval treasure, and is probably the *mihrab* built by the Mufti in the 1930s as part of his campaign to keep the Jews from the wall; it will be preserved nonetheless, out of local sensitivities. (The late date of the *mihrab* was not reported with the excitement that its original discovery occasioned.) One story that reflects the grim cynicism of all this is that the *waqf* actually asked the Israeli archaeological authorities to use some of the stones from the dig for repairs to buildings on the Haram, while the fuss about the dig was being orchestrated—though the deal, not surprisingly, fell though in the end. (All parties who told me the story said they would deny it if I published it.) From the Israeli side, the initial plans to rebuild the walkway included grandiose schemes to construct a huge bridge from the entrance of the plaza to the entrance of the Haram—a design that would have added a grotesque touch of flyover architecture to one of the best-known public spaces in the Middle East.

UNESCO attempted to broker a deal between the Israelis and the Jordanians, who run the *waqf* of the Haram. Twice, UNESCO organized secret "encounters" for the two sides with international mediators, but twice the Jordanians pulled out at the last minute. The Israelis eventually produced a less worrying set of plans for a new walkway (actually, and typically, five sets of plans were circulated before the final one was cantankerously agreed upon: architects and archaeologists rarely find it straightforward to agree). The Jordanians have responded with a counter-proposal. A Jerusalem newspaper published a mock-up of the Israeli-proposed walkway, which included canopies to give shade to the waiting tourists. The Jordanian proposal reproduced the fuzzy picture—and identified the canopies as tanks, to prove the Israelis' military agenda. Even though the mistake has been pointed out to them, the Jordanians have kept the misidentification in the proposal, because it represents accurately enough their fear. Indeed, because they see the Israeli plan as the beginning of some sinister further development, the Jordanians have proposed a fixed concrete edifice, sacrificing aesthetic and archaeological principles to their political fears. At the time of my writing, no solution has been agreed on. There are no heroes in this sorry story.

THE FIRST AND FURTHEST MOSQUE

As you enter the gate, immediately in front of you is a stone bench that marks the Station of Burâq (the mosque of Burâq is on your left as you enter the gate). This is the traditional site where al-Burâq, the magic steed of the prophet Mohammed, was tethered (in contrast to modern claims for the Western Wall). But turn to the right and there, against the south wall of the Haram, stands the al-Aqsa mosque, one of the two most important buildings in Islamic Jerusalem. It is a single-storey building, with seven open arches at the front, creating a narrow porch, and recessed, blocked arches around the sides, above rectangular iron windows, all edged in bright green, the color of Muslim affiliation and Palestinian nationalism. The middle arch of the façade is the largest and has a set of six recessed niches above it, and thin pillars inside the more massive doorway, rising into unfussy, geometric decorations above the door (Figure 15). The three central bays are crusader and surprisingly recall the Church of the Holy Sepulchre in design; the outside four were added in the fourteenth century by the Mameluks, to a similar model. It is a broad building, with a central, raised section leading back to a gray dome. The front roof is decorated with a parapet of delicate crenellations (added by Al-Ashraf Qaytbay in the late fifteenth century). A pair of dedicatory inscriptions on the front façade, also in recessed niches, records repairs to the building. This is the central congregational site of worship on the Haram and

Figure 15. The al-Aqsa mosque.

one of the oldest mosques in the world. Although al-Aqsa, like so much in Jerusalem, has found its current form due to centuries of rebuilding to different agendas, it remains a simple building. It has little decoration on its facings, compared with a grand cathedral or the Dome of the Rock; it has no soaring minarets or striving for grandeur, even though the inside achieves an impressive, open monumentality. A simple building, but its history is complex and deeply interwoven with the religious history of Islam and the status of its holy texts.

The seventeenth *surah* (chapter) of the Qur'an tells of Mohammed's Night Journey. The Qur'an is, as so often, oblique and even obscure: Mohammed was carried, it says, "from the sacred mosque to the furthest mosque *[al-aqsa]*, whose precincts we have blessed, that we might show him of our signs." This bare narrative, which has no precise geographical coordinates, was filled out by Ibn Ishaq, the first biographer of the Prophet, who wrote in the eighth century: "Then the messenger of God was carried by night from the Mosque of the Ka'aba to the Aqsa Mosque, which is in the Holy House of Aelia" (Jerusalem—using the Latin name, a common practice in early Arabic sources). The story is further expanded by Ibn Ishaq and by other *haddith*—stories of the life of Mohammed, passed down by tradition, which have an authoritative status below that of the Qur'an, but are nonetheless authoritative. The angel Gabriel came in the night to where Mohammed was sleeping, took out his heart, purified it, and filled it with faith and science. He kicked Mohammed awake (according to Ibn Hisham in the name of Al Hassan, it took three kicks to awaken Mohammed properly). Gabriel led him outside to where al-Burâq, a white steed, awaited. He was transported to Jerusalem on al-Burâq, and there found Abraham, Moses, Jesus, and the company of prophets. Two bowls were given to Mohammed, one of milk and one of wine. Mohammed chose the milk, and Gabriel praised him for his choice: "You have been guided to the true religion, and your community will be so guided. Wine is forbidden to you." This is why Muslims, in contradistinction to Jews and Christians, for whom wine is an integral part of worship, do not touch alcohol.

The story continues with Mohammed rising to heaven on a ladder of the finest gold. He rises through the seven heavens finally to the throne of God, where he receives the rule that Muslims are to pray five times a day. In this way, the story of the Night Journey provides the basis for two of the most publicly evident elements of Islam, abstinence from alcohol and the pattern of daily prayer.

In the early traditions of Islam, it was often argued that the Night Journey was to a heavenly city and not to a literal, physical Jerusalem. In Shi'ite literature, this tradition is particularly evident: "Abu 'Abd Allah was asked which mosques are meritorious. He answered: the mosque of Mecca and the mosque of the Prophet [Medina]. The man asked: And what of the mosque of al-Aqsa? He answered: This mosque is located in heaven, to it Mohammed was carried in the night. The inquirer persisted: People say that this is located in Jerusalem. He answered: The mosque of Kufa is better than that of Jerusalem." The polemic against Sunni lore, and the status of Jerusalem in it, is clear, especially as Kufa is a Shi'ite holy site. But gradually such interpretations were sidelined by Islamic teachers (though not by modern scholars). One such lost story is that Mohammed was asked to describe Jerusalem to the as yet not-quite-faithful audience of the Night Journey. Since he had not properly seen it in the dark, the angel Gabriel uprooted the city and brought it before the Prophet unbeknownst to his listeners. This was a popular subject for fourteenth-century Persian Islamic art, which had no problem with representing the prophet (despite the vitriolic response to modern drawings of Mohammed by contemporary Muslim protesters). The intricate dynamics of the earlier traditions of Islam are one victim of the move toward increasing fundamentalism in modern public expressions of religious belief.

Jerusalem is a holy city, the third most holy city after Mecca and Medina, in part because of this journey and its place in Islamic tradition; and in part because for the first seventeen months of Islam, as the second *surah* of the Qur'an records, Muslims were instructed to pray toward Jerusalem, before Mecca became the *qibla,* the direction in which a Muslim must face to pray ever since. Jerusalem is the first *qibla.* ("Mecca and Jerusalem are constantly linked," as one modern commentator has put it.) The buildings of the Haram are all constructed in response to these rich, expanding stories—and stories in turn swirl in new directions in response to the buildings.

The al-Aqsa mosque was built between 709 and 715 by Caliph al-Walid, the son of Caliph Abd al-Malik, who built the Dome of the Rock. It replaced a wood structure that had been built by Caliph Omar, the conqueror of Jerusalem. When Omar captured Jerusalem in 638 (only six years after the death of the prophet Mohammed), the story goes that he entered the city on foot dressed in a simple camel hair tunic, the sort of gesture that only the truly powerful can make. (Allenby remembered this, no doubt, when he chose to enter Jerusalem on foot to take possession of the city for the English and the Christians in 1917.) Omar was asked if he wished to pray in the Church of the Holy Sepulchre, but he refused: "Had I prayed in your church, the church would have been lost to you forever, for after my death, the Muslims would have taken possession of it arguing that Omar had prayed there" (a gesture from which modern warmongers and peacemakers could learn a great deal).

Instead he asked the patriarch Sophronios to be shown the place where King David had prayed *(mihrab Dawood)*. He was taken to the Haram al-Sharif, where he identified the rock and began to clear the debris with his own hands, forcing the patriarch to join him in the work. (Arab writers from the Middle Ages onward have referred to the Church of the Holy Sepulchre as *Qumama,* "dung heap," a scatological pun on the proper Arab name for the church, *Kanisat al-Qiyama.* I can't help wondering whether this story of Omar forcing the patriarch to clear the filth from the rock helps motivate the pun. It certainly gives it a deeper resonance.)

Omar decided to build a mosque on the deserted site, and the Jewish convert Ka'b al-Ahbar suggested that the mosque should be built north of the rock. Omar refused because no Jewish sign or symbol—the rock with its associations of the sacrifice of Isaac—should come between Muslims at prayer and Mecca. It should be built south of the rock. (There are many different versions of this story, as so often with medieval narratives, and there are many embellishments and varied emphases.) So Omar built a wooden structure to the south, of no great merit, but big enough to house 3,000 worshippers. By a strange chance, we have a Latin description from a Christian pilgrim, the French bishop Arculf, who visited Jerusalem in 680. He dismissed it as "crude work," "beams laid across a ruin." Because of Omar's role and fame, however, both the al-Aqsa, and especially the Dome of the Rock, have been known as the

Mosque of Omar, and that is how they appear in most Victorian travelers' accounts.

This wooden mosque was turned into a large stone structure—al-Aqsa holds 5,000 worshippers—by al-Walid, continuing his father's monumental building program on behalf of the new regime. It was rebuilt or restored after devastating earthquake damage between 775 and 785 by al-Mahdi. In 1033 it was rebuilt again to a slightly narrower footprint by Caliph al-Dhahir. In the twelfth century the crusaders added a rose window, which can still be seen on the east window, a surprising Christian touch in this center of Muslim decoration—as well as the bays of the façade, and the chapels on either side of what they construed as an apse. Most crusader work on the Haram was removed by Saladin; though, since this historical reconstruction must have been based on the memory of three generations before, it must also have been a somewhat unreliable exercise. But the al-Aqsa still shows some signs of the crusader occupation. Most likely the basic shape of the building at least has remained constant since the fourteenth century; but repairs have been regular, and major elements have also been changed, as we will see as we enter the building itself.

As with so much in Jerusalem's Jewish, Christian, and Islamic religious worlds, it is not easy to rationalize a historical account of accretion and change and interaction, with the participants' passionate claims of what has always been the case. Many Muslims view the al-Aqsa simply as the mosque mentioned in the Qur'an, though even in its earliest, wooden form it was built well after the death of the Prophet, and cannot therefore have been visited by him. More nuanced Muslim historians have argued that the term *musjid* need not literally mean "mosque" but could imply any place of prayer, and therefore the Qur'an could be referring to the site of the Temple, on which the al-Aqsa was subsequently built. Less apologetic and more critical historians embrace the development and embellishment of *haddith* over the centuries, and see the building and naming of the al-Aqsa mosque as a retrospective authorization of the text of the Qur'an, which then takes on a life of its own in story and in religious practice. But the most common story is that the mosque has been there since before the time of the Prophet. In conflict-torn Jerusalem it is especially depressing to read the wilder claims of the ideologues—journalists, politicians, historians, and their followers—which ride roughshod over history, which they inevitably claim to support their extremism. Perhaps it is just the naïve idealism of a historian to hope that a better understanding of the past could put a small brake on the careering machine of shrill ideology, even in Jerusalem.

The first impression on entering the al-Aqsa is space (Figure 16). Unlike a Christian cathedral in Europe, or the Church of the Holy Sepulchre with its shrines and altars and divisions, the mosque has a set of seven aisles, divided by marble pillars and rounded arches, with small windows above. The original, eighth-century building had fifteen, more constrained aisles. The central aisle is the widest and is covered with a brightly painted wooden roof donated by King Farouk of Egypt. The pillars on the east side are of the finest Carrara marble and were donated to the mosque by Mussolini in 1938, partly in a gesture to appease Muslims after his military violence in Africa. The mosque had been severely damaged by earthquake in 1929 and 1937, and this was part of the restoration. The pillars on the west side did not need to be replaced, and so they were not. There is certainly no fetish of symmetry here, but a rather haphazard lopsidedness between the aisles. Between the columns, high up in the hazy sunlight, birds fly around.

The long walk down the central carpeted aisle leads toward the *mihrab,* the prayer niche, on the southern wall. The *mihrab* was donated by Saladin and is the one piece of the great general's restorations still surviving. It is framed by a monumental arch; above is the Dome, supported by four arches and eight pillars. To the east is a crusader chapel, known as the *Mihrab* of Zacharia, with the pretty

Figure 16. The interior of the al-Aqsa mosque, flooded with early morning light.

rose window; to the west is another small chapel, also crusader, now used for women's prayer. It is here that King Abdullah of Jordan was assassinated in 1951 by a young tailor, Mustapha Shukri Ashu. The future king Hussein survived only because of the heavy decorations on his chest, a good enough reason for wearing medals again. There are still bullet holes in one of the pillars. By another pillar, on the west side, a small shrine of collected bullets and empty tear gas canisters has been set up—a modern shrine to the rioting and military responses around the mosque. On August 21, 1969, part of the mosque was burned, and the irreplaceable *minbar* (pulpit) of carved cedar wood, donated by Saladin and brought from Aleppo, was destroyed. (A replica, donated by King Abdullah II of Jordan, has just been built and installed, and it looks very new: "a step towards liberating the mosque from occupation," declared

Adnan Husseini, on behalf of the *waqf,* adding the usual political gloss to restoration work.) The fire was set by a mentally deranged Australian Christian called Dennis Rohan, who belonged to an evangelical Christian sect, and who declared in court that by destroying the al-Aqsa he believed he would hasten the Second Coming. This act of madness prompted serious rioting, as well as the accusation that the Jews were trying to destroy the Haram al-Sharif. The identity and motivation of the criminal are clear enough, but this has not stopped repeated manipulation of this dire event as so-called proof of Zionist plots. The Western Wall is a permanent reminder of the violent destruction of Jerusalem by the Romans, and a history of Jewish persecution. The al-Aqsa is scarred with its own shrines of violence, violence from inside and outside the Arab world. The edginess and suspicion that one feels around the Haram al-Sharif and the Temple Mount plaza are fully explicable, as tense, religiously committed groups circulate through carefully framed memorials of political conflict, psychotic aggression, and an imagined past of peace, now lost.

The al-Aqsa is not built on bedrock, which means that it is more prone to earthquake damage than the Dome of the Rock. It is built above the archways that originally supported Herod's Royal Portico, strengthened by later Muslim regimes. These vaults are known as Solomon's Stables. They have now been turned into an underground mosque, to extend the covered area for prayer, and renamed in honor of Abd al-Malik's father, Marwan. In the current political climate, this new mosque is difficult for non-Muslims to visit. Its long, vaulted hallways are carpeted in red and lead out through massive green wooden doors to a new set of polished stone steps back up onto the Haram. This entrance was excavated by bulldozer and the ancient remains driven out by the truckload over a single weekend, a process that produced an outcry from archaeologists around the world: it has been impossible to dig on the Temple Mount for obvious religious reasons, and many would give their eye teeth to explore properly during such building work. The likelihood of any major discoveries may be slight, as most of whatever came out must have been the soil and debris Herod's workmen put in when they built the Temple Mount, with the accrued silt of generations. Rubbish can be archaeological gold, but in this case it is important not to overestimate the vandalism. The truckloads of dirt have been collected by the Israelis from where the Muslims dumped them, and retransported to a site where they are being sifted: a host of coins, including a nice French gold piece from the nineteenth century, parts of a column, and many other small finds, have been recovered. This painstaking and repetitive salvage work will take years to complete. A bulge has since appeared on the southern wall, and the accusation that the new mosque has threatened the survival of the Haram has been dismissed by the Arab authorities with the same speed and aggression that they accuse any Israeli activity near the Haram of being precisely such a threat. It is very hard to be an archaeologist in Jerusalem without becoming embroiled and implicated in what feels partly like a fight between playground bullies, and partly like a threat to world peace.

In the southeast corner of Solomon's Stables is a wooden shrine set above a stone trough, lit by a small window looking out over the Mount of Olives—a window that gives an extraordinary view of the cemeteries from what looks like a blank wall from the outside. This shrine is the so-called Cradle of Jesus. Now here is not the site of Jesus' birth in any story, of course, but this cradle has been here since the Middle Ages. It seems to be a tourist attraction constructed to give the visitor to the Haram a chance to see a relic of the full collection of prophets in one place. It has rather drifted out of favor these days and sits in dusty seclusion—a reminder of a past age of capacious myth-making.

THE MOST BEAUTIFUL BUILDING IN JERUSALEM

When you leave the al-Aqsa and walk on upward, the view of the Dome of the Rock that emerges is one of the most splendid sights

in Jerusalem, which changes with every step. It is framed and punc-
tuated by arches and steps and fountains, and each moment pro-
duces a new vista, a new angle. You go past *el-kas,* the Cup or Chalice, a fountain strategically placed in the direct line between the
central entrance of the al-Aqsa and the steps up to the Dome of the
Rock, used by worshippers for ritual washing before entering the
al-Aqsa mosque. You approach the steps with their colonnade of
four pillars, flanked by trees. The colonnade acts like a frame, and as
you climb up each step, the frame changes what you can see of the
beautiful building ahead of you.

It is hard to take full notice of the *minbar* and two small domed
shrines on the left as you approach the Dome of the Rock, but they
are an integral part of the overall effect of the platform here. The
two-tiered dome of the *minbar (minbar Burhan al-Din)* is the "summer pulpit," used for outdoor services. It was restored in the late
fourteenth century and is made up of some exceptionally fine crusader sculpture: the re-use of materials repeatedly layers monuments with their enemies' work. There are eight smaller domed
shrines around the Dome of the Rock, each with its own name and
design. They are from a range of periods, mainly from the thirteenth to the nineteenth century. Each was built to honor a particular ruler or group, as well as to provide a focus for prayer. They act
like satellites or little images of the central dome, and the visual effect of these small monochrome shrines around the vast and multicolored central edifice is pleasingly to punctuate the symmetry of
the monumental Dome of the Rock and to provide points of visual
focus to assess the scale of the platform. In the same way that a person in the foreground of a photograph of a building provides a
sense of scale, a human focus, and a sense of perspective, so these
shrines from different angles help locate the viewer before the
Dome of the Rock.

Two of these shrines are particularly interesting. To the east of
the Dome of the Rock is the Dome of the Chain (Map 3). It is a
striking design—a domed hexagon with open arches surrounded

by an eleven-sided polygon with eleven open arches, with elegant, slim columns (Figure 17). The Jerusalem myth is that all seventeen columns can be seen from any position: it is not strictly true, but it does nicely evoke the engrossing symmetry of the building and the desire it gives to walk around and around it. Oddly, the first description of the building from 903 says that it has twenty columns, which has led some architectural historians to suggest that the design was changed perhaps in the fifteenth century (though it is hard to see how the alteration could have been made). Unlike the other, smaller shrines it is tiled on a frieze beneath the dome, with light blue tiles that shimmer against the colors of the Dome of the Rock, which dwarfs it. The building is particularly beautiful, but it is also a mystery. It seems to have been built very early, probably by Abd al-Malik in 691–692. But its purpose, and its significance, remain deeply obscure. It is placed at the exact center of the Haram al-Sharif, leading some modern scholars to suggest that it marks the *omphalos,* the navel of the Haram, which is the center of the world. (Another competition between the Church of the Holy Sepulchre and the Haram al-Sharif: to be the location of the center of the world.) Jamâl ad-Din Ahmad stated in the middle of the fourteenth century that it was a treasury, though the open sides make this hard to envisage. Some have suggested that it marks the site of the Holy of Holies, and may even predate the Islamic rule of the area, though this seems highly unlikely, not least because the oldest sources say it was built by Abd al-Malik. It has even been suggested that it is a sort of architectural model for the Dome of the Rock, though it has a quite different design (which does in its symmetry and angularity at least echo the larger form). It is best to say here that we simply do not know the history and function of what is the third largest religious building on the Haram: and enjoy looking at it.

The story of why it is called the Dome of the Chain is not much help—though it is a great story. King David, it is said (or, in some versions, Solomon), hung a chain from the roof of this shrine, and

Figure 17. The Dome of the Chain, used by Arab mothers and their children as a shaded picnic area.

anyone who held it and lied under oath would be killed by lightning. So he used it as the place to give judgment. A man—in some versions, inevitably, a Jew—had borrowed a sum of gold from a friend, and when the friend asked for it back, the man falsely claimed to have returned it already. The friend demanded they go to the Dome of the Chain to resolve their case. The cheat had the gold melted down and fitted into a walking stick, which he used to walk to the Haram. When he was called on to take an oath that he had returned the gold, the man duly accepted the challenge to hold the chain and swear, and so gave his friend his walking stick to hold. He swore that he had returned the gold to his friend—which at that precise moment was technically true. The man was not struck by lightning. He took his stick back and walked off; but the chain fell and was never used again. It is not a story that greatly helps us with the history of the shrine, but it does show the religious imagination at full tilt, trying to provide a background for the mysterious construction.

The second small shrine is more typical in form and sits in the northwest corner of the platform. It is usually called the Dome of the Spirits, or *Qubbat al-Arwah* (Map 3). This is a sixteenth-century construction, a little dome held up by eight pillars. As a piece of architecture, it is standard and easily passed by. But it has become the center of one of those Jerusalem disputes that cannot quite be silenced. The dome here covers a small piece of bedrock, and it was proposed in 1975 by an Israeli physicist that this is the site of the Holy of Holies, and that this therefore is the rock on which Abraham offered Isaac as a sacrifice. Although archaeologists and religious writers have in general completely dismissed this claim, there is no theory in Jerusalem so crazy that some people will not embrace it. It is a revealing episode. An obsessive theory, motivated by religious desire, fixates on an object—in this case a piece of bedrock—and it becomes an issue of holy war. And changes the perceived importance of an otherwise minor if elegant little shrine, and its bit of bare stone. In its own small way, this rumbling academic argument epitomizes the large-scale vectors of Jerusalem's history.

The Dome of the Rock is not a mosque but a shrine (which can, of course, also be used for prayer). It is octagonal, with a golden dome rising above a circular drum, from the center of the octagonal base (Figure 18). The octagonal shape reflects Byzantine church architecture most closely and is unlike mosques elsewhere. It has four doorways, on the north, south, east, and west walls, each with a pillared porch of multicolored marble, with a small arch above. The doorway to the south, which marks the *qibla,* has an extended porch of eight columns, built by Sultan Mahmud II in 1817; the other doors have two columns, as they all did originally. Otherwise,

Figure 18. The Dome of the Rock—glorious, but on a human scale.

all four doorways are the same, and all restored in the twentieth century. The bottom level of the building, up to doorway height, is decorated with inlaid marble, with a moderately austere geometric pattern. The upper levels of the octagonal building and the drum beneath the Dome are decorated with the most lavish of intricate geometric patterns in a profusion of blue and white and gold. The upper level of the hexagonal base and the upper level of the drum have calligraphic inscriptions of texts from the Qur'an. Each wall has six tall, thinly recessed arches, which pre-announce the internal structure of piers and spandrels.

It is a building of immense splendor, and quite different in its opulence from anything else on the Haram or indeed in Jerusalem. As the Arabic historian and traveler Muqadisi wrote in the tenth century: "At the dawn, when the light of the sun first strikes the cupola, and the Drum catches the rays; then is this edifice a marvellous sight to behold, and one such that in all Islam I have never seen its equal; neither have I heard tell of aught built in pagan times that could rival in grace this Dome of the Rock." Mujir al-Din more whimsically wrote that happiness is "eating a banana in the shade of the Dome of the Rock." A lot has happened since the tenth century, but the Dome of the Rock remains one of the marvels of Islamic architecture, matched perhaps only by the exquisite palace of the al-Hambra in Spain.

Unlike so much in Jerusalem, the shape of the Dome of the Rock seems to have changed very little since it was first built. It is set on bedrock, and though it has inevitably suffered from earthquake damage and from disrepair over the centuries, it has survived much more sturdily than the al-Aqsa (or the attacked, burned, and redesigned Church of the Holy Sepulchre). The shape was recognized from the earliest records as something extraordinary. Ibn Batuta from Tangier wrote around 1355: "This is one of the most fantastic of all buildings. Its queerness and perfection lie in its shape, though it has more than its fair share of other charms. It is so amazing it captivates the eye." Neither Muqadisi, nor Ibn Batuta, nor Jamâl ad-Din Ahmad saw the amazing tiles: they were set in place in 1552 by Suleiman the Magnificent, who also built the city walls of the Old City. (These tiles replaced the original mosaics.) The tiles have needed repeated repair, most recently in the 1960s, but the designs have continued in the same form.

The roof, too, has maintained the same design, and though Muqadisi's description of it glowing at dawn suggests it was burnished in the tenth century, in the nineteenth century at least it was a dull gray lead. It was turned a gold color in 1964 when Egyptian engineers put gold-colored anodized aluminum sheets on the roof. Unfortunately, these were not watertight, and the roof leaked whenever it rained. But it was not until 1994 that the necessary repairs were paid for by King Hussein of Jordan, who had formal responsibility for the upkeep of the Muslim holy places. Although some members of the *waqf* argued for a return to the traditional lead, it was decided to keep what by now seemed the iconic gold. King Hussein hired an Irish firm, headed by one Patrick O'Hare, who used an electro-chemical metallizing technique. Copper and nickel are layered onto brass plates, and a thin film of gold—2 microns thick—makes the final layer. The copper and nickel shine through the gold, giving a matte finish that prevents the viewer from being completely dazzled by the glare from the reflected sun. It is yet another twist in the ironies of Jerusalem that it should be a Catholic Western firm that made the roof of the Dome of the Rock safely iconic again.

The strangest story of the repair of the tiles comes from the days of the British Mandate in 1918. Ronald Storrs, the military commander of Jerusalem, and Charles Ashbee, the civic advisor of Jerusalem, decided that the evident damage to the tiles should be put right. They remembered visiting a Turkish bath in Yorkshire, in North England, that had tiles of the sort they were looking for. So they wrote to Yorkshire to get the name of the tilemaker. He was David Ohanessian, an Armenian, who was summoned from Aleppo, where he was now living. He brought in tilemakers from Kutahya who knew how to make and fire in the old style to match the old tiles. They brought the right clay and other materials with them. For color, they sent for a recipe to London, to William de Morgan, a now elderly potter of the Arts and Crafts movement. Ohanessian set up his workshop and was ready to proceed. His wonderful work is evident in numerous sites over Jerusalem, most prominently in the Rockefeller Museum and St. Andrew's Scottish Church. The tradition he started of Armenian pottery is one of the still-thriving businesses of the Old City. But he was not allowed to produce the tiles for the Dome of the Rock. I was told the reason for this in the Armenian quarter. There was one Turk on the *waqf,* and in line with his country's genocidal treatment of the Armenians, he vetoed the employment of an Armenian. Whether this story is true or not, the work did have to wait several years to get under way, and then, in 1928, it was with the Turkish architect Kemalettin directing the project from Istanbul, with Rushdi Bey Ahmad as the architect on the ground. There is politics in every tile in this city.

The Dome of the Rock is entered through any of the doors that are open at the time. It is an overwhelming sight of splendor and sheer profusion of color and shapes (Figure 19). The Dome was built in part to express Muslim supremacy over the Jews by building on this site, and supremacy over the Christians, not only by architectural dominance over the Church of the Holy Sepulchre, but also by the inscriptions on the inside (as we will see shortly). It is designed to be seen from far and wide as a glittering monument. When the viewer is close up, however, it is easy to feel lost in the mass of detail. But there is a clear structure to the building that is connected to its function and focus. Map 3 (top) is a plan. At the center is the rock itself, which determines the size of the dome built over it. Around the rock is a carved wooden screen to keep away the zealous worshipper. Around this is a circular set of square piers and marble columns, holding up arched spandrels. Around this is an octagonal arcade of square pillars and columns, again supporting arched spandrels. These two arcades form two ambulatories.

These ambulatories help provide a second explanation of the purpose of the Dome of the Rock. Muslims are instructed to make pilgrimage to the three holy cities of Mecca, Medina, and Jerusalem at least once in their lifetime. The Dome of the Rock is the central focus of that pilgrimage, and the ambulatories encourage a sense of procession (which we saw so much in evidence in the Church of the Holy Sepulchre). The building can be entered at any point and has to be viewed by circling around it. What is more, there are calligraphic inscriptions around both the outer octagonal arcade and the inner octagonal arcade. These inscriptions can only

Figure 19. The outer ambulatory of the Dome of the Rock. (©1992 Said Nuseibeh Photography.)

be read by walking around the building. The building encourages its viewers to process ceremoniously around it.

These inscriptions contain selections from the Qur'an, interspersed with pious phrases, and remarks on the original construction of the building. The outer inscription, starting from the *qibla* and moving clockwise, begins, "In the name of God, the beneficent, the Merciful . . . No God exists but God alone, indivisible without peer. Say, God is One; God is central—birthing no child, nor birthed in turn—nothing and no one is comparable." This critique of the familiar stories of polytheism, which love to talk of the birth of gods, also contains a veiled attack on Christianity, which is made fully explicit on the inner arcade: "O People of the Book! Don't be excessive in the name of your faith! Do not say things about God but the truth! The Messiah Jesus, son of Mary, is indeed a messenger of God: the Almighty extended a word to Mary, and a spirit, too. So believe in God and all the messengers, and stop talking about a Trinity. Cease in your own best interests! Verily God is a God of unity. Lord Almighty! That God would beget a child? Either in the heavens or on earth?" When the worshipper processes around the building, reading the inscriptions, he is also performing a polemic against Christianity and a defense of the faith of Islam. It is fully religious architecture.

The circular ambulatories and the four equal doors create a focus on the center of the building, the rock itself, and this provides a further reason for the building. The rock is invested with the most symbolic value of any object on the Haram—the place where Abraham offered his son as a sacrifice; where David sang; where Solomon prayed. Nasir-i-Khusro, a Persian Muslim from the Ismaili sect, visited Jerusalem in 1047 and wrote down his response to the rock:

> This stone of the Sakrah is that which God commanded Moses to institute as the *qibla*. . . . Then came

the days of Solomon—upon him be peace!—who seeing the Rock was the *qibla* built a mosque around it
[the First Temple] . . . So it remained until the days
of our Prophet Mohammed, the Chosen One—upon
him be blessings and peace!—who likewise recognized
this to be the *qibla,* turning towards it at his prayers;
but God—be He exalted and glorified—afterwards
commanded him to institute as the *qibla* the House of
Ka'aba [Mecca].

Nasir-i-Khusro, when he looks at the rock, sees the whole history of the prophetic tradition from Moses down to Mohammed
instantiated in this one spot. He sees indentations in the rock and
sees the marks of Abraham's and Isaac's feet. The pilgrim is condi-
tioned to view the rock like this, and by writing of his experience
he encourages others in the same perception. It is a place where religious history is set in stone.

Nasir-i-Khusro does not tell the most celebrated story linking
the rock to the revelation of Mohammed—a story that does not
appear in the written record at least until the fourteenth century
(we have no access to the oral tradition, of course). According to
this tradition, as Mohammed rose toward heaven, the rock tried to
follow him, and he had to press it down with his foot. The footprint of the Prophet is duly to be seen still on the rock. It is perhaps
no surprise that this story of a miraculous journey with its relic is
written down in the medieval period: so, too, were so many Christian and Jewish stories of a similar timbre. The three religions share
the habits of the age as much as they fight to assert their differences
from one another. There is a screen in front of the spot, and you
can put your hand through a hole in it and touch the place, which
is perfumed daily. It is curiously reminiscent of the kissing of the
Stone of Unction in the Church of the Holy Sepulchre, and the
worshippers' faces pressed to the Western Wall. Stones take on a

power of their own in Jerusalem. But I also saw a group of school-girls, drawing and writing about the Dome on a day trip, run back again and again, giggling, to put their hands through the hole, and then skipping back to their friends. The building felt very homely at that moment.

Perhaps the strangest kink in all this history is the fact that the rock is not mentioned in any Jewish source. And yet there are so many stories about the Temple Mount. There can be little doubt that it was there and a distinctive feature of the topography. Was it so familiar or obvious that no description felt the need to specify it? This seems unsatisfactory, to say the least. Or was it in fact unseen by almost everyone and not suitable for description—within the Holy of Holies? Was it somehow enclosed and only revealed at a later stage? No one has managed to find a wholly convincing explanation for this mysterious silence.

Beneath the rock is a cave, which you can climb down a short set of stairs to reach. There are, of course, some old stories here: that you can hear the voices of the dead (hence the name *Bir el-Arweh,* the Cave of Spirits); or that you can hear the rushing of air, which shows that the rock is suspended in space. A pregnant woman was so frightened when she entered the space and saw the floating rock that she had a miscarriage: after that, a wall was built to prevent more terror among the faithful. The cave was used for prayer as early as 902 (when Ibn al-Faqih mentions it), and the *mihrab* here is one of the oldest surviving anywhere. Some would even date it back to Abd al-Malik in the seventh century, which would make it the oldest *mihrab* existing in the world (though this has been contested in the usual way of academic matters). It is more likely from the late ninth century. Its design is architecturally unparalleled and rather rustic in its carving. Below the luxury of the building above, this is a small moment of an older, simpler gift of piety.

The decorations inside the Dome are unique (Figure 19). The arcades are decorated with mosaics of elaborate abstract design in gold, red, blue, and turquoise. Stained-glass windows give a mottled light. The ceilings of the ambulatories have large gilded panels in the forms of rosettes and interlacing star patterns. These were almost entirely refashioned in the 1960s in imitation of the patterns created in the thirteenth century. The piers are faced with single, split-faced, and quartered panels of marble and stone. Perhaps the most impressive sights of the whole design are the mosaics in the circular arcade and the drum. These combine exuberant floral designs against a gold background, in between arched windows of delicate white latticework, all bordered with friezes of elaborate circular designs below, and square boxes with diamonds and circles above. This mosaic work is wonderfully lavish and intricate; but it also suggests another explanation of the Dome of the Rock as a building. Here is the place, an image of paradise, where Mohammed will return to earth at the Day of Judgment.

Jews, Christians, and Muslims all have elaborate, folkloric accounts of the end of the world. The Muslim story goes that there will be a rope as thin as a hair stretched from the Haram to the Mount of Olives opposite, where the Garden of Eden will "be led like a bride on the Day of Resurrection." Beneath the rope will be the fire-filled pits of Hell. The assembled mass of Muslims will be made to walk across this rope. The scales will be placed on the Haram: "the mustering and accounting will take place in the Holy House." The pious and faithful will walk calmly from the Haram across toward the Prophet, secure that their guardian angels will save them if they slip. The evil will fall to their eternal doom. Those who cower behind on the Haram are the Muslims who have realized the error of their ways, and who will be saved through repentance. For this story—in all its varied forms—the Dome of the Rock and the Dome of the Chain are central. The Haram mediates not just between man and God but between life and death, or between transitory life and eternal life. So modern scholars have seen in the flamboyant floral designs and in the sheer exuberant wealth of the Dome of the Rock an image of paradise connected to these eschatological stories. There was indeed once a metal plaque over the door facing the Mount of Olives (now to be seen in the Museum of the Haram), which calls on Mohammed to intercede with God on behalf of Muslims. This is the earliest example of Mohammed in this role, and this, too, emphatically declares the Dome to be the place of judgment and the end of days.

There is one final explanation for the function of the Dome of the Rock, and it takes us away from paradise and back toward the messy business of politics and power. Already by the time of its construction there were political divisions in the Arab world, and conflict about the legitimate line of authority. It was argued, particularly by the enemies of Abd al-Malik's Umayyad dynasty, that the very building of the Dome was a gesture asserting the authority of this region over and against Mecca. But perhaps the clearest sign of the Dome's political status is the inscription on the building, on the outer hexagonal ambulatory, which records its founding. The name of the founder, Abd al-Malik, has been removed and replaced by the name of the Abassid caliph al-Ma'mun—but strangely the date of the foundation, 691–692, has been left untouched, even though al-Ma'mun ruled from 813 to 833. This is unlikely to be just a crass mistake. It may indicate, rather, that the time of the building's foundation is not to be forgotten and remains unchanged, but that the ownership of the building can change—and can be used to give authority to a regime. Decorating the Haram, and the Dome of the Rock preeminently, became a sign of a regime's self-promotion and declaration of legitimacy. Contemporary talk of custodianship of the holy sites has a long history, a constant tale of the interweaving of politics and piety.

STROLLING ON THE HARAM

The Dome of the Rock, with its nexus of varied functions and meanings, and the al-Aqsa mosque, the congregational center of Islamic worship, provide the defining points of the physical and spiritual topography of the Haram. But built up around them over the centuries is a range of other buildings that reflects the changing status of Jerusalem as a city. No regime is more important for this development than the Mameluks, who tend to get rather short shrift in the standard history books, caught as they are between the glory of Saladin and the coming of the Ottoman Empire with Suleiman the Magnificent. They may lack the glory and the magnificence, but they were instrumental in making the Jerusalem we see today.

The Mameluks were originally slave soldiers and mercenaries from the Caucasus who served the Abbayid dynasty from the tenth century, and who converted to Islam. From the thirteenth to the sixteenth century they took over the caliphate and ruled from Egypt. They found Jerusalem a poor backwater, with barely a religious life. Already in the tenth century Muqadisi had written of Jerusalem: "Few are the learned there, many are the Christians, and these make themselves distasteful in the public spaces . . . The Christians and the Jews predominate here, and the mosque is devoid of congregations and assemblies." But when the Ottomans took over Jerusalem in 1517 they found a flourishing city centered on religious education and practice. In part this came about because Jerusalem was used as a place of political exile during the Mameluk period; exiles from the political centers of the empire were expected to work their way back into the favor of man and God by expenditure on the fabric of the holy city.

Mameluk architectural motifs are easy to spot. The Mameluks loved to build with white, pink, and black stone, often in striped bands known as *ablaq,* and almost every door, often tall, and highly decorated, has a pair of facing stone benches in a narrow porch, often with an inscription (sometimes there is only one bench). And they built up the structures that make up the north and west sides of the Haram al-Sharif today, as well as many structures in the immediate vicinity, including the Market of the Cotton Merchants, the *suk al-Qattanin.* They added several of the small cupolas and *minbars,* which we have already mentioned, but, more importantly, they also constructed a religious and social infrastructure for the Haram: religious and legal schools *(madrasas),* pilgrim hostels, hostels for sufi mystics *(khanqaks),* libraries, drinking fountains *(sabils),* and so on. They built the four square minarets around the edge of the Haram from which the call to prayer is proclaimed. They restructured (and renamed) the gates. The Mameluks gave the Haram its physical sense of being an enclosed garden, and they turned it into a center of religious and legal learning.

Al-Nasir Muhammad, who ruled (three times) between 1294 and 1340, had perhaps the most extensive effect on the compound. He built the portico along the western edge of the Haram—a set of vaults, one bay deep, which are open onto the Haram and give some cool in the heat of the summer. He built the colonnades on the north end of the terrace of the Dome of the Rock, and he built the Bab al-Silsila minaret, and the Gate and the *suk* of the Cotton Merchants. The Gate of the Cotton Merchants, as its name suggests, is a secular structure that links the Haram to the *suk,* which is one of the finest medieval covered markets in the Middle East. The gate itself (Figure 20) lies under a splendid vault and sits in a trefoil arch set in a larger recess, which is topped with a semi-dome and pointed arch above. The alternating red and cream stone bands of the topmost arch, and the pattern over the door, are typical of Mameluk *ablaq* design. The vaulting, which looks like the stone has been scooped out, is called *muqarnas* (or sometimes "stalactite") corbelling, and is also typical of Mameluk design. The boldly articulated passage between the gate and the *suk* links the religious life of the Haram and the commercial life of the city, just as the Mameluk buildings just outside the perimeter of the Haram itself tie the Haram into a civic setting. The continuity of religious, political, and military life for the Mameluks is expressed in their architectural planning.

Just to the south of this gate is one of the most important

Figure 20. The Gate of the Cotton Merchants, leading from the Haram al-Sharif
out into the Old City through the Cotton Market.

madrassas, the al-Ashrafiyya. These schools were central to Mameluk policy and were built all along the west and north walls of the Haram. Typically, a *madrassa* would have four domed rooms (*iwans*) built around a central hall, often with a *mihrab* in the southern wall. The door to the al-Ashrafiyya reveals the particular flamboyance of Mameluk architecture. The porch opens through two pointed arches. Red and cream-colored *ablaq* designs are enclosed with complex moldings. The vaulting is an elaborate folded cross vault, which is a popular design from Cairo at the time of the sultan Qaytbay, whose royal inscription can still be seen on the column. The design and the inscription in this way link the *madrassa* with the imperial center and its ruler—which is the role of state-sponsored architecture of the empire: to visualize and enforce the structured unity of imperial power. There is a cruciform-decorated panel in the crown of the vault and a stone bench along one side of the porch. The porch frames the doorway itself, which revels in an over-the-top profusion of just about every decorative device Mameluk architecture uses. There is black, red, and cream *ablaq,* separated by thin black lines of lead rather than mortar; moldings with palmettes; elaborate corner pieces (squinches) with *muqarnas* corbelling; a semi-dome inlaid with a fantastic pattern of scrolls and palmettes; and an inscription detailing the completion of the building's construction. This door gives some sense of just how extensive and gaudy Mameluk architecture could be (and scholars have tried to reconstruct the frontage of the whole building accordingly). The geographical writer Mujir al-Din, the best guide to Jerusalem of this period, lovingly lists the splendid windows of Frankish glass, the walls and floors covered with cut marble, the ceilings of wood, covered with gold leaf and azure, and the lamps of unparalleled beauty. It was, he said, "the third jewel" of the Haram.

The assertion of Mameluk authority was stamped gloriously around the platform of the Haram al-Sharif. The rather dull brown frontages that now provide a more muted background to the splendor of the Dome of the Rock and al-Aqsa are still the signs of the religious infrastructure of local Muslim society that the Mameluks put in place—and perhaps there is a hint of a better future in the contrast between the familiar newsroom image of stone-throwing children and the laughing girls in the schools, which today are in the *madrassas,* or the boys playing soccer in the gardens.

There are four final sights that shouldn't be missed. First, in the northwest corner of the Haram, between the towering Mameluk buildings, you can still see the striations on the rock face of the hill—testimony to where Herod's engineers cut away the mountain. This was the site of the Antonia, the fortress of Herod, which overlooked the Temple Mount—the military force that backed Herod's rule and was suitably named after his Roman patron, Marc Antony.

Second, as you walk around the outside edge of the Haram, in the east wall is the Golden Gate, a double gate that has been sealed since the time of Saladin, and that was probably built in its current form by Abd al-Malik in the late seventh century. It is through this gate, the story goes, that the Messiah will enter (and presumably the Messiah will be able to unseal it easily enough, unlike any one of the false messiahs who dot the landscape of Jerusalem's history, all too keen to fulfill a prophecy). Most scholars think this was originally the Shushan Gate, used at the time of the Temple for the ritual of the Red Heifer, one of the stranger biblical purification rites, which required a perfect, red, young cow for sacrifice and burning. The breeding of this flawless animal has become an obsession of some American evangelical Christian groups, to hasten the Second Coming and the unblocking of the gate. So far, without success. According to a story that became very popular in the medieval period, the emperor Heraclius brought the True Cross back through this gate: when he tried to enter in magnificent robes, "the stones of the gate descended to make a solid wall"; but when he humbled himself, they opened again. Under the crusaders, the gate was unblocked twice a year for the festivals of Palm Sunday and the Exaltation of the Cross, a memorial of the emperor's victory. But as usual, the story is almost certainly untrue, and Heraclius entered through St. Stephen's Gate (without any supernatural drawbridge). Even the name of the gate changed in a mistaken way in this period. It is called the Golden Gate probably because "aurea," the Latin for "golden," is a corruption of the Greek "oreia," which sounds very similar and means "beautiful," the name attested in the previous, Greek-speaking period.

Third, in the southwest corner of the Haram is the Museum of the Haram. Here you can see, among other treasures, the crusader wrought-iron screen that went around the rock (until it was replaced in the 1960s by the present, wooden one); the copper-plated doors donated to the Dome of the Rock by Sultan Qaytbay in 1467; and the seventh-century cypress roof beams of al-Aqsa, removed from the mosque in 1948. Like all museums, it records the difference of the past. Yet its very foundation is part of the competition over the past. The collection that became the Rockefeller Museum (see Chapter 6) was founded in 1890 by Ismail Bey, the director of public instruction in Jerusalem, and by Frederick Bliss, the archaeologist who failed to find the map of Madaba for the Palestine Exploration Fund (and who was the son of the founder of the American University of Beirut), working with the director of the Istanbul Museum of Antiquities, Osman Hamdi Bey. This was a classic nineteenth-century project. It aimed to service the new influx of tourists, of course, but also to make a point about the Bible, archaeology in the Holy Land, and the relation between the new sciences of the Victorian academy and the old world of buried history. When it moved to the Rockefeller Museum in 1929, it included in this mix the massive gift of the American philanthropist, which made the building possible, and the fact that now the Ottoman Empire had collapsed, and Jerusalem was under the Mandate. It is against this background that the *waqf* decided to build its museum in the 1920s, to parade its own treasures and give its own view of history. Both the Islamic Museum on the Haram and the Rockefeller Museum have carved beams from the al-Aqsa—a division of the spoils of the past that can only remind us how intensely the past is both shared and struggled over in this city. The museums are part of this fight.

Finally, between the Gate of the Cotton Merchants and the steps up to the platform of the Dome of the Rock is the Fountain of Qaytbay (the sultan we have already seen decorating the al-Aqsa). This is a super example of Mameluk design and is still in use as a fountain. It is actually one of the first things you see on entering the Haram, but the eye is drawn away by the splendor of the Dome ahead, so it is better to view it on the way out. The fountain was built by Egyptian craftsmen under a Christian master-builder in 1482 (and restored in 1883, as the inscription tells us), and it has the dignity and prominence usually associated with tombs rather than fountains. Figure 21 is the south elevation. Set on steps, the rectangular tower with retained pillars frames a grill that lets light into the shaft. (The inside is just as carefully decorated.) Above, a second level with a little arch is topped by a dome with a detailed floral design. The water, which is pumped up from the cisterns below, is poured into troughs under the windows, and cups chained to a bronze ring are fitted into two holes in the windowsill. The modern troughs and pump inside the shaft are unattractive additions. The *sabil* is a public fountain founded as a charitable act to gratify God. *Sabil* means "pathway" and indicates the proper flowing of water; it can also imply "purpose." Some modern commentators refer to the verse in the Qur'an that talks of good deeds earning a pathway to heaven, and thus make giving a *sabil* a specially meritorious good deed. The *sabil* of Qaytbay has an elegance and stature that make it one of the most aesthetically attractive buildings in Jerusalem.

Oleg Grabar, the finest modern commentator on the Haram al-

Figure 21. The *sabil* (water fountain) of Qaytbay on the Haram al-Sharif.

Sharif, recalls how in the 1950s the Haram was a deserted and rundown place, with only a few old men at prayer. When he battled through the not yet open Western Wall tunnels at that time, his Jordanian guide suggested that the vaults and passageways would make a great disco. He was not alone in imagining an increasingly secular future. Now the Haram scarcely seems big enough for the worshippers, for whom nationalism and religion have combined, just as the Western Wall plaza seethes with a mix of the pious, the military, and the tourists (and many combinations and in-betweens). The Haram and the space around and outside it have become polarized into a political, religious, and national opposition. But they share a great deal, apart from their physical closeness and long intimacy. They are both sites of great beauty. They are both sites that have embodied noble ideals of charity, education, and spirituality, in the schools, hostels, and shrines built for them. They are both sites that have scarred those ideals with violence and bigotry and small-minded nastiness. They are both sites where myth is interwoven with sanctity, where stories spin, enthrallingly, murderously, inspiringly, debasingly—where history's claim to truth struggles to survive.

But above all, this whole area is a place where not only Jewish, Christian, and Muslim but also religious and secular architecture, lives, and stories are irrevocably mixed together—in time and in space. And yet it is increasingly filled with people who insist on the impossible demand that this complex interweaving should be simple, clear, and separate. And who try to declare that history is on their side. Amid this political clamor, how can the beauty and awe of the religious combine with an understanding that comes through generous, critical history? How can the delicate intricacy and complexity of truthfulness be respected? How can a seriousness of commitment escape the lures of extremism? How can acknowledgment of others emerge from over-certain knowledge? The Western Wall plaza and the Temple Mount/Haram al-Sharif pose these questions—the questions of Jerusalem—in the starkest and most challenging manner.

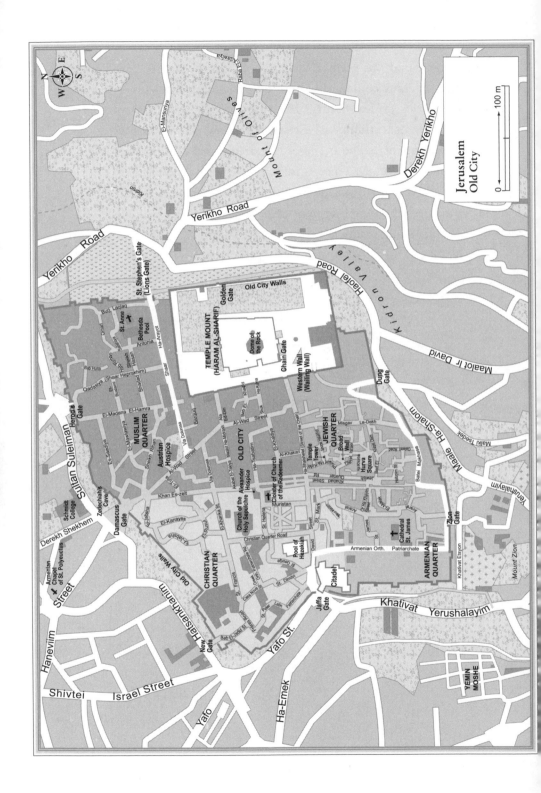

Jerusalem
Old City

0   100 m

4 The Old City

ROBERT RICHARDSON WAS A DOCTOR who traveled to Jerusalem with the Countess of Belmore in 1822. He cured the Ottoman governor of an eye disease while he was there and thus became one of the first Europeans to be granted permission to visit the Haram al-Sharif. His is one of the earliest of what would become a flood of nineteenth-century travelogues of the Holy Land by European visitors. Like almost all travelers at that date—and for many centuries before—he approached Jerusalem from Jaffa on the coast over the long, rolling, and continually rising hills. The series of ridges creates a fine sense of anticipation that just over the next summit, the Holy City will loom into view. Richardson was typical of many later travelers, even those who were emotionally overwhelmed to be where David and Jesus had walked, when he confessed that his first sight was actually a bit of a letdown: "These plain embattled walls in the midst of a barren mountain track, do they enclose the city of Jerusalem?"

For many Victorian pilgrims, the small, brown-walled city was surprisingly unlike their romanticized expectations, fed so long on praises of the beauty of Jerusalem from the Psalms to grand art to travel brochures. George Curtis, the American political journalist and one of the founding figures of the Republican Party, is positively lyrical in his disappointment when he writes in 1852: "There lay Jerusalem dead in the white noon. The desolation of the wilderness moaned at her gates . . . There were no sights or sounds of life. The light was colorless; the air was still. Nature had swooned around the dead city. There was no sound in the air; but a wailing in my heart 'O Jerusalem, Jerusalem, thou that stonest the prophets, and killst those that are sent unto thee.'" The author of *Moby Dick,* Herman Melville, depressed, commented laconically that Jerusalem "looks at you like a cold, gray eye in a cold, old man."

Until quite late in the nineteenth century, there were no buildings outside the walls of the Old City, and the walled city was precisely what you saw from the hills. The walls were a necessary protection against Bedouin brigands and the casual robbers and animals of the desert. As we will see in Chapter 6, the first building project outside the walls, Montefiore's windmill and workers' cottages of Mishkanot Sha'ananim, was far from an instant success, though now these are some of the most desirable residences in Jerusalem (with a great view of the walls). Mrs. Spafford, founder of the American Colony, which eventually took up residence in an isolated but palatial Ottoman estate outside the city walls, recalled that when she came to Jerusalem in 1881 it was still possible to count on the fingers of her hands the number of buildings beyond the wall's protection. It requires a real effort of imagination to remove a century of urban development from our mind's eye view of the city, though nineteenth-century photographs can be wonderfully evocative of this lost time.

These days, the walls of the Old City are one of the most familiar and loved sights of Jerusalem, and few travelers look on the walls with such gray disappointment as the long line of nineteenth-century pilgrims. Especially in contrast to the urban sprawl through which the modern visitor arrives in Jerusalem, the walls have become an image of Jerusalem the antique, of Jerusalem the golden. S. Y. Agnon, the Israeli Noble Prize winner for literature, has a quite different color palette from the disappointed Victorians: "Before him, the walls of Jerusalem suddenly appeared, woven into a red fire, plaited with gold, surrounded by grey clouds, blended with blue clouds, which incise and engrave it with shapes of spun gold, choice silver, burnished brass and purple tin." (Saul Bellow, the American Nobel Prize winner for literature, finds a dark undertow even in the Jerusalem sunlight: "Late afternoon light on the stones only increases their stoniness. Yellow and gray, they have achieved their final color. The sun can do no more for them.") The very phrase "walled city" resounds with notes of romantic tales of the East, or Talmudic laws, or old epics of siege and spectacle. The yellowing stones change color in the different lights of the day and the different seasons, and from many vantage points in the modern city, to look up and see the walls of the Old City is for a second to feel a different sense of historical perspective.

Yet the very fact that we can look up and see the walls in this way depends on a quirky and charming history of the Mandate era. The walls were built by Suleiman the Magnificent in the sixteenth century. He began in the north in 1537, and the south wall was completed in 1540. There was a dispute—as ever with building in Jerusalem—in this case whether Mount Zion should be included within the boundary. The architects were uncertain that the expense of so much extra wall was worth it for one building, the cenacle, the room where Jesus was said to have had the last supper. Consequently, the walls were built excluding the hill. Suleiman was infuriated by their decision and had the architects put to death—the graves just inside the Jaffa Gate, said to be the graves of the architects, are nothing of the sort: just the memorials of two mildly distinguished citizens of a later date—but that's why the walls have the scope we know today. The walls were largely untouched over the next centuries, and eventually they were allowed to fall into some disrepair. Buildings were erected up to the walls and incorporated into them—until the arrival of the British Mandate.

Ronald Storrs was the first military governor of Jerusalem. He appointed Charles Ashbee as his first civic advisor (city planner) in 1918. Many years before, when he was a boy, Storrs had heard Ashbee give a lecture at Charterhouse, his high school, and was so impressed with it that now with no further ado he invited Ashbee over from Cairo, where he was working, and made him head of civic development for Jerusalem. No need for a job search or c.v. in those days.

Ashbee is a fascinating man. He had made a name for himself back in the 1890s as a leading figure in the Arts and Crafts movement, as a disciple of John Ruskin. He was actively gay but had married a seventeen-year-old girl. She had a nervous breakdown after six years of a non-consummated marriage and a non-consummated and aborted love affair. But this crisis seems to have changed their relationship for good, and they had four daughters together. (The whole family eventually joined him in Jerusalem, though now husband and wife had separate bedrooms.) Ashbee was involved throughout the 1890s in all aspects of the politics of the Arts and Crafts movement. He was active in the conservation of old buildings in London and founded the publication that is still the basis on which ancient buildings are listed for protection and preservation. He was passionate about the Garden City movement: he traveled to lecture on it to America, where he became great friends with Frank Lloyd Wright; he designed a plan for a garden city himself (though it was not built); and wrote books and lobbied politically to bring more garden spaces into the modern urban landscape. He was also passionate about guilds: groups of young men working together to produce designed objects of beauty. (His guild workers were chosen for "what art could do for them, not for what they could do for art," and there are lovely accounts of Ashbee, Mrs. Ashbee, and his young men shocking the staid citizens of the Cotswolds with their bathing parties and picnics.) When Ashbee arrived in Jerusalem, he brought these two great passions, the Garden City and the guild, with him.

He immediately declared that Jerusalem was the finest medieval walled city still standing, and he made the walls his first project. For Ashbee, with all his 1890s pre-Raphaelite baggage, the medieval world inevitably had the greatest pull on his imagination, and it was the medieval walled city he wanted to preserve. Consequently, Ashbee not only repaired the walls but also built the rampart walk, which has been so popular a tourist route to see the city from above. The walk was to enable every visitor to appreciate the fine scope of the walls and Jerusalem as a walled city. But with his Garden City principles in mind he also cleared away all buildings from the immediate vicinity of the outside of the walls, and planned a series of gardens and walkways to enable the Old City to stand out like a jewel in a green setting. He even lovingly designed and planted gardens for the Citadel of David (though these have since been redesigned). The green spaces around the Old City, the clarity with which the walls can be seen, are the product of an 1890s aesthetic program, brought to Jerusalem in the 1920s because the governor remembered a good school lecture.

Ashbee also brought his guild principles with him. He repaired the *suq,* the roof of which in particular was in a terribly poor state. He established a guild of weavers, where Arab boys might be trained in the handicrafts that their family tradition had not passed on. ("Better for these lads—the sons of weavers, potters, glass-blowers, cabinet makers—to be practising the crafts they love and studying their much needed service to Western Industrialism than shouting catchword politics in the streets and class rooms," he wrote, with no worry about the role of Arab workers for Western

Industrialism.) He furnished the shops along the *suq* for small craft workshops. Figure 22 is a marvelous image of the ceremonial presentation of indentures to the boys who are becoming apprentice weavers—the very image of an imperial occasion. On one side of the *suq* are the British dignitaries lined up for the occasion in their hats. On the other side—for they should not mingle—the Arab parents and officials. In the middle is Ashbee, grandly overseeing his project. But Ashbee and Storrs also passed a law that no stucco and no corrugated iron could be used in Jerusalem—all buildings had to be faced with local Jerusalem stone. (This is a law of which Jerusalemites are very proud, and they often boast, mistakenly, that it was an Israeli policy.) Ashbee's insistence, based on his Arts and Crafts principles, that only local building materials should be used in the city, and Storrs's summary decision to enact it, have been one of the most influential moments in making the Jerusalem we see today. They also enacted a law that no building projects would be allowed within a zone around the Old City—preserving the integrity of the city's prospect. And, in decision after decision at the most local level, the committee Storrs and Ashbee set up and ran, the Pro-Jerusalem Council, guaranteed that the fabric of old Jerusalem—traditional wood windows, old cisterns, wells, and so on—was preserved. When you reflect on what Victorian and later planners have done to the centers of so many old cities across Europe, Storrs and Ashbee, grandees of the British Empire both, emerge as enlightened heroes.

The rampart walk is still an excellent way to see the roofs and towers of the Old City and to appreciate how poor a defense the wall is against genuine military attack, especially from the north: it is good enough protection against marauding bandits, but would, I suspect, be precious little help against the cannons and siege-craft even of a sixteenth-century army. A British sea captain named Nathaniel Crouch, who was imprisoned on suspicion of spying, did write an account of the fortifications in 1699 that concluded: "Jerusalem is the strongest City that I saw in all my travels from Grand

Figure 22. C. R. Ashbee presenting Arab boys with their indentures to become apprentices in the weaving trade: the Mandate at work in organizing society.

Cairo hither," but his estimation of its strength was never put to the test. Jerusalem from the sixteenth century until the twentieth was a backwater over which no one seriously fought in military terms. This did not stop the authorities from being extremely suspicious: any non-Muslim visitors had to unbuckle their swords, await formal escort through the gates into the city, and pay an entrance fee.

The rampart walk is just over two miles in full, and there is no point in rushing it, even if the narrow path did encourage speed (which it doesn't). There are stunning and constantly changing views in both directions, out across modern Jerusalem as well as across the Old City. You can go up at Jaffa Gate, the Citadel and Damascus Gate; but you can only leave the ramparts at St. Stephen's Gate, Herod's Gate, New Gate, Zion Gate, and near the Dung Gate (Map 4). In the best of all possible worlds, a visitor should do the walk twice, once early on just to get a sense of the city and to work out the relations between the quarters and their most distinctive buildings and specific atmospheres; a second time later, when the city is more familiar, and when each of the spires and monumental structures has a name and a history in the imagination.

This walk provides a very particular vista. It lets the visitor see how the monuments of the Old City, churches, mosques, or hostels, are all locked into the jumble of everyday life. From the walls, you can look into courtyards from above, seductive with an orange tree and bench, or squalid with the detritus of modern urban living; you can look through windows of administrative buildings or into little roof gardens and dark passageways; glance toward children playing and staring at you, mothers avoiding your gaze, kids playing football. It is sometimes easy for the sightseer to forget that the Old City is a proper city, but from the ramparts both the privacy and the face-to-face closeness of old Jerusalem are open to view.

The walk also gives a good sense of the different quarters, as the austerity of the Armenian quarter contrasts with the bustle around the Jaffa Gate, the quiet authority of the Christian ecclesiastical buildings, then the exuberance of the Damascus Gate, and the more evident poverty of the Muslim quarter. But the contrast that I always find most striking here is another one. When you look into the Old City your eye is drawn immediately to the tall buildings punctuating the skyline and demanding attention: the old and newer churches, the minarets. This is the city where religions compete for attention in architecture as in politics. But when you turn away from the Old City and look out over new Jerusalem, the Old City is ringed by a series of large, monumental Victorian edifices, as well as some more modern monstrosities. The French, the Italians, the English, the Germans, and the Russians all began building here in the nineteenth century, as each strove to extend their empires over the territories of the failing and fading Ottoman regime. There is an eerie sense of the different European empires gathering around the Old City, waiting to move in—massing outside the gates. Yet most of these buildings—the French hospice, the Italian hospital, the Russian compound—are no longer used for their original purpose. These empires, too, have now passed away. Walls are boundaries, and, when you stand on the walls between the Old and the New City, there is a strong sense of the contrast and the complications of secular and religious power in the history of Jerusalem.

THE GATES OF THE CITY: INSIDERS AND OUTSIDERS

There are seven gates to the Old City—that is, seven that are open and used—each with different names, depending on religious group and history, and each with its own story (Map 4). The gate that most visitors these days use to approach the Old City is the Jaffa Gate in the Western Wall. It is known as Bab al-Khalil, "Gate of the Friend" in Arabic; this refers to Abraham, "friend of God," and the road that leads from this gate toward the west and Jaffa (which is why it is known to the westerners as Jaffa Gate) also leads to Hebron, the site of the burial place of Abraham. Walls divide, and it is a telling difference that the gate through the wall here orientates the Arabic community inland toward Hebron, the western community toward Jaffa and the port to Europe. Each and every gate in this way doesn't just "have a different name" but also expresses a different story about a community, a different relation to Jerusalem.

The gate originally had an L-shaped entranceway—as did all of Suleiman's original gates, except the Damascus, which has a double L—and it is still there through the gate tower, but a road has also been opened just next to it. The L-shaped entrances made a simple defense against onrushing troops or transport, but modern needs of access—the all-powerful lobby of the automobile, against which Ashbee raged unsuccessfully: "the enemy of architecture," he called the car—have made these gates seem too awkward. Hence the road. The Jaffa Gate is where two of the most famous modern entrances to Jerusalem have been made, by Kaiser Wilhelm II and General Allenby, Wilhelm at the height of German imperial ambition, Allenby as Britain began to win the war that would result in the kaiser's abdication.

In 1898 Kaiser Wilhelm II, emperor of Germany and Prussia, made his journey to Jerusalem. In some ways, he was a perfect nineteenth-century Protestant tourist. The approach to Jerusalem and the condition of the holy places "cut him to the quick." While "the thought . . . that His feet trod the same ground is most stirring to one's heart," he also found that, as he wrote to his uncle, the tsar of Russia, "the Holy Land is simply terrible in its arid dryness and utter want of trees and water." Above all, he hated "the race for the highest towers or biggest churches" and the "free fights and battles in the churches." He confessed finally, like so many Protestants before him: "I return home with great feelings of disillusion and with the firm conviction that our Saviour's grave *quite certainly is not* beneath that Church of the Holy Sepulchre." Jerusalem, he lamented angrily, was full of "worship of stones and wood," "fetish adoration."

But no emperor, especially not this emperor, could be an average tourist. He was the first foreign sovereign to make a state visit to Jerusalem, and it caused huge international excitement. In what the Victorian English novelist G. K. Chesterton called "a mixture of madness and vulgarity which literally stops the breath," he wore a crusader outfit for his arrival on his white horse (his autobiography and letters show him to have had more than a passing self-interest in ceremonial and, indeed, in dressing up). In part because traditionally only a conqueror could enter Jerusalem's gates on horseback, and in part for the more mundane reason that the empress Augusta's grand carriage couldn't easily handle the bend of the gateway, a section of the wall was torn down and the sixteenth-century moat filled in—to form the road we see today. (The empress had to use the carriage because she was feeling rather weak from the travel anyway; and the emperor had put her on his patent "anti-fat" treatment, though she was already quite slim.) He may have expressed a dislike of the "race for the highest towers or the biggest churches" in a private letter, but he was in Jerusalem precisely to dedicate formally the Dormition Abbey, whose dome dominates the skyline of Mount Zion opposite the Old City, and for the opening of the Church of the Redeemer, near the Church of the Holy Sepulchre, whose huge tower gives the best view over Jerusalem ("Willy's extinguisher," the British called it). For the opening of the Church of the Redeemer he arrived in a parade with his entourage all dressed in white as Teutonic knights to a band playing Handel's "See the Conquering Hero Comes." *Punch,* the popular British satirical magazine, wickedly depicted him in a cartoon as "Cook's Crusader," after the travel company Thomas Cook's—a jibe that so hit home that the German press had a hissy fit, and years later in the First World War, *Punch* was one of the targets threatened with destruction after the intended capture of London. The Augusta Victoria Tower, named for Wilhelm's wife, is set on the hill between Mount Scopus and the Mount of Olives, and is another huge landmark to navigate by. "Two German towers will raise their towers into the blue sky," crowed the Cologne press, recognizing the imperial triumph.

The property on which the Dormition Abbey is built was given to Germany when Wilhelm visited the sultan in Constantinople just before traveling to Jerusalem. Wilhelm, who had recently paid a grand visit to the pope, gave it to the German Catholic community, and in his speech he promised to support Germans of all Christian persuasions. This gesture was seen by the *Times* of London as a "political masterstroke," as the pope had been distinctly unhappy with German moves in the Holy Land, and had temporarily broken off diplomatic relations. At the same time, the newly built Church of the Redeemer became the center of the German Lutheran community. Wilhelm cared about religion and actively worked for Protestant unity. But this trip was certainly not solely about religion. He was given this prime land by the sultan because Germany was building the Anatolian Railway for the Ottomans, and the emperor was looking to expand Germany's imperial influence. German-Turkish relations were being cemented by this royal tour. Even the apparently bland promise to support Germans of all Christian persuasions was a political firecracker. The French for centuries had claimed the right to be the sole and official protector of all Catholics in the Holy Land. Germany was muscling in on the imperialist arena where politics and religion intertwine. The British press noted and deplored the show (as the long buildup toward the First World War continued). There were around thirty articles in the *Times* on Wilhelm's progress. "His pilgrimage to Palestine is invested politically with [the] most significant international character," it noted; "the influence of German finance and German commerce in the East has mightily increased," it worried, underlining the material concerns behind the spectacles; and, it concluded, "The pacific crusade . . . will mark a new and memorable starting point . . . in the advance of Teutonic power and influence in the East." The road through the Jaffa Gate is a memorial to this spectacle of power.

Allenby's entrance nearly twenty years later in 1917 was no less self-conscious about the symbolic value of spectacle. The surrender of Jerusalem had been slightly farcical. The Ottoman governor asked the Arab mayor to make the official surrender. With a sheet taken from the American Colony as his white flag (he had visited Mrs. Spafford to tell her the news first), the mayor had looked for several hours before finding an officer of suitable status to accept the surrender (and he caught a cold that developed into pneumonia, from which he died three weeks later). But there was nothing left to chance about the ceremony of entrance. The War Cabinet discussed the issue at length, and the main figure deputed to devise the event was no less than Sir Mark Sykes, the leading foreign af-

fairs official who also negotiated and signed the infamous and originally secret Sykes–Picot agreement between Britain and France
(which was an agreement to divide the Middle East between these
two imperial powers after the war; the border between Syria and
Iraq still follows the Sykes–Picot line). The British government had
two aims to achieve in Allenby's great moment. The first was to
score a propaganda victory over the Germans. Allenby was informed by the War Office: "It would be of considerable political
importance if you, on officially entering the City, dismounted at
the City Gate and entered on foot. German Emperor rode in, and
the saying went round 'A better man than he walked.' Advantage of
contrast in conduct will be obvious." It was certainly obvious to the
British press. The *Daily Mirror* duly noted the contrast with "the
German Emperor's swagger into Jerusalem (and all over the East)
before the war," and the *Daily Sketch* crowed that this was "a staggering blow to the German dream of domination in the East and to
the Kaiser's pretensions."

The second aim was more tricky. The War Office was frightened
about how the millions of Muslim subjects of the empire would re-
act to the capture of Jerusalem. On November 15, 1917, the British
government's Department of Information published a private and
confidential memo to the press that stressed "the undesirability
of publishing any article, paragraph, or picture suggesting that military operations against Turkey are in any sense a Holy war, a modern Crusade or have anything whatever to do with religious questions. The British Empire is said to contain a hundred million
Mohammedan subjects of the King and it is obviously mischievous
to suggest that our quarrel with Turkey is one between Christianity
and Islam." Modern attempts to control the "mischievous" language of holy war are no more successful than this one was: on De-
cember 9, less than four weeks after the government memo, *Punch*
published a cartoon showing Richard the Lionheart looking down
at Jerusalem contentedly: "My dream come true!" The cartoon was

headed "The Last Crusade." Books like *Khaki Crusaders* (1919), *With Allenby's Crusaders* (1920), *The Modern Crusaders* (1920), and *The Romance of the Last Crusade* (1923) took up the theme, as did a string of newspaper articles. But in 1917 the British government was desperate to avoid any implication of a holy war, and this led to the form the ceremony finally took.

There was a wildly misguided first plan to stage the entrance in accordance with an old Arab prophecy, which claimed that a prophet from the West would enter Jerusalem through the Golden Gate and bring an end to Turkish rule when Nile water was brought to Jerusalem. The ingenious but politically dim major-general Guy Dawnay pointed out that Nile water was carried to Palestine by a British-built pipeline, and that Allenby's name could be written in Arabic *al-nabi,* "the prophet." But this half-baked scheme would have required not only opening the long-sealed Golden Gate but also the general's marching through a Muslim graveyard and right across the Haram al-Sharif. And so this plan was "unfortunately" scrapped, as Allenby ruefully wrote to his wife. Instead, Allenby entered on foot (Figure 23) and made a proclamation on the steps by the Citadel of David: he declared martial law, guaranteed freedom of religious worship, put the Haram and Hebron under Muslim control, and specifically announced that the hereditary Muslim gatekeepers of the Church of the Holy Sepulchre "have been requested to take up their accustomed duties," in remembrance of the "magnanimous act of Caliph Omar who protected [the] church."

Allenby's entrance is often remembered as a moment of spontaneous and natural humility, the mark of a true English gentleman and soldier. But at this historical moment, the walk itself and every word were carefully scripted by London with a careful, manipulative gesture toward the long history of Jerusalem's conquering heroes, in order to assuage the potentially difficult subjects of the empire. And the British government's plans worked. T. E. Lawrence—Lawrence of Arabia—dressed in a borrowed major's uni-

Figure 23. Allenby walks into Jerusalem in 1917 at the head of the conquering British Army.

form rather than his usual Arab headgear, was at Jaffa Gate and, in on the plan, cynically noted the success of "Sykes' catholic imagination." There was hardly any reaction from the empire; and at home the British reveled in the moment precisely as a triumph of Christianity: in the Temple Church in London, to celebrate the arrival of a Christian army in Jerusalem, "the first since 1239," the barristers processed around the church and put laurel wreaths on the effigies of the crusader knights buried there, and after a sermon on the duties of empire, sang the hymn "Gird on Thy Conquering Sword."

Not all the entrances to Jaffa Gate were full of such historic significance. Flaubert, the great nineteenth-century French novelist, was prepared to be disappointed, and records merely that he farted very loudly as he entered (ever in search of the *mot juste,* he was not one for the clichés of Romantic tourism): "I was even annoyed," he wrote dyspeptically, "by this Voltaireanism of my anus." Charles Warren, imperialist archaeologist and adventurer, with brisk distaste records a public execution in the 1870s, events that usually took place by the Jaffa Gate. The inexperienced executioner swerved in his first blow: "You are hurting me!" was the incongruous complaint from the victim. The executioner struck wildly, and after sixteen blows, turned the victim over and sawed at his neck as if he were sacrificing a sheep.

Jaffa Gate is the place to enter the Old City, then. It is a place of buried memories. Above the gate in 1917 rose a huge clock-tower (Figure 23) in white stone. It was erected by Sultan Abdul Hamid II as an icon of municipal modernization in 1907. R. A. S. Macalister, the archaeologist who was director of excavations for the Palestine Exploration Fund, stormed that the gate "has been utterly spoilt by the erection above of an ultra-hideous clock-tower, which is in itself a perfect eye-sore." Ashbee and the Pro-Jerusalem Council agreed (the color of the stone was enough in itself): down it came immediately after the Mandate took over, though it was reassembled in Allenby Square near the post office, so that the inconvenienced citizens could tell the time at least. Post offices were also part of the imperial struggle. Each of the major empires at the end of the nineteenth century established its own postal system in Jerusalem. The Austrian was most efficient, by repute, and was in the little square onto which Jaffa Gate opens; it is now a tourist office. (The British Post Office, on Jaffa Road, remains a dominant municipal building and a sign of past glories.) The Imperial Hotel on the left as you come into the square is a charmingly ramshackle affair, swathed inside with pictures and posters. From the balcony of the tiny bar, you can look out over the square (hard to imagine a more intoxicating place to stand); from the roof, there are extraordinary views of the Old City (though you need permission from the hotel to go up there). It has been run by the same delightful Palestinian family since 1949. It was once the Grand New Hotel, built by the Greek Orthodox treasurer of the Church of the Holy Sepulchre, for the arrival of Wilhelm; it became a hospital in the First World War and then a British Army Headquarters. This was where Sari Nusseibeh met his team of Palestinian intellectuals and activists associated with the new al-Quds University. The Swedish Bible Study Center on the corner of David Street opposite the road's entrance has a large sign on it. This building, owned by the Armenian community, was where the American consul lived in the nineteenth century. From his front room he could look out over the square and have a wonderful view of who arrived and who left and who met whom. Jaffa Gate is still the place for that. For all too many visitors, the historical richness of the Jaffa Gate is lost in the rush of modern life.

The Zion Gate—Bab el Nabi Daoud, Gate of the Prophet David—to the southeast of Jaffa Gate (Map 4), leads from the Old City to Mount Zion. It was badly damaged in the fighting of 1948. Zion Gate was the old entrance to the Jewish quarter, and where the lepers sat. Early Victorian tourists were much taken—usually with a shudder—by the biblical resonance of the "lepers by the gate." They particularly noticed the foul smell, which was not mentioned in the Bible. The Dung Gate, further around to the east (Map 4), was widened by the Jordanians in 1953 to get cars through (it was originally only a postern). It is called the Dung Gate by Jews because of a reference in the biblical book of Nehemiah to a southern gate used to take out dung from the Temple Mount (though this gate is certainly not that!). The Arabs call it Bab el-Magharbeh, "Gate of the Moors," because this part of the city was populated by North African immigrants in the sixteenth century. Each name of each gate records a community's different sense of history.

The whole stretch of wall between the Jaffa Gate, the Zion Gate, and the Dung Gate has been well excavated. It is clear that the sixteenth-century wall of Suleiman followed the line of a Hasmonean (second-century B.C.) wall, and that Herod built a wall just outside the Hasmonean wall, using it as an extra support. The towers still standing here are all medieval, but perhaps the most interesting archaeological discovery is the massive stones, five courses of wall, which were once the corner of the Nea Church. The Nea ("New") was built by the Roman emperor Justinian (under whose name Roman law was codified; the "Justinian Code" has influenced European law ever since). It was the largest church in Jerusalem—115 meters long and 57 meters wide, with four rows of columns supporting the roof. It is described for us in awestruck eulogy by the Byzantine historian Procopius, who adds the detail that they had to make special wagons to transport the stones, each wagon the size of one stone and drawn by forty oxen. Certainly the huge stones of the wall here suggest something of that magnificence.

A bare image of the church is on the Madaba map, at the end of the cardo (Figure 8), an image that actually led the archaeologists to find the site of the church. A large cistern that was part of the church compound was also discovered nearby in 1977 in the dig in the Jewish quarter of the Old City. The archaeologists were incredibly excited to discover a Greek inscription on it (Père Benoit, by then one of the oldest archaeological experts on Jerusalem, whose subject changed beyond recognition in these post-war years, wandered around it mumbling, "Unbelievable! Unbelievable!"). The inscription, unseen for more than thirteen hundred years, identified the date and the provenance of the building precisely: "This is the work which our most pious emperor Flavius Justinian carried out with munificence, under the care and devotion of the most holy Constantine, priest and superior, in the thirteenth year of the indiction" (549 A.D.). The Nea did not stand long; it was destroyed, probably by the Persians in 614, and unlike the Church of the Holy Sepulchre, it was never rebuilt. Only with the opportunities for excavation after the 1967 war were archaeologists able to find and describe its ruins. The bare traces of the destroyed monument of a great emperor were revealed after thirteen hundred years, because modern destructive violence allowed scholars the chance to pick over the bones of the city.

To the north of Jaffa Gate, the New Gate (opened in 1887 to service the new northern suburbs) and Herod's Gate (or Bab el-Zahr, "Flower Gate") flank the most elaborate of all the city gates, the Damascus Gate, opening into the heart of East Jerusalem. It is the only gate to have been properly investigated by the archaeologists. The first gate here was built in 41–44 A.D., but it was extensively rebuilt by Hadrian in 135 with the founding of Aelia Capitolina after the Bar Kochba revolt. It was a free-standing monumental entrance to the city which opened onto a semi-circular plaza, from which the two main arteries of the city extended. The Madaba map (Figure 8, to the far left of the map) gives a strong impression of the importance of what has always been the main entrance to the city: it shows two towers on either side of the gate, the plaza with the cardo leading off it, and what appears to be a monumental column in the plaza (the gate was also traditionally known in

Arabic as the Gate of the Column, Bab el-Amud). Hadrian's Gate had a large central arch for traffic, with two smaller entrances on either side for pedestrians. It was incorporated into the wall by the end of the third century; but by the eighth century the side entrances were completely blocked by debris, and the medieval gate was several meters higher than the Roman. You can see something of the Roman remains exposed below street level on either side of the present gate. Jerusalem has always grown up on the debris of the past.

The Ottoman towers now with their arrow slits and crenellations are the most warlike part of the whole circuit of the wall (Captain Crouch, the supposed spy, counted twenty-five cannons in position there in 1699), and you can investigate the guardroom and tower. Inside and outside this gate is the most crowded market: the exhilarating noise, colors, smells, press of bodies can also be overwhelming, and it is not the easiest place for detailed archaeological touring. But opposite the gate is the four-square and solid Schmidt's College, a German Protestant hostel (which has a super historical model of the Temple in the basement made by Conrad Schick, the German Protestant designer of Me'a She'arim). The roof here provides the best view by far of the Damascus Gate, its full frontage, now with the Dome of the Rock and the rest of the city behind it. There is something poignantly telling about Jerusalem, too, in the contrast between the view and the place of viewing: the heaving and shouting Palestinian market around the Ottoman towers; the cool, wide corridors of the hostel with its quietly swishing nuns, behind the heavy doors of the Victorian building. Inside and outside, East and West, Christian and Muslim, sixteenth century and nineteenth century, public and private, exuberance and silence—walls are boundaries that divide.

Slightly further around the city walls to the east, opposite the bus station, the authorities have just reopened the Cave of Zedakiah, closed previously for many years. This is a Herodian quarry that extends a natural carstic fissure in the bedrock 250 meters down under the city. It is a long, manmade cave. But how could an underground space in Jerusalem be free of stories? Because it looks old, it was easy to associate it with the time of Solomon: so from the 1860s it was adopted by the Freemasons as if it were a secret Solomonic chamber (and even when the cave was closed to the public, by special permission it was used ritually by them). But even before this, the religious imagination was at work. It is called the Cave of Zedakiah because Zedakiah, king of Israel, was said to flee through it to escape his enemies, and to emerge on the plain of Jericho, where he was captured anyway. This is a story that turns up in Rashi, the great eleventh-century French commentator on the Talmud and the Bible. Muqadisi, the Muslim travel writer whom we have already met, tells the story that this was where Korach and his followers, rebels against the authority of Moses, were dispatched: the Bible says a hole opened in the ground to swallow them. But Muqadisi knows this is a quarry and doesn't believe the story, though he is interested enough to tell it. Since Korach perished when the Israelites were wandering in the desert, it is hard to know quite how the story could be attached to a site by the walls of Jerusalem. Even in 1887, a guidebook reports the tale that it was an endless tunnel, and that an old woman had entered it and never returned (the sort of story told of every deep mine). Barclay—of Barclay's Gate fame—was the first to explore it. Worried about local feelings, he and his two sons came at night dressed as Arabs, and one of the first things they found was a human skeleton . . . So the stories multiply. When I visited shortly after it opened, I heard violin music more and more clearly as I reached the back of the cave. Then in one of the larger excavations to one side, I saw a table laid out for a luxurious lunch, complete with tablecloth and candles— and a violinist practicing for the guests about to arrive. It turned out that a government official was entertaining his Ukrainian government counterpart to lunch here. It was an extraordinary sight, and as bizarre a place for an official function as I have seen. Perhaps the tale of ghostly diners under the city will soon be in circulation.

THE FOUR QUARTERS

The four quarters of the Old City have grown up in response to the pressures of cultural, political, and religious conflict over the centuries. To the inhabitants, the boundaries between them are significant markers, and the few recent attempts to cross these boundaries—mainly militant radical Jewish settlements in the Muslim quarter—have resulted not only in deep anger and resentment but also in the need for permanent military protection (which is no way to live). Although these quarters are recognized by all sides as a reality on the ground, it never stops the ideologues from claiming that the Old City (and Jerusalem as a whole) is really, absolutely, and properly a Jewish city or really, absolutely, and properly an Arab city (while the Christians are unhappy with all the depredations of Muslim or Jewish sovereignty). The problem of Jerusalem . . .

THE ARMENIANS: SECRET DOORS AND STONES THAT CRY OUT

The Armenian community is the oldest Christian community in Jerusalem, but it is by far the hardest quarter to get to know. The Armenians as a kingdom converted to Christianity even before Constantine made the Roman Empire Christian, and they came to Jerusalem as pilgrims from a very early date indeed; they began to build dedicated hostels and churches probably in the fifth century. Armenia itself has been subject to brutal treatment across the centuries, and in particular in the early part of the twentieth century, when the Turkish Ottomans slaughtered up to two million Armenians in a vicious exercise of ethnic cleansing for which the Turkish government still shamefully refuses to acknowledge culpability. The Armenian community is a community of the diaspora. But the

Armenian quarter in Jerusalem, unlike the other quarters, is a formally established, highly conservative, inward-looking community,
whose thick walls and closed doors maintain its privacy firmly.

The community centers around the Cathedral of St. James and
the monastery attached to the cathedral, which has extensive housing in which the lay community lives. The Armenian patriarch,
whom we have already met in the ceremony of Greek fire in the
Church of the Holy Sepulchre, is the titular and spiritual head
of the community, but there are very few monks—around sixty
worldwide—while no more than two thousand Armenians live in
the Old City. The ordinary families live in houses once designed
for pilgrims or monks—white terraces and alleyways around open
squares. It is a face-to-face society, a village within the city, with its
own institutions and fiercely protected education system. (It can
only be visited with an Armenian host, and the gates to the compound are still locked every night at 10.00 P.M.) The patriarchate
owns all the property of the quarter, and plenty of other commercial sites around the city, which are let out on peppercorn rents to
their occupants. Houses change hands only by "key money." An
amazing collection of early Armenian manuscripts is now housed
in a specialized modern library, but it is used only by a few scholars
of Armenian religious and cultural history. Behind its walls, the
quarter is a quiet place; many of the young are leaving for a more
exciting life, and there is a palpable sense of the old living with their
history here.

The Cathedral of St. James (Map 4) is only open for services and
to tourists for short periods each day, but it combines the splendor
of a baroque cathedral with nooks and crannies of surprising and
homely treasures. It was created over many centuries, as with so
many religious buildings in Jerusalem. The oldest part of the cathedral is a fifth-century chapel—the Chapel of St. Menas, which is
only open to visitors once a year; there is a tenth-century sacristy
around it, but the bulk of the church is twelfth century, though

many of the decorations come from the eighteenth century and later. It has a wholly different atmosphere from the Church of the Holy Sepulchre—not only calm, but also the home of a single, thriving community with a passionate artistic and intellectual tradition, rather than a bunch of communities jammed together in conflict.

The entrance way (with a prominently displayed 1432 Mameluk inscription on the wall granting the Armenians tax-free status) leads onto a porch decorated with inscribed crosses in relief, called *khatchkars,* which are the archetypal sign of Armenian pilgrims (which we also saw on the steps down to the Armenian chapel in the Church of the Holy Sepulchre). The oldest here are from the ninth and tenth century. But when you enter the cathedral itself, after these simple signs of piety, a dazzling forest of ornate lamps of silver and gold, hanging from the ceiling, bursts into view. Each of these lamps *(ganteghs)* was donated, many by villages that no longer exist in Armenia; some by guilds, others by rich individuals. As early as 1422, John Polomer, a pilgrim, was amazed at the "two hundred or more lamps" and a single chandelier with more than 120 lights. They hang in the air of the wide nave under the dome all the way to the altar, which is decorated from the floor with a band of ornate Armenian tiles with fabulous colors and designs, as are each of the four square pillars (Figure 24). Above the tiles are paintings of bearded saints, simple against rich and elaborate backgrounds. The floor itself is covered with luxurious carpets. There is no iconostasis (screen of icons) in the Armenian liturgy; instead, at the most dramatic moments of the year's religious ritual, the altar is concealed with an immense curtain, normally furled away. It is light blue silk, woven with images of the life of Jesus and the saints. It dates back to 1756,and took twenty-five years to make. The curtain makes a very striking sight as it swirls across the front of the altar, the size of a small house, with its delicate colors and weaving. The floor in front of the altar is a seventeenth-century stone marquetry

Figure 24. The interior of St. James, the Armenian cathedral.

(opus sectile) with elegantly aging marble inlaid patterning. The monks in black cowls sing the service in rich harmony, and the officiating priests in yellow copes intone a distinctive melody against the plain chant in swirls of incense. Against the gloom of the cathedral light, the baroque splendor is muted into a gorgeous blend of textures and colors, which makes this one of the most impressive and engaging interiors in Jerusalem—and the service an aesthetically powerful experience.

To the left as you face the altar are a set of three small chapels and the sacristy. There are some very fine doors to the Chapels of St. James the Apostle and St. Macarius (a fourth-century bishop of Jerusalem), inlaid with tortoise shell and mother of pearl, dating from the eighteenth century. The Chapel of St. James, covered by an elaborate small dome set into the wall, is said to hold the head of the apostle St. James, who was beheaded by Herod Agrippa: you can look through a grill to its resting place beneath the floor level. Between and behind these two chapels is the fifth-century chapel dedicated to St. Menas. St. Menas was an Egyptian soldier in the Roman army in the realm of Diocletian, who retreated to become a hermit but then sought to declare his faith publicly and was martyred for it. (Diocletian's reign, 285–310 A.D., was the time of the great persecution of the Christians.) Around his burial site in Bumma, Egypt, a large monastic complex developed from the fourth century onward, and holy water from its well was transported all over the world as the "oil of Menas"—it cured ailments, of course. Thousands of little inscribed oil flasks have been dug up by the archaeologists. The rise of Islam put paid to the monastery and its cult. The shrine to Menas here in Jerusalem was built by a Roman lady called Bassa. She came to Jerusalem with the empress Eudocia, wife of Emperor Theodosius. Eudocia had been born a Greek called Athenais and took the name Eudocia when she converted to Christianity; in 444, after a sexual scandal, perhaps false and a result of court politics, she was exiled from Constantinople to Jerusalem, where she built the Basilica of the pool of Siloam (which can be seen on the Madaba map [Figure 8]) and the Church of St. Stephen; added to the walls; and, against anti-Jewish legislation, allowed the Jews to come and celebrate the festival of Succoth in Jerusalem. She is renowned as a great patron and doer of good deeds, as well as a poet whose poems in Greek still survive. Her companion, Bassa, less powerful and less wealthy, had become the abbess of a convent in Jerusalem; she built this little shrine (as we are told in a single sentence of Cyril of Scythopolis, modern Beth She'an: otherwise the connection would be quite unknown), a shrine to a distant Egyptian martyr, then the figure of a spreading cult, now almost entirely ignored, except by the Copts, Egyptian Christians, who still celebrate their own Egyptian saint. The simple shrine is still there in Jerusalem, its history made up of such a patchwork of tiny, almost forgotten fragments.

As we move toward the altar, the entrance to the sacristy is the last exit in the north wall. It is a Chapel of St. Stephen, and in the corner over the baptismal font is the chain of Gregory the Chain Bearer, an eighteenth-century patriarch and culture hero of the Armenian community. Gregory built the porch of this cathedral, and many of the decorations within it come from this time. The story goes that he wore this chain for four years, a symbol of the church's burden, while begging in Constantinople for 800 bags of gold to relieve the Armenian church of its debts to the Muslims. Thus he saved the church for the community. The chain is surprisingly neither gigantic nor displayed with any pomp and circumstance. But perhaps fund-raising is not the most impressive saintly task, either.

As you cross over the nave to go into the side chapels on the southern wall of the cathedral, just before the door itself (originally the main door of the cathedral) on the left about four feet from the floor is a panel inlaid with mother of pearl. This is one of the nicest secrets of the building. Behind the panel is a magnificently carved wooden door, decorated with eight ornate interlaced crosses, surrounded by foliage scrolls, which was donated by Jovannes and Thoros in 1371, as the inscription declares; behind the door is a hidden passageway that climbs inside the wall to a small chamber, the Chapel of Peter and Paul. I was told only half earnestly that this secret room had been a necessary protection against the fierce and evil Ottomans, who might invade the cathedral without announcement; this was the way for the priest to escape and hide. There is a similar concealed doorway in the northwest corner of the nave. The Armenians have good cause to be paranoid about the Turks, but I don't know how much this story is the familiar spinning of historical imagination around the blankness of objects.

The Chapel of Etchmiadzin, the southside chapel, is another reason for visiting the cathedral: it is distinguished for its superb Kutahya tiles, which are unlike anything else in Jerusalem. The painted tiles were made originally as dedications for the Church of the Holy Sepulchre, from the crusader period in the twelfth cen-

tury, and were set up in their current sequence here in the eighteenth century. Each of the painted images takes a religious subject,
often with a dedicatory or identificatory inscription, set in a frame
of elegant blue abstract patterns. Figure 25 shows four of these tiles
with their frame. The top shows the virgin and child, and the inscription underneath records that five tiles were dedicated at the
Church of the Holy Sepulchre in memory of Agh-Gul, an inhabi-
tant of Kutahya; her mother, Anna; her father the chief, Usep; and
her son Thoros Nuridjan in the year 1168. Behind the virgin, large
bunches of rich blue and yellow flowers bloom, against a cream
background dotted with red abstract design. Below the virgin are
three angels, Gabriel, Michael, and Uriel (as their scrolls state), each
with a drawn sword (as befits crusader times, when guardian angels
needed to be more warlike than ever). Each has yellow boots, a blue
tunic, and rather fetching red-spotted undergarments, with a design
that spreads onto their wings. I don't know of any other image of
angels with spotty wings. Below the angels rides St. Theodore,
calmly killing the dragon. The dragon is curled like a large snake
around a fruit tree, and the red fruit is picked up in the red design
of the background and the red gash of the dragon's mouth. This tile
also has a dedicatory inscription, to Abraham, the father of the cho-
rister Thoros. Finally, the prophet Isaiah sits holding the scroll of his
book open to a page from which you can just read in Armenian
script: "Behold a virgin shall conceive and give birth and thou shalt
call his name Emmanuel," the prophecy taken by Christians to announce the birth of Jesus Christ. With these four tiles, the announcement of Jesus' birth and Jesus as a baby in the arms of his
mother frame two images of a more militant Christianity, angels
and a saint with weapons drawn. The whole sequence is framed by
three different sets of blue patterned tiles. There are forty-seven of
these pictured tiles, and the combination of the detailed inscriptions with the bold colors and direct style of imagery, like manuscript miniatures transferred onto ceramic, opens a unique window

Figure 25. Kutahya tiles from the Cathedral of St. James.

onto the pilgrim society that linked Armenian towns and the religious center of Jerusalem, in a shared artistic and religious tradition.

The Convent of the Olive Tree is nearby in the Armenian quarter. It has a fine chapel built in the thirteenth century in classic Armenian style, but the real reason for visiting this spot is to admire how the religious imagination creates its own memorials. The convent houses my own favorite relic in Jerusalem. In the Gospel of Luke (19.40), when some Pharisees rebuke the disciples for singing out their halleluias to Jesus, Jesus replies: "If these should hold their peace, the stones would immediately cry out." Built into the wall of the chapel as a relic is one of the stones that would have cried out. (One can't help feeling that whoever first set up this relic had a precarious grip of the subjunctive.) I suppose you could see a mouth and an eye on the stone, if you have a fecund imagination. In the corner of the courtyard is a still surprisingly youthful looking olive tree, which according to fifteenth-century tradition is the tree against which Jesus was tied for the scourging. (It is not clear where Pilate's palace would have been if this is to be that spot.) But the identification is proven by the fact that built into the northeast corner of the chapel is a well-cut stone with a shallow cavity at its rough center. This cavity was made by Jesus' elbow as his body jerked at the pain of the first blow of the scourging. Our distance from the medieval imagination is once again all too apparent.

One of the most memorable treasures of the Armenian community is to be found outside the Old City walls in the Musrara district a short distance from the Damascus Gate, where there was an apparently extensive Armenian religious community living from the fifth century. In the Chapel of St. Polyeuctus (Map 4, top left) is a mosaic from the mid-sixth century with breathtaking colors and precision of design (Figure 26). It shows many different species of birds enclosed by a trailing vine with bunches of grapes. The caged bird is a Christian image of the soul in the body (especially for the Christians influenced by the philosophy of Plato in its neo-Platonic

Figure 26. A detail of the mosaic from the Mortuary Chapel in the Church of St. Polyeuctus.

guise). The dove of the Holy Spirit flies from the martyr's body at the moment of death. So, to continue the bird symbolism, the eagle at the top of the mosaic (not shown in Figure 26) indicates the threat of evil; the peacocks are drinking the elixir of eternal life. But it is the inscription that gives this allegorical picture its full weight: it reads, "For the memory and salvation of all Armenians whose names are known to God alone." The beautiful imagery of the eternal life of the soul honors the unknown Christian soldier, the nameless, fallen, and lost to history. For the Armenian community, this chapel has grown in bitter significance in the twentieth century.

THE JEWISH QUARTER: MAKING A MUSEUM OF THE PRESENT

The Armenian quarter, behind its walls, has a long, unbroken tradition and established institutions and rituals to support it. The Jewish quarter, in contrast, is a history of repeated destruction, exile, and rebuilding. The jumble of twisting streets and tiny squares leads down to the Western Wall, but there is no longer a unified community here, no central synagogue or shared social life. Almost every inhabited building here is new, though the pattern of old streets and the use of Jerusalem stone create a nice feeling of how the old quarter may have felt—though without the emaciated and rag-covered beggars, the horrid smells, non-existent plumbing, and pile-up of refuse and dead animals that so disgusted Victorian visitors, even those used to Dickens's London. This is a cleaned-up and historically re-created image of an older life. The quarter was badly damaged in the fighting of 1948, when Jews fiercely defended and eventually lost the area. After 1948, when the Jordanians took over, the whole quarter was looted, the synagogues destroyed, and many buildings left to ruin. In 1967, when the Israelis returned, archaeologists again took the opportunity of war's destructiveness to make some remarkable discoveries, before the reconstruction of the area started (Figure 27). There are now well–sign-posted and well-explained historical sites throughout the quarter. History is very much on display in the Jewish quarter.

This is all part of the area's current, rather odd atmosphere. The twists and turns of the streets and the variety of shapes of the courtyards certainly make this an enchanting area to wander in. The carefully preserved and highlighted archaeology allows an engrossing vista of the long history of the space. But the clean stones and polished scientific display of the past also cannot help emphasizing the newness of the Old City—with a touch of the theme park about it: the past neatly packaged for the visitor. From the end of the nineteenth century most Jews

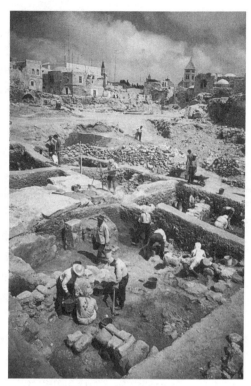

Figure 27. The destroyed Jewish quarter is laid bare by the archaeologists.

who could afford to do so moved out of the Old City, which was dirty, without facilities, and cramped—just as with the Lower East Side in New York or the East End in London. In a familiar pattern, poor, new immigrants moved in. Some impoverished religious groups insisted on staying near the Temple Mount. But the quarter now is clean, houses are expensive, and the religious groups well supported. In a museum, it is usual to contemplate the far past in a modern setting; it is rather more disconcerting to experience that contrast in a living city. There is a strange sense in the Jewish Quarter of a city turning into a museum of itself.

The cardo was the main street of the Byzantine city and stretched from the Damascus Gate straight through the town to the Nea Church, as the Madaba map shows us (Figure 8). Roman builders, who liked straight lines and good order, usually organized their towns around a main street (the cardo) and a cross street (the decumanus). About 180 meters of the Byzantine cardo were excavated in the 1970s and now form the centerpiece of the quarter's view of the past. The whole thoroughfare was about 25 meters wide. The roadway itself was originally about 12 meters wide, easily broad enough for two good-sized wagons to pass; a row of columns right along both sides were covered with a wood canopy to keep shoppers on the pavement cool and dry, and shops lined both sides of the thoroughfare. This was a grand arcade. The paving stones, columns, and one shop with its arch still in place have been excavated and worked into a modern shopping area, which is actually built down the middle of the ancient street. (One continuity of Jerusalem is its commercialization of the past.) The cardo is now fully six meters below the current street level—a figure that gives a good idea of how the ground level of Jerusalem rises over the centuries thanks to compacted deposits of rubbish. There are five glass-covered wells along the cardo, down which you can see to the lower levels still.

The look underground here is not just a silent glimpse through layers of old levels of city life down to bedrock. The excavations here solved one of the most contentious arguments about the ancient history of Jerusalem, and the solution turned on what has been called, not least by the excavator himself, the most important archaeological discovery of twentieth-century Jerusalem. For at least a century before the 1970s, scholars had debated where the Jerusalem of the First Temple really was, how far it stretched, and whether it was anything like as important as the Bible suggests. Maximalists (as they are known) suggested that it was a large city, incorporating not merely Mount Moriah, where the Temple was, and the eastern hill (the City of David) but also the western hill, beyond even the southern wall of the current Old City. The minimalists argued that it was a tiny hill town that did not stretch beyond the Temple area and the City of David.

Dame Kathleen Kenyon, the outspoken and autocratic British archaeologist who more than made her way in a field dominated by men, while bringing modern stratiographic science to biblical archaeology, had shown that previous scholars had overestimated even the size of the City of David; she further claimed from her limited trials to have found no evidence for any inhabitation of the western hill before the second century B.C. It seemed that her authority had won the case for Jerusalem to be seen as a small town on just the eastern hill. But the 1970s dig gave archaeologists the opportunity to open up a large territory previously impossible to excavate on the western hill; they found, not only pottery, statuettes, and inscriptions that were evidence for a permanent settlement in the eighth century B.C., but also, most surprisingly and conclusively, a 7-meter-thick monumental defensive wall. They uncovered an unbroken stretch of it running some 65 meters in length, with a maximum height of 3.3 meters. This had to be the Israelite wall—the broad wall—that is mentioned in the Book of Chronicles and built by Hezekiah. Even the doughty Dame Kathleen was convinced. A piece of the broad wall is displayed just off the cardo (Map 4).

The Palestine Exploration Fund was set up in part to bring a better water supply to Jerusalem, but most Victorian archaeology was motivated by a desire to find proof of the Bible's veracity in the face of the growing weight of a more cynical and scientific criticism. Kenyon's own much-publicized, scientific excavations at Jericho claimed to show that there was no archaeological evidence for Joshua bringing the walls a-tumbling down. Here in the 1970s was a modern scientific excavation, which almost inadvertently found itself arguing that the Bible's history was ratified by archaeology. It is no surprise that the excavators were at first extremely cautious about advertising their find—and when it did become known, the whole design for rebuilding the area was changed, thanks to a command from the government to preserve the historical and now religious site.

But there was more. In digging to the north of the broad wall, looking for the expected site of a Hasmonean wall (which was duly found), the same excavators were amazed also to uncover a massive Israelite tower, more than eight meters tall, surprisingly well preserved and apparently part of a further fortification system here at the north wall of the city, traditionally its weakest point. With much excitement, the excavators found that the surface of the foot of the tower was covered with charred wood, ashes, and soot, and amid these signs of a conflagration, arrowheads. They wrote: "If we fit these discoveries in with known historical data, it seems likely that they are direct evidence of the siege and final conquest of Jerusalem in 586 B.C. by Nebuchadnezzar, king of Babylon," as related in the Book of Kings. Here, amid the modern ruins of the Jewish quarter, were the traces of the first and foundational destruction of Jerusalem, still lamented in Jewish liturgy. The rebuilding of the Old City would echo the old history of return and rebuilding.

It is difficult to get orientated before the remains of the tower, physically or historically (Map 4). As you look at the fortification and across it into the Old City, you are actually looking out across the final barrier of the eighth-century city, toward the enemy, as it were. The overlapping historical topographies of the different cities of Jerusalem need a shift of bearings. But here just off the cardo, center of the Byzantine city, in a fully modern setting, it is startling to see the boundary of the eighth-century B.C. city, fought over so long ago. The archaeologists are obsessed with walls in part out of a desire to find where the ancient space of the city lies; but ever since the time of the Victorian excavators, the search for walls has remained such an obsession because of the inflammatory relationship between Jerusalem and the holy scriptures of the Bible. There is always a politics of archaeology, wherever the dig is, but in Jerusalem there is also a theology of excavation.

The Hurva Square (Map 4) takes us to another scene of destruction, reconstruction, and politics. The square is one of the more open spaces in the quarter, light and airy. There are three buildings in the square, jammed up against one another, and the relation between them and the history of the quarter is emblematic. One is the Ramban Synagogue. When Nachmanides, known as the Ramban, came to Jerusalem in 1267, he found two Jews and no synagogue. He established a synagogue, which moved to this site around 1400, and in 1523, it is said, this was still the only synagogue in Jerusalem. In 1599, Jews were banned by the Muslim authorities from praying there, and the building was used over the next three centuries for a range of menial purposes (though in the Mandate, with precise historical aggression, the Mufti turned it symbolically into a little mosque). In 1967, with a self-conscious sense of history, it was once again restored as a place of Jewish worship. It is a simple, stone building, vaulted, with few decorations but an impressive austerity. In the center of the square is a tall minaret, the second building, the minaret of Jama Sidi Umar, built in 1397, the only minaret in the Jewish quarter, and its position in the middle of where the Jews gathered to pray is pointed: as with the minarets on either side of the Church of the Holy Sepulchre, there is an evident architectural message of supremacy.

The Hurva Synagogue, the third building, gives its name to the square. This synagogue was founded by Yehuda ha-Chasid, who arrived in Jerusalem from Europe with great hullabaloo in 1700 and died five days later. The community he led collapsed into financial and social disarray, and as they fell into debt, their building fell into ruin. Hence its name: "*hurva*" means ruin. Gedaliah, a Polish immigrant, describes the horror of being an Ashkenazi Jew at this time. The Ashkenazis (Jews originating from northern and western Europe) were forced to pay special taxes—basically an extortion racket—for building the synagogue, which crippled them with debt; it was hard to trade as they did not know the language; if they sold some wine to an Arab and the Arab was seen drunk, the Jew was imprisoned and beaten and fined: "If a Jew makes a Turk angry, then the latter beats him shamefully and dreadfully with his shoe, and nobody delivers the Jew from his hand." Simon van Geldern fled the city at night in 1766: "On my journeys," he lamented, "I see how contemptible we are in the eyes of those who dwell in the land. We are, after all, great fools . . . But I can tell you that in fifty years' time no Ashkenazis will be living in the land any more." Despite this grim prophecy of an impoverished, humiliated, and frightened immigrant, in 1838, the Pasha granted the site to the Ashkenazi community again, and the synagogue, which became the center of the Ashkenazi Jewish community, was finished in the 1850s. It was a large, domed structure, and for Jews between the Dome of the Rock and the dome of the Church of the Holy Sepulchre, this was the dome of the Jewish quarter. It became a ruin again, however, in 1948, when it was deliberately dynamited by the Jordanians. For many years after the recapture of the quarter in 1967, a simple thin, high arch stood over the site as a memorial to the once-thriving synagogue. Now this arch has disappeared, too, since the government announced a plan for the reconstruction, once more, of the building.

They had a great opportunity here. One of the century's leading architects, Louis I. Kahn, was fascinated by ruins, though his completed buildings have a clean line and hard sense of light. He was inevitably drawn to "the ruin" and made a complete set of designs for the Hurva; they have been computerized so that you can take a virtual walk through the proposed building. From Kahn's bold modernist invention, there was plenty of encouragement to consider the space in a creative way. But the competition to rebuild the Hurva was won by a firm that offered to reconstruct it in its nineteenth-century form. Another dome to dominate the skyline, another large building trying to re-create the lost past. It is hard to predict who the community for such a building could possibly be, besides tourists looking to experience that past vicariously. It is unclear whether this exploitation of fake authenticity is naïve or cynical. It is certainly aesthetically uninspiring.

The four Sephardic synagogues are nearby down Mishmarot Street, in a sunken courtyard. The Sephardi community—eastern and Spanish Jews—was the dominant Jewish group in Jerusalem from the fifteenth century until the massive increase of Ashkenazi immigration in the late nineteenth century. The tension between Ashkenazi and Sephardi worlds remains one of the insistent internal tensions of Israeli society. The four synagogues are each small prayer rooms dating from the seventeenth or eighteenth century, which were allowed to be restored and set up as synagogues again in 1835. The Prophet Elijah Synagogue is so named from the legend that one year on Yom Kippur Elijah turned up to make the necessary tenth man for the quorum for prayer *(minyan)*—which also gives a sense of the smallness of the community in the difficult years of Muslim rule. All the rooms were looted under Jordanian rule, and they are now equipped with furniture taken from the wreckage of Italian synagogues destroyed during the Second World War. Once again in the Jewish quarter, overlaid histories of persecution and violence, the physical remnants of destruction, make up the very fabric of the reconstructed space.

On the corner of Hurva Square is the small entrance to the Wohl Archaeological Museum. The nondescript entrance gives little notice of the remarkable treasures the museum houses—the second great discovery of the 1970s excavation in the quarter. The archaeologists uncovered six houses of the Herodian period, the time of the construction of the Temple Mount, and they give a fascinating insight into Jerusalem in the Roman Empire. The houses are, first of all, luxurious and finely designed and finished. They are built on a terrace going down the hill, with what must have been fine views. The masonry is of excellent workmanship, and they were two-storey houses, though some may have been higher still. One has an elegant peristyle around a courtyard; another, the grandest, is large enough to deserve the archaeologists' name for it, the Palatial Mansion. These were houses for wealthy and secure Jerusalemites.

But what was most surprising was the image of life provided by the interiors of these homes. Each house had at least one and usually at least two ritual baths *(miqva'ot)*. These baths are for maintaining ritual purity, and purification from uncleanliness was a particular concern of Temple worship. According to strict law, a ritual bath has to have no less than 198 gallons of pure spring or rainwater, which has to be drawn directly into the bath and not carried in containers. This law can be observed by bringing some fresh rainwater or spring water from a "store-pool" next to the immersion pool. But none of the *miqva'ot* excavated had such a store-pool. They must have been filled and emptied by hand, which not only raises the question of whether they were used for strict ritual use but also indicates the likelihood of a goodly number of servants to draw the water. The baths, like the hallways and other rooms, were decorated with high-quality mosaics of a simple and elegant abstract pattern. There were frescoes painted on the walls. The mosaics, the frescoes, and the peristyle courtyard with its marble fluted columns show just how much Greco-Roman culture had been absorbed by the wealthy in Jerusalem. As Jerusalem was becoming an important city under Herod in the eastern Roman Empire, the Jerusalemite elite seemed to have combined Jewish ritual life with the classy luxury of empire social life. Many people like to think of the Jews as being quite different from the other subject peoples of the empire. But for Jews as for everyone else, from Britain to Damascus, the lures of Greco-Roman life—its literature, its baths, its entertainments, its sheer successfulness—were a powerful attraction. These houses show this cultural assimilation at work.

There are signs that these houses were destroyed by fire. But the most evocative record of the Roman destruction of the urban life of Jerusalem is a few yards away up Hakarim Street, in the Burnt House. What makes the Burnt House so gripping is the precision of the finds and their link to one of the most celebrated stories of the history of Jerusalem. These rooms—an entrance corridor, four rooms, a kitchen, and a bath—were evidently the basement of a larger establishment. Everything had been burned to the ground, but in the debris lurked some telling evidence. The latest coin found here is dated to exactly 69 A.D. There was an unused spear in the corner. The bones of the hand and arm were all that was left of a seventeen-year-old girl. There was a stone weight with the inscription "Belonging to Bar Kathros," which tells us who owned the house. The Kathros family turns up in the Talmud, in an attack on the high priests, who were clearly not very popular with the writer: "Woe is me because of the House of Kathros, woe is me because of their pens. Woe is me because of the house of Ishmael, son of Phiabi, woe is me because of their fists. For they are High Priests, and their sons are treasurers, and their sons in law are trustees, and their servants beat the people with staves." With the classic cry of the disempowered ("the people"), this lament bewails the writing—legal cases?—the violence, and the nepotism of the powerful priestly families. Not that such authority helped Bar Kathros. His house, along with the whole area, was burned by the Romans in their assault on the city in 70 A.D. As Josephus writes: "When they went in numbers into the lanes of the city, with their swords drawn, they slew without mercy those whom they overtook, and set fire to the houses from where the Jews had fled and burnt every soul in them." The Burnt House seems like an illustration to Josephus' grim account.

THE CHRISTIAN QUARTER: CONFLICT AND MEMORIAL

The citadel by Jaffa Gate marks the border between the Armenian and the Christian quarters, but it scarcely belongs to either. It has been the military stronghold of the city since it was built, and it has always been occupied by whichever group is in power at the time. It now houses a museum that traces the history of the city from the earliest times to the present, starting with broken curse tablets and ending with video footage. In the basement is a lovely detailed model of the whole Old City, built by Stefan Illes for the World's Fair in 1873, where the scale is subtly altered so that each building looks slightly taller than it was. That the military base should now have become a display of history (with models that are slightly distorted) seems to capture rather well the role of telling the story of the past in the current battles over Jerusalem.

The citadel is often called the Citadel or Tower of David. The Byzantines christened it the Citadel of David because they thought that this western hill was Mount Zion and that the biggest building on it should be King David's Palace; it was probably the Ottomans, later, who attached the name Tower of David to the Muslim minaret. The fortress was actually first built up to its current strength by Herod, but the name of David has stuck. Herod built three huge towers by the earlier Hasmonean wall, and he named them after his wife, Mariamne, and his friend Hippicus, and his brother Phasael. They looked over his palace, which stretched through some of the current citadel into the Armenian quarter. (It was from here that Pilate judged Jesus.) The palace, by then a symbol of Roman rule, was burned by Jewish revolutionaries in 66 at the beginning of the first Jewish Revolt. The Tower of Phasael still stands in the middle of the citadel today, a four-square building that exudes a sense of strength, from its squat dimensions and huge Herodian stones. From the roof, its strategic position is palpable, as it dominates the approach to the Old City. Its imposing military structure is evident, with its corner towers and walls enclosing its central courtyard. Seen from below, during the day or lit up at night, the citadel has become one of the most familiar, iconic images of Jerusalem.

The fort was destroyed and rebuilt several times, especially during the crusader period. The basic form we see today is the product first of the Mameluk sultan al-Nasir Muhammed, who set out the line of the walls and the internal courtyard in 1310, and second of Suleiman the Magnificent, who added the monumental entrance

and the platform for cannon along the western wall in the sixteenth century. The minaret was added in the late seventeenth century. Each of the structures here is a mish-mash of development.
The Phasael Tower has massive Herodian masonry below, but the
small stones of the upper levels are Mameluk. The mosque, repaired
by Suleiman, constructed by Mameluks over a crusader hall, is built
on the site of Herod's palace, remains of which can be seen at the
external base of the wall. The main entrance just to the south of the
Phasael Tower, with its L-shaped passage to slow attackers, was built
by crusaders and restored by Mameluks: the stone benches in the
guardroom are crusader, as are the slits for the portcullis; but the
iron-plated doors are sixteenth century. The iconic image of Jerusalem is made up of the full jumble of its history.

The excavations in the courtyard are equally a mess of buildings
from different dates, and they are very hard to appreciate except as
the visible if confused record of centuries of fighting and collapsing
and rebuilding and fighting again. The Hasmonean wall, which was
strengthened and extended by Herod, runs in a sweeping curve
from the Phasael across the courtyard toward the mosque. The ruins here greatly attracted Ashbee, who laid out gardens to make
them into a pleasant oasis at the edge of the Old City, and they do
have the dilapidated romanticism beloved by the pre-Raphaelites
and their Romantic forebears. In recent years, this vista has been
perverted or brilliantly played with—depending on your artistic
taste—by the post-modern addition of brightly colored contemporary abstract sculptures. I suspect Ashbee and the Pro-Palestine
Council would have had a collective fit.

The museum exhibition leads the visitor through the buildings
and through the history of the land with a good deal of care
(though the graffiti show the dissatisfaction of modern zealots with
this and any but their own account of affairs). The buildings themselves as much as the displays are the repository of this history. It
was here that the Roman procurator Florus unjustly condemned

and crucified politically uninvolved citizens of Jerusalem, an act that helped fuel the passions of the Jewish Revolt, which led to the sacking of Herod's Temple. It was from here that Saladin sent off two columns of Christian prisoners, one to slavery, the other, the rich, for ransom. It was on the steps of the citadel, with full consciousness of the symbolic associations, that Allenby read his speech as conqueror of Jerusalem. It remains a good place to contemplate the military and political history of the city of peace.

The Christian quarter itself, the northwestern section of the Old City (Map 4), has grown up around the Church of the Holy Sepulchre. Some of its largest compounds of buildings cannot be visited by tourists: the Greek patriarchate, which are the offices of the Greek Orthodox Church; and the Latin patriarchate, which are the offices of the Catholic Church in Jerusalem. The Greek patriarchate, as one might expect, is a fine mess of passageways, balconies, and courtyards, with surprising vistas and turns—very much with the feel of a rather grand Greek village full of black-robed and bearded priests. The Latin patriarchate, as one might also expect, is a more severe, symmetrical, northern European palace, which you pass on the rampart walk. The Latin patriarchate was founded when the crusaders took Jerusalem. As Jerusalem became firmly established under Muslim rule, the patriarch fled the city, and the Guardianship of the Holy Places was granted by the pope in 1342 to the Franciscans, who had remained, and are still very much in evidence in the Church of the Holy Sepulchre in their brown habits. In 1847, as Europe geared up for the dismantling of the Ottoman Empire, the Latin patriarch returned to Jerusalem, and since then has been responsible for the Catholic Church in the Holy Land (and Jordan and Cyprus). It is a familiar part of the street life of the Old City to see the clerics walking the crowded streets between the patriarchates and the Church of the Holy Sepulchre, and to stand aside for their formal religious processions trailing down the narrow lanes.

In recent years, both patriarchs have been much in the news. The Latin patriarch who took up office at the beginning of 1988 is Michel Sabbah, who has become a well-known politicized figure in Israel: he was born in Nazareth, educated in Bethlehem and Paris, and speaks with great eloquence as a Palestinian in a way that upsets some Israelis—and some Palestinians—but that is well suited to the church's history of radical engagement with social reform, a history often easy to forget in Jerusalem. Those who bitterly denounce Sabbah's views see him in another history: the long tradition of Catholic anti-Semitism and, in particular, opposition to Zionism in Palestine. (Sabbah will be replaced in due course by Fouad Twal, archbishop of Tunis, who was born in Madaba—of map fame—and who began as a priest in Ramallah.) Arab Christians have played an increasingly large role in the higher echelons of the Anglican and Catholic Churches of Jerusalem since the 1920s: one of the striking changes since the heyday of Victorian European imperialism.

The Greek patriarch Irineos, elected in 2001, was so embroiled in financial scandals by 2004 that he was attacked on Palm Sunday outside the Holy Sepulchre by an angry crowd, and afterward he did not even attend the ceremony of Holy Fire. There is a secret passageway in the Church of the Holy Sepulchre, opening into a shop on Christian Quarter Road, designed for a quick getaway from attack (like the hidden corridors in the Cathedral of St. James). Irineos was the first patriarch to have to use this passageway for a long while—but to escape from his own congregants! He had been accused of selling to Israelis church-owned property near the Jaffa Gate in the Old City, an act that would deeply upset the fragile balance between the quarters of the Old City. The explosive symbolic impact of Jews' buying ancient Christian property lived in by Arabs was magnified by inflammatory headlines in the newspapers of all sides, and the story has spun into increasingly intricate tales of corruption. Irineos was deposed as patriarch by a vote of bishops, which he refused to recognize, and he continues to live, holed up in strange isolation in a small apartment in the Greek patriarchate, while the controversy over the property grumbles on. For every group in Jerusalem, it seems, the intermingling of religion and politics reaches a combustible state with hectic rapidity.

If we stroll from the Jaffa Gate up the little alley to the left, where four covered streets meet, we come to a column that is the grave marker of a Roman military governor, Marcus Junius Maximus, who bossed things here in 200 A.D. (Map 4). Turn right along St. George's Street toward the Holy Sepulchre. After the road turns a sharp right and before it crosses Christian Quarter Road, we are following the edge of a large rectangular reservoir, hidden behind the houses on the right. It can be seen only from one of Jerusalem's high vantage points—the citadel, or the roof of the Imperial or Petra Hotel. It is completely surrounded by houses and workshops. It is now dry, though Sir Richard Temple painted it full of water as the foreground to his view of the Holy Sepulchre in 1888, and photos from the period do show it with glimmering reflections in the water (Figure 28). In fact, it is now being used largely as a rubbish tip by the businesses and dwellings around it. In the Middle Ages it fed the baths near the patriarch's palace and is known therefore as the Pool of the Patriarch's Bath. Others call it Hezekiah's Pool. Back in the first century A.D., Josephus called it Armygdalon, the Almond Tree Pool. It has not proved feasible to excavate this empty site, simply because for any one building to grant access to the archaeologists might be thought to grant privileges of ownership. For one brief moment in the late 1990s it seemed possible. One of the buildings finally allowed access to archaeologists, who immediately started to clear the rubbish. Within a week the Palestinian who leased the building had been threatened with the loss of his lease; the archaeologists were banned; and the rubbish was left to build up again. Given that so much of the past is lovingly tended in Jerusalem, and so much emotion is invested in the imagined past

Figure 28. Hezekiah's Pool in the late nineteenth century, when it still was full of water.

through archaeology and relics, it is something of a shock to find so large a site with so continuous a history left to dilapidate because of the bitterness of local politics. But this, too, is fully part of Jerusalem.

On the far side of the Holy Sepulchre, past the two minarets (which are equidistant from the edicule itself, and stand as a Muslim exclamation point to the Christian shrine), are two Victorian buildings, both products of European imperial projects, and yet quite different in feel and outlook: the Church of the Holy Redeemer and the Alexander Hospice. The Church of the Holy Redeemer is Kaiser Wilhelm's home for Lutheran worship in the holy city. The church itself is bare, simple, and to my eyes undistinguished. The tower, however, is one of the highest spots in the Old City—a stiff climb—and the view from it is simply extraordinary:

360 degrees and with that strange intensity that comes from staring down from a height at the life below. The church was built over the ruins of the eleventh-century Church of St. Mary of the Latins, and the medieval cloister has been kept (along with some fine Victorian photographs of the ruins in an earlier age when property in the Old City was not in such demand). It cannot be reached at present from the church, but the main door of the church's hospice is just outside on the street. Not many tourists visit the cloister, and it is a pleasant space of quiet calm of the sort one learns to seek out and appreciate in Jerusalem.

Nearby on the other side of the street is the Alexander Hospice. It is not immediately clear that this is a public building (and most parts of it are not). The door is often unmanned. It shuts for long lunches. The room on the right as you enter is a rather overstuffed Victorian parlor, full as it is with mementos of Grand Duke Sergei Alexandrovitch and his family. But the corridor opens into an unexpectedly large and airy chapel and hall of archaeological remains, which are crucial to understanding the development of the city in the Roman times of Hadrian and Constantine. Nineteenth-century explorers recognized that there was a significant archaeological site here—remains of the original Church of the Holy Sepulchre—a fact that led Russia to buy the property in 1859. This is the same time as the major development of the Russian Compound, which we will look at in Chapter 6, buildings all made possible by the relaxing of former rules against foreigners' holding property in the Holy Land. But it was not until 1882 that Grand Duke Sergei Alexandrovitch and his pious and beautiful wife, Elizabeth (Ella), granddaughter of Queen Victoria, funded the excavations and the construction of the building over them. The religiously motivated search for the historical Jerusalem of Jesus, combined with imperial expansion and the excitement of the new scientific archaeology, made this an archetypal late nineteenth-century project. It brought the wealthy and lionized Russian noble couple on a visit, which drew 5,000 Russian pilgrims to line the route of their carriage. As we will see in Chapter 6, it was a journey that led eventually to Elizabeth's becoming a saint of the Russian Orthodox Church, and to a set of buildings that have helped define the Jerusalem landscape.

The pier of an archway on the right (up some stairs), as you enter, is part of the remains of a triple arch, which marked the entrance of the forum of Aelia Capitolina, built by Hadrian in the second century. The forum, with its temple of Aphrodite, was built over the site of the burial place of Jesus, according to Constantine's rediscoverers of the Holy Sepulchre. Here, then, is where the Romans haggled and strutted, before the city became a Christian center, a sign of the Romans' attempt to wipe out Jewish Jerusalem. At the far end of the remains of the forum is another gateway, with the holes for the pins of the door still visible, and the worn-down sill on the floor. The sill is enclosed with glass because the Russians, keen to find the biblical, declared that this must be the Gate of Judgment through which Jesus left the town toward crucifixion. But it is actually Constantinian in date (late fourth century A.D.) and is probably part of the atrium of that first compound (Figure 7). (The main door of the atrium is in the backroom of Zelatimo's sweetshop in the alley nearby. For a couple of coins, the baker will let you view it, and if you have never paid a few coins to go into the backroom, one of the great gestures of gangster movies, this is your chance to do so with complete piety.) The Alexander Hospice has little interest these days in displaying its important finds; and throughout the Communist era the building represented a community in exile. It has the feeling of a place that does not quite know its role in the order of things. The massive numbers of Russian pilgrims that were such a feature of Jerusalem before the Russian Revolution have not returned with Glasnost; the long-exiled White Russians are uncertain of their position under the new regime. The museum built to contain the relics of Jesus' Jerusalem turns out to hold major remains of Hadrian's and Constantine's cities, and now to have become in itself a monument of the changing place of Russia on the world stage, and of religion for the Russians.

THE MUSLIM QUARTER: FROM THE *SUK* TO THE ROOFTOPS

The Via Dolorosa runs through the Muslim quarter from the Gate of St. Stephen, also known as the Lion Gate. It is called the Lion Gate because of the relief sculptures of four podgy lions on it. Suleiman is said to have dreamed that he would be devoured by lions if he did not build the walls and the gates of the city, and the lions record this inspirational threat. This is also one of several places said to be where St. Stephen, the first Christian martyr, met his death. Just inside the gate on the right, as you enter the Old City, is the Church of St. Anne's and the Pool of Bethesda. The church is one of the most aesthetically satisfying buildings in Jerusalem (Figure 29). It is a simple but elegant Romanesque design, built by the crusaders in 1140, and as good an example of crusader architecture as any in the Holy Land. As usual there is a biblical story attached to the structure: the house of Joachim and Anne, the parents of the Virgin Mary, is said to have been where the crypt of the church now is. The church's story is a microcosm of the histories we have been tracing in the Old City. The crusaders built over a Byzantine church; when Saladin conquered Jerusalem it was turned into a *madrassa,* and the inscription recording this is still over the door (July 25, 1192). A host of Arabic manuscripts attest to the importance of this school for Jerusalem in the next centuries. But by the nineteenth century the building was no longer in use and was filled with rubbish literally to the roof. But in 1856, in thanks for France's help in the Crimean War, the Ottoman authorities granted it to the French government and hence to the Benedictines (the White Brothers), who have restored and run it ever since. It has the most beautiful acoustics of any of the Jerusalem churches.

Figure 29. St. Anne's Church, by the Pool of Bethesda, one of the finest crusader buildings in Jerusalem.

Any voice sounds better here, and singing from near the altar reverberates around the church with a rich echo. Jerome Murphy-O'Connor, the author of the excellent *Oxford Archaeological Guide to the Holy Land,* comments with reproachful piety that "the church deserves silent contemplation," no doubt because everyone sings in St. Anne's.

The Pool of Bethesda, the remains of which are in the grounds of St. Anne's, was dug and dammed as early as the eighth century B.C., and was part of a temple to Asclepius, the Greek and Roman god of healing in the Egyptian guise of Serapis, by the second century A.D. The Gospel of John says that Jesus cured a man here who had been ill for thirty-eight years. Hence the archaeological care with which a rather unimportant pagan religious site has been excavated and incorporated into the church's compound. (The contrast with the rubbish tip of the Pool of Hezekiah/the Pool of the Patriarch's Bath is marked.) Here is one place where the connection between a Gospel and the stones on the ground is secure, and these ordinary foundations have taken on their significance from that fact alone. Whereas the Via Dolorosa itself has so little connection to history, the truth of archaeology brings its own consolations for the faithful of the scientific age.

The Via Dolorosa zig-zags through the Muslim quarter. The Church of the Flagellation was built in 1929 to mark the station where Jesus was beaten; the Ecce Homo arch is another entrance way to the Roman Forum of Aelia Capitolina (and hence cannot have been seen by Jesus). The impressive stone pavement known as the *lithostratos* is partly in the Church of the Flagellation and partly in the Convent of the Sisters of Zion. For many years this was said to be where Pontius Pilate condemned Jesus, and the board game scratched in the floor by Roman soldiers was added evidence of the callousness of the legal system that condemned him to death (and easily associated with the dicing of the soldiers for Jesus' clothes in the minds of the pilgrims). The floor was authenticated as a first-century floor at the beginning of the twentieth century by Father Vincent, one of the finest archaeologists of his generation. Unfortunately, it has been conclusively shown now to be at least from the second century, and therefore this relic again has nothing to do with the life of Jesus—except, as the sisters of the convent sadly reflect, that it has now been sanctified by so many prayers. It is still an exceptional ancient floor. The third station, where Jesus fell for the first time, is marked by a little chapel finished by Polish soldiers during the Second World War; each of the remaining stations is marked by a small chapel, except the ninth, for the third fall of Jesus, which is marked by a Roman column outside the Coptic Monastery of St. Anthony (which is where the monks live who tend the little shrine behind the sepulchre in the Church

of the Holy Sepulchre). There is no place where the disjunction
between being a tourist and being a worshipper is more strongly
felt than on the Via Dolorosa. For the pilgrim, this is a journey of
faith, a ceremonial and passionate route that is often the completion of a longer journey in religious experience as much as across
the world to reach Jerusalem. For the tourist, it is more likely to
look like a set of thoroughly undistinguished and shabby marking
points that record a modern recapitulation of a medieval misunder-
standing.

One of the nicest stories of the Via Dolorosa actually concerns a
Jewish *yeshiva* and its Arab caretaker. The *Torat Hayim* synagogue
and study hall was founded in 1894, but in the Arab riots of 1936
the students fled for their lives, leaving their books and the hall in
the care of their Arab janitor. The janitor died, and his place was
taken by his brother. In 1967, the library of 3,000 books was found
to be exactly as it had been left. The janitor was asked: "Were you
not afraid to watch over the synagogue when all the other synagogues in the Old City were demolished?" He replied: "The holy
place watched over me more than I watched over it."

By the ninth station is one of the places where you can climb up
onto the roofs of the *suk* and follow the paths around toward the
Ethiopian convent, Deir es-Sultan, on the roof of the Holy Sepulchre. The paths above the Old City are a fantastic change of perspective. The Muslim quarter is a mixture of two very different atmospheres. Most obviously, there is the liveliness and color of the
suk itself, which is a working market with animal carcasses, fish,
vegetables, piles of spices, sweet cakes and savory falafel, and *foul*
hawked all around, as well as the touristy gewgaws nearer to the
Church of the Holy Sepulchre. It is a public life, a life on the street.
But most of the Muslim quarter is behind doors. There are shadowy and dusty streets, with façades that conceal the life within.
Near the Haram, the façades are often Mameluk, and impressive.
Elsewhere, tenements look blankly on the outside world. The

Figure 30. A group of policemen on the rooftops listening to a lecture about Jerusalem's multicultural life.

Muslim quarter is one area where the slow decline of Jerusalem under the Ottomans and the stagnation of the economy through this period, as well as the lack of social and scientific development (especially in contrast to Europe), are most strongly in evidence. Unlike much of Jerusalem, the Muslim quarter can still seem like an impoverished, rather backward Arab town.

So to reach the roofs above is to enter another plane. It is messy, for sure, with ramshackle huts, illegal third stories, illegal corrugated iron roofs, and television satellites everywhere. But unlike the rest of the Old City, it is not overlooked and shaded by buildings. It is a make-do place where everything seems to be part of the marginal, but the walk opens a new vista—the market looks and sounds different from above; the roofs feel more homely when you are among them; the lack of crowds and the lack of religious monuments are suddenly noticeable. Figure 30 is a snapshot of police recruits on the roofs being given a lecture about the city, and about the need for understanding its different elements and aspects. Perhaps the instructor felt it was the only place from which you could see the city as a whole. Perhaps the marginal seemed a good spot from where to think about the job of being a policeman. Perhaps she felt it was time to sit in the sun and take in the view.

Map 5

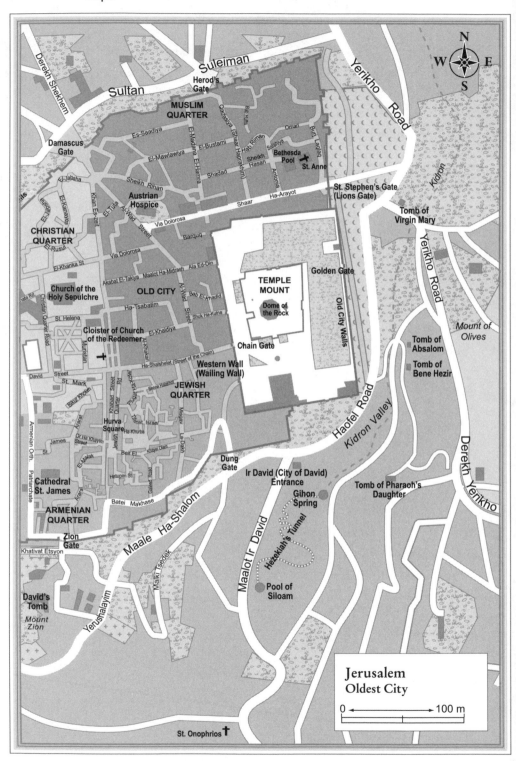

N W **E** S

Derekh Shekhem

Sultan · Suleiman

Herod's Gate

MUSLIM QUARTER

Es-Saadiya

Damascus Gate

El-Madana · El-Hanra · El-Bustami

Qadısiyya (Shaar Haprakhim) · Bet Hulū

El-Mawlawiya

Omari · Buri Laqlaq

Hab Rima · Salahiya

Sheikh Hasan

Antonia

Bethesda Pool · St. Anne

El-Jabsha

Sheikh Rihan

Austrian Hospice

Shadad

Shaar · Ha-Arayot

St. Stephen's Gate (Lions Gate)

CHRISTIAN QUARTER

El-Kanaya · El-Tula · Al-Wad Street

El-Khanka St.

Via Dolorosa

Barquq

Yerikho Road

Kidron

Tomb of Virgin Mary

Yerikho Road

Via Dolorosa

Akabat El-Takiya · Maalot Ha-Midrash · Ala Ed-Din

Golden Gate

OLD CITY

Church of the Holy Sepulchre

St. Helena

Cloister of Church of the Redeemer

Mustanan

David Street

St. Mark

Ha-Tsabatim

Bab El-Khadid

El-Khaldiya

Al-Wad Street

Shuk Ha-Kuna

Al-Khakan

Ha-Shalshelet (Street of the Chain)

TEMPLE MOUNT

Dome of the Rock

Old City Walls

Mount of Olives

Tomb of Absalom

Tomb of Bene Hezir

Chain Gate

Western Wall (Wailing Wall)

Bitur Khayim

Khabad Street Quarter · Jericho-Jeru

Shone Halahat

JEWISH QUARTER

Misgav · Le-Dakh

Or Ha Khayim Street

Hurva Square

Ha-Khurba · Tiferet. Israel

Jewish

Khaye Olan

James St. · El-Malak

Beit El

Haofel Road

Kidron Valley

Derekh Yerikho

Hatupim St.

Batei Makhase

Dung Gate

Ir David (City of David) Entrance

Gihon Spring

Tomb of Pharaoh's Daughter

Cathedral St. James

Armenian Orth. Patriarchate

ARMENIAN QUARTER

Ararat · James

Maalot Ir David

Hezekiah's Tunnel

Zion Gate

Khativat Etsyon

Maale · Ha-Shalom

Malki Tsedek

David's Tomb

Mount Zion

Yerushalayim

Pool of Siloam

St. Onophrios

Jerusalem
Oldest City

0 ————— 100 m

The Oldest City

JACOB ELIAHU WAS FORMALLY adopted by the Spaffords, leaders of the American Colony, at family prayers on July 9, 1883, when he was eighteen years old. He had been born a Sephardi Jew in Ramallah and was a rave success story of the London Mission to the Jews, one of the main organizations of evangelical Christians who set up shop in Jerusalem in the nineteenth century expressly for the conversion of the Jews of the Holy Land. He was a bright boy with a keen interest in archaeology. He had already lived with the Spaffords for a good time. A couple of years before, Jacob had become very excited by the thought of Hezekiah's Tunnel. Parts of the tunnel had been explored by Captain Warren, who was lionized in London for his bravery. Father Vincent, the great scholar of Jerusalem, had written of Warren's feats: "If this audacious attempt had been made in classical times it would have been celebrated by an epic poem as important as that which sang of the heroic enterprise of Diomedes and Odysseus when they stole the Palladion of

Troy." What is more, it was always said, especially among the boys with whom Jacob played, that the tunnel was haunted by a genie, or by a dragon. Jacob knew this would be an adventure. Nonetheless, he managed to persuade a friend, Sampson, to join him in exploring the tunnel for themselves.

They did not know how long it was or how deep the water. They prepared floats with candles and matches attached, which they tied around their necks. Jacob started from one end and Sampson from the other, intending to meet in the middle. Quickly, Jacob found himself in muddy water up to his chin. The light blew out, but the matches were already too damp to relight it. He kept going, however, guiding his way in the dark by running his hand along the damp stone and feeling the chisel marks of the ancient construction workers on the wall. Feeling his way like this, Jacob suddenly became conscious that the chisel marks had changed direction. He realized he must be in the precise spot where the two sets of workmen had met under the city. As his fingers ran over the wall in the tunnel—he had slipped into the water and was helping himself up—he became aware that he could feel not chisel marks but letters: there was an inscription on the wall. He hurried forward through the passage to tell Sampson. Sampson meanwhile had taken off and run back to school. As Jacob emerged, covered in mud and dazzled by the light, he dimly saw a boy whom he clutched, yelling, "Sampson, I have succeeded!" The overwhelmed local lad thought the genie had got him, and he promptly fainted and fell into the water. The Arab women who were washing clothes around the pool nearly tore Jacob to pieces: he ran for his life back to school and there—almost good Christian that he was—he confessed to his escapade.

Instead of being punished as he expected, Jacob found that his announcement of the discovery of an inscription in the tunnel caused a sensation not only in the school but also in the whole city. Conrad Schick, the great German archaeologist and designer of

Me'a She'arim, immediately took over and published the discovery for the Palestine Exploration Fund Quarterly to immense excitement from biblical archaeologists across the world. Ten years later, while plans were still being made for it, a Greek fellow with an eye for the main chance went into the tunnel at night and cut the whole inscription out of the rock (breaking it in the process). Before he could get away, the Turkish authorities captured and imprisoned him; from then on, the inscription, with the crack through the middle, has been in the Istanbul Archaeology Museum.

The inscription is one of the oldest extended pieces of early Hebrew that exists, but unless you are interested in ancient philology and letter formation, what makes it so transfixing is the fact that it was evidently scratched on the wall by one of the men from the digging team: it is testimony to the triumphant moment of the completion of the tunnel (and everyone can see in their mind's eye that moment when two tunneling teams break through into each other's space); and it is the monument of the workers, rather than that of the king and court. There are no names or grandiose boasting, just pride in the achievement:

> Behold the tunnel! This is the story of its cutting. While the miners swung their picks, one toward the other, and when there remained only 3 cubits to cut, the voices of one calling his fellow was heard—for there was a resonance in the rock coming from both north and south. So the day they broke through the miners struck, one against the other, pick against pick, and the water flowed from the spring toward the pool, 1,200 cubits. The height of the rock above the head of the miners was 100 cubits.

This is one of the most visually gripping inscriptions of any ancient period: the image of the workers calling to each other in the echoing tunnel, just a few feet to go, and then their crashing through the last piece of rock, "pick against pick," and the sudden flow of water, makes for a wonderfully evocative picture.

Jacob Eliahu and the evangelical Spaffords were thrilled that this was another archaeological triumph that attested to the Bible's truth. It confirmed that this was the tunnel built by Hezekiah as described in the Book of Kings and Chronicles. Hezekiah ruled Judah for twenty-nine years at the end of the eighth century B.C. (716–687, or thereabouts). This is the period of the Assyrian Empire, and an attack from the imperialist Assyrians was expected: "Hezekiah and his officers and champions decided to cut off the water supply from the springs situated outside the city. His military staff supported the plan and numbers of people banded together to block all the springs and cut off the watercourse flowing through the fields, saying, 'Why should the kings of Assyria come and find much water?'" (2 Chron. 32). The water supply was at this point outside the main city walls and would therefore satisfy the besieging army and be of no use to the Jerusalemites. So they camouflaged all the sources of the water. At the same time, Hezekiah "constructed the pool and the tunnel to bring the water into the city" (2 Kings 20) and "directed the waters of Gihon down to the west side of the city of David" (2 Chron. 32). Thus the water from the disguised spring of Gihon now flowed through a rock tunnel into the pool of Siloam, inside the protecting wall of the city.

The Assyrians under Sennacherib duly arrived, viciously taunted the Jerusalemites with their impending defeat—and, according to a cuneiform prism from Assyrian records, made Hezekiah "a prisoner in Jerusalem, his royal residence, like a bird in a cage." But Sennacherib suddenly fled home without capturing Jerusalem— because thousands of the warriors died in the night at the hands of the angel of the Lord (according to the Book of Chronicles), after accepting tribute, for which Hezekiah despoiled the Temple (according to the Book of Kings), because a plague of mice attacked their bow-strings and shield straps (according to an Egyptian story told by the fifth-century B.C. Greek historian Herodotus), because of domestic political problems (modern historians, more dully). But Hezekiah's water supply remained an essential part of the daily life and military protection of the ancient city of Jerusalem. The apocryphal book Ecclesiasticus, a late Greek text, has this concise summary of the king's lasting achievement: "Hezekiah fortified his city, and laid on a water supply within it; with iron he tunneled through the rock and constructed cisterns."

Hezekiah's Tunnel curls around in a big S shape (Figure 31, Map 5). Why the shape is as it is, and how the two groups of miners navigated toward each other, are the sorts of problem that scholars fight over with gusto. The most probable solution (of the many suggested) is that the teams were following thin natural fissures in the rock, through which water and air could flow—so that the miners could be sure of reaching the other side and not suffocating while doing so. The tunnel is still full of water to about hip height, but it makes for a sporting expedition (light shoes, good spirits, and a torch highly advisable), best taken in summer when the sun will dry off the clothes quickly. Start at the Gihon Spring and travel down it to the Siloam Pool. Edward Robinson, of Robinson's Arch, the American archaeologist, was the first to wiggle through the silted tunnel in 1838 (it took two attempts before he managed it); Charles Warren cleared it in the late 1860s; Yigal Shiloh in the 1980s turned the whole system into a tourist site; the current, still ongoing dig of Ronnie Reich, as we will see, has really changed our whole view of the water systems. But it was the brave Jacob Eliahu's chance discovery of the inscription that really brought the tunnel to life and tied it firmly into the biblical history of Jerusalem.

The second tunnel system, Warren's Shaft, was discovered by Charles Warren in 1867. The entrance today is from above in the Ir David complex, now modernized and designed to give a safe and

Warren's Shaft Water System

Cross Section

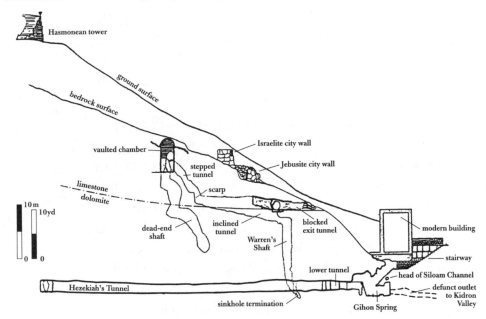

Figure 31. Plan of the Warren Shaft system.

dry trip (Map 5). The system consists of an entrance tunnel into a vaulted chamber, a stepped tunnel, a further sloping tunnel, and a vertical shaft down to the level of the spring (Figure 31). The trip continues on past the shaft to the Gihon Spring. Warren describes the excavation with his customary low-key emphasis on the danger and physical effort of his endeavors: "It was difficult work, full of hard mud, which had to be carried 50 feet through the water of the passage, and then taken up the steps of the pool. The men seldom have their heads above water when removing the soil, and sometimes the water suddenly rises, and there is danger of their being choked." Warren's derring-do is legendary; but the most dashing and ill-intentioned exploration of the tunnels was made by Montague Parker in 1909–1911.

Parker was a well-born and rather feckless young Englishman

who achieved the rank of captain fighting in the Boer War. He was persuaded (or at least tempted) by the theories of Walter Juvelius, a Finnish spiritualist and poet, who claimed to have located the site of the treasures of the Temple by a careful numerological interpretation of biblical texts, thanks to a mysterious manuscript discovered in a dusty library (that story again). Parker collected more than $100,000 from hopeful and gullible backers, and he was given permission from the sultan's court to dig, after some shady dealing and an agreement to share the profits. Parker reopened Warren's Shaft and laboriously cleared the tunnels. Surprisingly, he managed to persuade Father Vincent of the École Biblique, one of the world's most distinguished archaeologists, and a Dominican monk, to join him as an advisor. (Consequently, we have top-notch drawings and a scientific record of the whole process, though Parker was there only for the loot.) But they failed to find any secret chambers or buried treasure. So an increasingly desperate Parker bribed the governor to let him dig under the Temple Mount itself. He was discovered after only a few days by an unbribed guard, digging under the rock itself at night disguised in Arab dress, and had to flee the city for his life, as rioting broke out. He reached Jaffa, where he was stopped and his baggage was impounded. Thanks to some sharp talking, he escaped onto a yacht in the harbor and hurriedly made off for Europe. He returned to London and, after a quick burst of scandal at the hugely expensive failure of his expedition, lived out his days in ignoble obscurity—a victim of his own opportunism. One of his buckets, a rather sad memento of the intimate connection of archaeology and adventuring, can still be seen where he left it, now rusted, high on a ledge in the wall just before the metal stairs, in the Warren Shaft complex.

Until recently, the Warren Shaft system was thought to make perfect sense. The story went like this. The tunnel was created to bring water from the Gihon Spring to where it could be collected safely from inside the walls by bucket from the vertical shaft. The shaft was originally a natural feature of the rock formation but has been extended and widened by human hands. The Jebusite city wall and the Israelite city wall built just over it were excavated first by Kenyon (and more of it has been found since; Figure 31). This is the same broad wall we saw in the Old City, Hezekiah's massive eighth-century defensive works against the Assyrians (which were finally sacked by the Babylonians in the sixth century). The spring is clearly outside this wall, and Warren's Shaft system enables the inhabitants to go underground beyond the wall and collect water safely. It seems not to have been used after the eighth century, when Hezekiah's new tunnel made the collection of water at the Siloam Pool much easier. So this second tunnel system is older than Hezekiah's eighth-century project and dates back to before the coming of the Israelites in the tenth century.

An eminently practical shaft, then, for drawing water safely under siege; but it also raised a burning question: was this the route through which David captured the citadel of the Jebusites? This argument turns on the translation of one word in the Bible. In 2 Samuel 5, David sets out to capture Jerusalem, and he encourages his men to conquer the apparently impregnable city "through or up (to) the *tsinnor.*" No one is quite sure what *tsinnor* means in the Bible—it occurs only here—and the whole account of the conquest is hard to follow. The King James version has "whosoever getteth up to the gutter"; the Jerusalem Bible, "whoever . . . goes up by the conduit"; the New Jerusalem, "whoever gets up the tunnel"; the Revised Standard, "let him get up the water shaft"— where the modern translations are obviously affected by the recent archaeology. ("Dagger," "hook," "throat," and "penis" are less likely variants in the context, though all are suggested meanings for *tsinnor.*) Eliezer Ben-Yehuda was the founder of modern Hebrew, its first lexicographer and leading activist for its adoption as the national language of the modern Jewish community in Palestine. (His redoubtable granddaughter, in another era, was known as the

White Devil and was a leading figure in the Palmach, the Jewish underground army during the Mandate: a different Zionist fight.) Ben-Yehuda was fascinated by Warren's discovery. So, looking at Warren's Shaft, he decided that *tsinnor* would be the modern Hebrew for (water) pipe, and so it has become. He made the choice of word knowingly, and it has an obvious effect on the archaeological argument in Israel. For modern Israelis, *tsinnor* naturally means water pipe . . . Father Vincent, the Dominican, also understood *tsinnor* as water shaft, and immediately identified Warren's Shaft as the very place through which David captured the city (and thereby started everything in Jerusalem for the Jews, Christians, and Muslims). The combination of the archaeologist's identification and the lexicographer's linguistic authority was powerful. Warren's Shaft became another place where the feet of a figure from the Bible can be said to have walked, or at least scrambled; and so archaeologists, with the help of trained rock-climbers, have tried climbing the shaft (as if that would prove the issue), dated and re-dated the stone to an Israelite or pre-Israelite era, and argued vigorously and inconclusively whether this system is like other water-supply systems in Israel. Warren's Shaft was constructed before Hezekiah's Tunnel; that much seemed clear. But how the Bible's narrative is to be related to what we can now see of the rocks—that depends on the huge and thorny question of how the Bible is treated as history.

That was the story until the end of the twentieth century. And then suddenly a new set of excavations threw a heavy wrench into the works of this happy if cantankerous picture—and the certainties of a generation of archaeologists have been shatteringly undermined. (It is strange how archaeologists still express themselves with great certainty when the history of their profession is littered with the dead dinosaurs of discredited, previously certain theories.)

Although there had been so much excavation around this part of the City of David, surprisingly no one had yet dug around the spring of Gihon itself. Ronnie Reich, the chief excavator of the site, seems to have started digging here unenthusiastically because a "rescue dig" was needed for the preparation of a new visitor center. Before building in a site like this, archaeologists usually look underground first to see what needs salvaging (as with the *Kotel* plaza, as we saw in Chapter 2). Reich was without the greatest of hopes and free of grand theories. To the total amazement of everyone concerned, the excavators discovered a huge tower by the spring. It was built out of massive, rough blocks of stone, six feet long, three feet high, and three feet deep—the largest blocks used before Herod's great walls—and still stood to four courses high. The walls of the tower were twelve feet thick. Around the outside the tower measured forty-five by fifty-five feet. There was a conduit cut into the rock, which channeled the water out of the tower into the third tunnel system, the Siloam Channel (Figure 31). This, too, can be walked along, at least for a part of its length. It is dry now but originally also took water along the side of the Kidron Valley to the south; it has some small openings at regular intervals that look out over the valley. These may be irrigation channels that brought water to the lush agricultural gardens at the foot of the hill—the Gardens of the King, the orchards mentioned in the Book of Kings. For the first 600 feet this is not really a tunnel but a channel cut in the rock of the mountainside, over which huge rocks were later fitted to cover and protect it. Since the channel begins under the tower, it must have been built no later than the tower—which, from pottery shards in the foundations, is datable to the seventeenth or eighteenth century: the middle of the Bronze Age, when other huge walls and towers were also being built in the region. This channel is not built from the time of Solomon or David, then, but is very early indeed.

At the same time, Reich found by the tower a huge rectangular stone-cut cistern—the largest cistern from this period—with a rounded feeder pool attached. Just by this were the foundations of what was first thought to be another huge tower, which Reich named the "Pool Tower" to distinguish it from the "Spring Tower." By the summer of 2007 it had become clear that the second tower was actually a massively fortified covered walkway leading from the town to the tower—and that the cistern was outside its walls. Here was evidence of a large-scale defensive stonework around the Gihon Spring from the very earliest days of Jerusalem. The spring may have been outside the wall, but it was certainly not completely exposed in those days. The latest theory is that what had been thought a cistern functioned as a moat, defending the tower against attack. As the dig continues, it is possible that the details of this picture will continue to alter: they have changed each time I have visited, and the first publications of the site are already out of date. But our picture of the earliest city now certainly needs to add a huge tower defending the spring—and presumably facing the armies of the Israelites when they came to Jerusalem.

But more surprises were to come. Reich also found that the upper levels of the Warren's Shaft system were first dug to aim at this tower and were connected with them (and thus are very early, too). It was only when the tunnel was widened many years after its original construction, perhaps even during Hezekiah's time, that Warren's Shaft itself, the deep sink hole, was uncovered. It was not part of the original plan—and may never have been used for collecting water at all. And indeed it would be extremely hard, if not impossible, securely to lower a bucket down the irregular walls, especially from the difficult footing at the top of the shaft. The "practical" shaft turns out to be accidental and was probably never used for drawing water.

Nor was this the end of the new discoveries. Along the bottom of the Kidron Valley a further expanse of eighth-century wall was discovered. Military-minded archaeological theorists had always assumed that a wall would never be built here because it would be so vulnerable to attack from above, from the other side of the valley. But here was another defense, in the same style and from the same date as Hezekiah's wall above the spring of Gihon. This also delighted the biblical archaeologists: in 2 Chronicles (32.5) it says: "Hezekiah strengthened his defenses: he had the broken parts of the wall repaired, built towers on it, constructed a second wall on the outer side." This new wall at the foot of the Kidron Valley must be the second wall, argued those who follow the Bible. It added further protection for the Gihon Spring as well as for the city itself. There are other cities with such a double wall from this period—but it was unlikely to have been enough protection during an extended siege. Hence the need for Hezekiah's Tunnel, between the two walls of Hezekiah, which replaced the earlier systems of Warren's Shaft and the Siloam Channel.

It is amazing to think of the labor that went into digging out these passageways from the rock, in the earliest case without even iron. But this was necessary work. All three channels indicate the constant problem of water supply for Jerusalem, a problem that is still a crucial factor in the political negotiations over national boundaries and landownership in the region, and that has run throughout the history of the region since Abraham first quarreled over wells. The final section of the Western Wall tunnel is a Hasmonean aqueduct, to bring water to the Temple Mount. In the Roman period, extensive aqueducts brought water from far away to the city—and you can see remains of these in the new dig at the *Kotel,* for example. There is also a well-preserved underground stretch of several hundred yards' length, with added Ottoman pipe work, that runs under the Hill of Evil Counsel—though it is unfortunately not possible at the moment for tourists to get access to it. It was not until the British Mandate that adequate water was provided for the city. From the first tunnels, perhaps as early as the eighteenth century B.C., through Hezekiah's Tunnel in the seventh century B.C., to the aqueducts of the Hasmonean and Roman periods, and finally to the British Mandate's development of a modern pump-driven water supply, the need for water has changed the urban geography of Jerusalem—and has reflected the power and ambition of successive ruling authorities of the city.

THE CITY OF DAVID: THE LURE OF THE STONES

The City of David, a tiny town by any modern considerations, was built on a low ridge surrounded by the Kidron Valley to the east and the Tyropoeon to the west, with the Hinnom Valley further to the south and west. When Solomon built the Temple the city stretched further up the ridge onto Mount Moriah. The Gihon Spring produced enough water, just about, for the town's immediate needs, expanded by the collection of rainwater in cisterns. Without the Gihon it would have been impossible to settle this part of the mountains, and the position of the earliest city on what was otherwise neither the most defensible nor the most pleasant ridge was determined by the water supply. By the eighth century B.C. at least King David's city had expanded over to the western hill—hence that stretch of the eighth-century wall visible in the Old City (as will be remembered from Chapter 4). The western hill is still usually called Mount Zion because that is where it was assumed for many years the first city was built, though now everyone agrees that the first settlement was on the eastern hill: old names die hard. This eastern hill is the space of the oldest city, the city of the First Temple, and its remains are now a fascinating and still changing archaeological park, the Ir David complex (Map 5).

With this oldest city we are in a different sphere of evidence and speculation. Archaeology is the prime mover here, and without it we would have little to say about the City of David, except to repeat what the Bible says, and the Bible is more than usually opaque about the capture, settlement, and city planning of Jerusalem. For most scholars since the nineteenth century, to use the Bible as a historical text in such a way would be scandalously irresponsible to the historical calling. Even those historians who are thrilled to find elements of the Bible apparently confirmed by cold rocks, authentic inscriptions, and datable ashes from datable battles—and there are plenty of such scholars—even they would hesitate to declare that the Bible is the truth, the whole truth, and nothing but the truth in its picture of the kingdoms of Judah and Israel from the tenth to the sixth century B.C. But even so, some of the discoveries made by the excavators in the City of David have been disconcertingly precise in their biblical echoes.

Take the House of the Bullae. A bulla is a clay seal for a document, made by impressing a ring or other stamp into wet clay to fix together a scroll of papyrus or parchment. Each bulla is individualized as a mark of identification (Figure 32). The practice is familiar from throughout the ancient Mediterranean, and even the prophet Jeremiah in one of his less angry and denouncing moods describes a transaction in which he bought a field from his cousin: "I signed the deed, sealed it, got witnesses . . . I gave the deed of purchase to Baruch . . . in the presence of Hanamel . . . in the presence of the witnesses who signed the deed." The archaeologists in 1982 uncovered a cache of these bullae in a house in David's city, which

was dated around the end of the seventh century B.C. and the beginning of the sixth century, that is, in the period of King Josiah and the destruction of the First Temple, according to the Bible. In a fire the documents will burn, but the clay bullae can become harder and survive in a readable form. The archaeologists found forty-seven seals, all with the formula "(belonging) to x son of y": the house must have contained a cache of documents and may have been an official building holding deeds of transfer or property

Figure 32. The bulla (seal impression) of Azariah son of Hilkiah. (Collection of Israel Antiquities Authority. Photograph © The Israel Museum, Jerusalem.)

ownership. From this discovery, it is called the House of the Bullae. Now as one might expect, the vast majority of these forty-plus names are of figures otherwise lost to any form of history. But the shock was that two of the names were extremely familiar indeed.

The first is Gemariah son of Shaphan. This man appears in the Book of Jeremiah, a high-level official and scribe at the court of King Jehoiakim of Judah, eighteen years before the destruction of Jerusalem by the Babylonians in 587–586 B.C.: "In the fifth year of Jehoiakim the son of Josiah, king of Judah . . . all the people in Jerusalem and all the people who came from the cities of Judah to Jerusalem proclaimed a fast before the lord. Then, in the hearing of all the people, Baruch read the words of Jeremiah . . . in the house of the Lord, in the chamber of Gemariah the son of Shaphan the secretary, which was in the upper court, at the entry of the New Gate of the Lord's House." Gemariah, son of a senior palace official, had a well-known house near the entrance to the Temple, and from his chamber the Book of Jeremiah could be read so that everyone could hear it. The combination of a name and an address, as it were, gives this seal a particular resonance.

The second name, Azariah son of Hilkiah, is from the same period (Figure 32). Azariah himself appears merely twice in genealogies of priestly families, and he does nothing in the Bible's narrative. But his father, Hilkiah, is extremely important indeed. He was the high priest who discovered the book of the Law in the Temple. He said to Shaphan the scribe: "I have found the book of the law in the House of the Lord." Shaphan brought the book to Josiah, and this started the reforms of Jewish life in Jerusalem, which were lauded in the Book of Kings as bringing the people back to the proper worship of God, and were seen as a founding moment in the construction of the Jewish people as a nation. Shaphan and Hilkiah, the two fathers recorded on the bullae, are the main players in this turning point in Jewish history, just as Gemariah's chamber is used for the reading of the Book of Jeremiah. Another bulla appeared on the market in 1975, though its provenance is unknown—it was probably stolen from a dig rather than faked—which has the name of Baruch, the secretary, friend, and confidant of Jeremiah; a similar seal emerged in 1995, this time with a fingerprint on its edge still visible—the modern mark of identification accidentally impressed on the ancient.

In the City of David, the bullae were in a house that was burned down at the time of the destruction of Jerusalem by Nebuchadnezzar in 587–586 B.C. and refer to characters of genuine significance in the previous generation—as the Bible tells the story. It is hard not to be touched by the romance of such discoveries. Here are the seals, the very marks of identification of the men who made the Jewish world what it was in the seventh century B.C. The hypercynical might point out that these could be seals of other men of the same name with the same father's name in the same period—but this quickly seems like intellectual churlishness rather than caution. Indeed, in 2006 another bulla was found in the excavation of the so-called King David's palace, which names Jehucal, son of Shelemial. This is one of the ministers who also appear in the Book of Jeremiah (Jer. 38), calling for the death of the prophet because he advised the people to accept their inevitable slavery at the hands of the Babylonians. For the archaeologist who found it, this little lump of baked clay was proof of the historical reliability of the Bible. At the very least, it confirms that a political figure named in Jeremiah once walked the streets of Jerusalem, and hoped a document of his would remain safe and sealed. Such proof emerges from the other side, too: in 2007 a small Assyrian clay tablet in the British Museum was read for the first time, and, to the scholars' great excitement, it records the name of the chief minister of Nebuchadnezzar, who also appears fleetingly in the Book of Jeremiah. In this detail, the history of the winners and the losers agrees.

The connection between the biblical text and the ancient, chanced-upon, everyday object, when it is so precise a connection, brings its own historical thrill (which puts us moderns closer to the medieval love of relics). A different sort of vista into the past was opened by another discovery from the same period, this time from a grave near Ketef Hinnom, southwest of the Old City where the Hinnom Valley turns east toward the Kidron Valley. Most early graves have been looted years before modern archaeologists can excavate. But by a freak collapse of rock, this chamber had been concealed from generations of robbers. In it were the bones of more than 100 people (the excavator thought these were dead from the Babylonian sack of Jerusalem), more than 250 pottery vessels, a considerable amount of silver and even gold jewelry, arrowheads, bone and ivory beads, a rare early coin, and so on. But the most remarkable find was two pure silver rolls. It took three years of painstaking work for the experts in the Israel Museum to open them. The larger is not even four inches long and an inch wide when unfurled. They were probably amulets to be worn, and both were inscribed inside with the same text in tiny archaic letters. Both had in part and with some variation the text of what we now call Numbers 6 24–26: "May the Lord bless you and keep you. May the Lord cause his countenance to shine upon you and be gracious to you. May the Lord favor you and grant you peace." This is the priestly blessing, delivered in the Temple originally by the priests, and still used today in religious services by Jews and Christians. These are seventh-century texts—more than 300 years older than the Dead Sea Scrolls—and the oldest quotations of the Bible we have. Unless you believe in the perfect text of the Torah given to Moses on Mount Sinai and transmitted without loss down through the generations, it is highly unlikely that the Bible in the seventh century B.C. had the form we now know, or even the precise wording of our current texts (hence the variation of wording on these little scrolls). But even so, the vista of continuity here is astounding—the same prayer being offered from the seventh century B.C. down to today. I find this unbroken tradition of the words of human prayer far more moving, even awe-inspiring, than the constructed continuities at the Western Wall or the bizarre fantasies of al-Aqsa mosque standing before the existence of Islam.

It is not by chance that the wonderful finds I have been focusing on all have words on them. Language cements the link between the objects and the biblical texts. Where the stones are mute, the space is created for quite different types of argument and quite different fuss.

Some stones speak simply across the centuries. One of the structures excavated near the House of the Bullae was a storeroom with fifty storage jars in it, one of which had on it the name Ahi'el: so the building of which the storeroom was the basement is known as the House of Ahi'el. On one side of the storeroom was a small chamber with a plaster floor. In the floor is set a limestone toilet seat (Figure 33); and under it is a two-meter-deep plaster-lined cesspool. Two other such toilet seats have been found in the same area. The toilet seat is not labeled as such at the site, and it is fun to hear visitors wonder uncertainly if that is what it really could be— caught between instant recognition and a fear that misrecognizing a "ritual object" as a toilet would reveal some terrible triviality of mind: surely history, such ancient history, should be about grander events . . . (The Talmud, however, in one of its droller moments, poses the question of what's best for a happy human life, and finally chooses as its answer "a good toilet.") History feels rather homely here, and the stones, for once, free of political angst.

Archaeologists have also begun to piece together in very general terms the history of the small section of the city they have been able to excavate. Ahi'el's House and the House of the Bullae are built into an impressively excavated stepped-stone structure (Figure 34). This structure is typical of terracing across the Mediterranean to create platforms for house construction on hillsides (and it can be seen in a modern form in the Silwan Village, which is stacked up on the opposite side of the valley). This particular stepped-stone

Figure 33. A toilet seat, probably from the eighth century B.C. The cesspool below was identified by the biological remains in it.

structure was once thought to be very early, probably thirteenth century B.C., and to have been the foundation of a Jebusite citadel. Pottery finds from within it, however, now indicate that it is probably tenth century, and was most likely built to widen the ridge and provide foundational support for the building above (which we will look at shortly). It is still the height of a five-storey building and remains a seriously imposing structure. In the eighth and seventh centuries houses were built into it. (The tower and walls now visible above it are Hellenistic—around the second century B.C.) As usual for archaeology in so complex a site we have strata of different buildings laid one over the other, which can make the visual impression of the site confusing. And the description I have given here depends on more than fifty years of archaeological work, test-

Figure 34. The stepped-stone structure, with the pillars of the House of Ahi'el visible below.

ing, rejecting, and revising theories to reach this point of (temporary) general agreement. What we have here are the remains of a very early monumental structure, into which far later domestic property has been built. Four-room houses are typical of this period and place; and the seals, together with the Bible, help locate these domestic buildings within a seventh- and sixth-century historical context.

But with these fascinating bare structures, as soon as interpretation strives for more detail, things become more complicated—and then the brouhaha begins. The two very recent excavations from either end of Hezekiah's Tunnel show the delights and perils of Jerusalem archaeology clearly enough. At the Siloam Pool, the southerly end of Hezekiah's Tunnel, two new sets of Second Temple steps and roadways have just been uncovered and will soon be open to the public. The pool itself has been built around several times (as one might expect), with a Byzantine colonnaded square, with a church above it (the remains were found by Bliss, who missed the Madaba map), replaced by a mosque. Thanks to the excavations that have just been completed, we can now see ten stone steps up from the pool to a colonnaded plaza, and a fine road that probably went as far as the western wall of the Temple Mount. There is a second set of steps, uncovered in 2007, rising more steeply up the hill toward the Temple. This well-preserved stepped path has the pattern of alternating large and small steps that have been uncovered by the Hulda Gate of the Temple Mount, where guides always say that this odd pattern of steps is to slow your pace to encourage spiritual calm before entering the Temple: the story will have to change to include the journey to and from the Siloam Spring at least. From these new digs, we can gain further insight into the circulation of traffic in the Herodian city of the first century and Herod's city planning, with his extension of public amenities. This new discovery also allows the romance of imagining the journey from the spring up to the Temple, climbing, freshly washed, up a well-made set of stone steps, to make your sacrifice. Here is a simple, high-grade piece of archaeological detective work that helps us understand the city of the Second Temple period.

At the Gihon Spring, the source of the Siloam water systems, however, the new excavation of the eighteenth-century B.C. tower, covered passageway, and cistern, which we have just looked at, is significantly harder to comprehend, much as it has changed what seemed comprehensible about the site for a previous generation. With the scaffolding of the diggers still there, and the darkness broken by their arc lamps, the whole dig has an eerie mix of industrial modernity and the extremely ancient—the dramatic attempt to throw light on the hidden past. Is this a gateway to the ancient city? If so, from what period exactly does it come: which people built it? How long was it in use? How does what appears to be a moat fit into the defenses—why does it appear to have a feeder pool attached? Was it also used for water collection? How does this gateway fit into the history of the earliest city? As the excavation slowly proceeds, theories are tried, and tested, and revised. Perhaps a coherent narrative will emerge, finally. But for the moment, the immense stones and yawning cistern remain mute—reminding us how fragile our knowledge of the oldest city is.

The two ends of Hezekiah's Tunnel, the Herodian city from the first century and the very earliest strata of Jebusite inhabitation from the eighteenth century B.C., are potentially explosive investigations because of contemporary political fights over ownership of the land. Part of the Zionists' claim to the land of Israel is that this is the Jews' ancestral home, and each sign of Jewish life from the earliest days is viewed in such a context. Similarly, Palestinians who enter the archaeology wars need to deny all such evidence, it would seem, or read it as really evidence of an Arab population. (It would be nice not to have to point out that the Palestinian claim depends on denying the truth, the Zionist on promoting a terribly oversimplified argument.) The silent stones encourage both sides to increasingly fervid assertions. But where the sites are directly linked to biblical texts the arguments become even shriller. The latest, still unpublished excavations at the City of David are typical of this.

One of the missing links for biblical archaeologists has been the absence of any sign of King David's palace. That is, if we are to take the story of the Bible at face value, David makes Jerusalem his capital for the united kingdoms of Judah and Israel, and builds for himself a large palace to display to the world his prestige and authority. Yet until very recently there was no indication of any large-scale building in the City of David, and precious few signs of any buildings clearly placed in the time of David or Solomon. (Indeed, some archaeologists claim that the evidence currently available for population, building, and development makes it extremely unlikely that there was a large-scale kingdom in the tenth century ruled by a central power in Jerusalem.) It might be possible to explain away the absence of domestic building remains for David's city by assuming that the stones were re-used, or that the wrong areas had been excavated, or that the buildings were too undistinguished to leave much trace. But these arguments sound even more desperate when we are looking for a palace. So it was with incredible excitement that in 2005 it was announced that the foundations of a massive new structure from the First Temple era had been found. It was above the "stepped structure," and it appeared that the stepped structure had been built to provide the support for a new palace outside and above the Jebusite city wall. This was immediately dubbed "David's Palace."

The chief archaeologist on the dig, Eilat Mazar, comes from a famous archaeological family. Her grandfather Benjamin Mazar was a leading light in the first great generation of Israeli archaeologists, and it was he who led the excavations around the Temple Mount that uncovered such remarkable remains from the Second Temple period. Eilat cut her teeth as his assistant. She also has a very high public profile (not least for her well-publicized complaints about the Arab construction work on the Haram al-Sharif as the wanton destruction of an archaeologically important site). She is famous in the press for her copy of the Bible, heavily annotated, which sits on her desk, and in a series of interviews she let it be known that her discovery of the building was guided by a close reading of the scriptures. Since David went *down* to the town, she said, she knew the palace had to be north, *above* where the earlier digs had taken place. It was quickly added (to put a bit more sexiness into the already sexy story) that this set-up explained how David could look out and see Bathsheba bathing on her roof. The story was a scoop, and the dig has been bought up for publication by the *National Geographic* magazine in the same way that *Star* or *Hello!* magazine buys an exclusive on a celebrity wedding.

The squeals of protest were immediate (and well founded). It is difficult to be sure what date these stones are: without a secure floor it is hard to date buildings. Even if the building could be securely dated to the tenth century, it is far from clear that this is anything other than a conventional date for David, a figure whose story is touched with myth. Even if the stones were dated to the tenth century, and David was dated to the tenth century, there is nothing to connect the building to David. It is a large building, and we can always call a large building a palace, but we have no way of identifying its use, or of linking it to anything resembling a social system. To call it David's Palace is to replay once again the crass hopefulness of previous generations who named a mixture of Hellenistic and Byzantine buildings David's Citadel, David's Tower, David's Tomb—and so forth. Starting from the Bible, concluded Mazar's professional colleagues stridently, is no way to do archaeology.

The vitriolic dispute over the status of the Bible for archaeology is a classic Jerusalem row, touched as it is with so many personal issues within the small community of professional archaeologists, and laced as it is with the political charge of early history in this country. But it should not be allowed to obscure the fact that this is another discovery of signal importance. For the first time, it can be asserted that in the First Temple period there is evidence of a major building, with all the implications that follow for the social status of the town and its inhabitants. As this dig and the dig near the Gihon Spring progress over the next few years, the textbooks on the early history of Jerusalem will all need to be rewritten. Again.

THE KIDRON VALLEY: THE DEAD WHO GET A VOTE

Archaeologists love graves. The discovery of the Tomb of Tutankhamen is one of the most celebrated archaeological stories of the century, and the treasures from it are marveled at, not only because of their beauty and luxury, but also because of stories of "the curse of the mummy," "the pharaoh's hand," and so forth. Opening the tomb is a story with deep cultural resonance for us. It is one way for an archaeologist to become a hero.

Tombs were tourist sights from the beginnings of travel for pleasure. The Great Pyramid was visited and discussed by Herodotus, the Greek historian, in the fifth century B.C. Mausolus built his tomb near Halicarnassus, and it became known as one of the Seven Wonders of the Ancient World—the Mausoleum. Cicero, the Roman statesman, describes looking at the now overgrown and difficult to read gravestones in Athens, as he reflects on the passing of empires. As the great men constructed great monuments to memorialize their greatness, tourists indeed gawked, and poets contemplated the fragility of fame, as did Shelley, whose traveler from an antique land looked on the ruined statue of Ozymandias, which proclaimed: "My name is Ozymandias, King of Kings: Look on my works, ye mighty, and despair!" while

> *Nothing beside remains. Round the decay*
> *Of that colossal wreck, boundless and bare,*
> *The lone and level sands stretch far away.*

It is through gravesites that many of the objects we view in museums were preserved, and every society expresses something essential about itself in the way it chooses to dispose of its dead. That
in itself would make the graveyard a fine hunting place for the archaeologist. But Jerusalem is also the only city where, as the Hebrew poet Amichai brilliantly put it, "the dead get a vote." It is not
just that there is the immense pull of the past here, nor just that the
burial place of Jesus is so central to the city's topographical imagination. Jerusalem is also where religious Jews, Muslims, and some
Christians believe the final judgment will take place. To be buried
in Jerusalem is to be on hand for the end of days. If you stand in the
Kidron Valley, you can see the Jewish graves on the Mount of Olives, the Muslim graves by the Golden Gate, and further down the
valley the Christian cemeteries. Back up the Hinnom Valley there
is even a Karaite cemetery—the sect of Jews who deny the authority of the Talmud and the oral law, and who were a major force in
the Middle Ages, though barely surviving today. These places of the
dead are integral to the layout of the city. And graves, because they
are so emotionally charged, become an overheated part of the politics, too. (The dead may get a vote, but they are also subject to insult
and aggression.) The desecration of thousands of Jewish graves on
the Mount of Olives by the Jordanians after 1948 remains a source
of burning rage among some Israelis. The decision to build a Museum of Tolerance over an ancient Muslim cemetery, whatever the
legal position on the treatment of disused graveyards offered by
Muslim clerics, is a ruling of the Israeli planners that will ironize
the mission statement of the museum forever. Perhaps the most
outrageous act of Dr. Merrill and Reverend Wallace, the American consuls who opposed the evangelicals of the American Colony
at the end of the nineteenth century, was to allow the American
cemetery on Mount Zion to be sold, and the bodies disinterred
and thrown into a general heap in the British cemetery—primarily
out of malice toward the colony. (The Reverend Wallace sued

Appleton's magazine, which reported this story; he lost and was forced to give up his position amid great scandal.) In Jerusalem in a different way from most other cities, graves are part of the physical and imaginative landscape.

Around the city you come across plenty of graves from the First and Second Temple period that have been excavated, including the family grave of Herod. Even Herod's empty and smashed sarcophagus was discovered in the summer of 2007. These sites are usually marked with a laconic sign, and few have much to reveal, as they were looted many centuries before. They follow a similar pattern of a bench or usually a series of benches on which the body was laid out to decompose, sometimes with a special headrest, and then an ossuary where the bones were collected after a year to make way for further burials. (That is why the bones of 100 people were found in the single tomb at Ketef Hinnom.) There are rarely any ways of identifying the owner, and certainly not in the case of the earlier graves. But the Kidron Valley has distinctive grave markers that have been visited as landmarks for centuries.

The Tomb of Absalom (Figure 35) has a surprising and curvy conical top, like a Persian hat in Greek vase imagery. It is a *nefesh* (funerary monument) that marks an eight-chambered catacomb behind it in the cliff side (though it also has a tomb inside it). There is a fine pediment over the doorway. The tomb must have been for a wealthy family and probably dates from the latter part of the first century B.C. It took on its present name after Benjamin of Tudela visited Jerusalem in about 1170. Benjamin was a rabbi from Tudela in Spain who journeyed the world for thirteen years and wrote a fascinating traveler's account of the places he visited, and especially the Jewish communities he saw. Fame outside the circles of those who could read rabbinic Hebrew came late, however. Only when his book was translated into Latin in the sixteenth century did he become a truly influential figure. When he came across this monument, he remembered the line in the book of Samuel: "And Absa-

Figure 35. Absalom's Tomb in the Kidron Valley.

lom in his lifetime set up for himself a pillar that is in the King's Valley: 'I have no son,' he said, 'to preserve the memory of my name.' So he had given the pillar his name, and it is called to this day the Pillar of Absalom." This monument seemed to him to be that very pillar, and in the absence of any other owner, the name has stayed with it.

A few steps away from Absalom's Tomb is a pair of buildings that form a single complex (Figure 36). To the right is the pyramid-roofed *nefesh,* with Doric columns against a blank wall. This marks the catacomb to the left, which is lit inside through the Doric columns above. This is called in the Christian tradition the Tomb of St. James. According to the standard martyr narrative, St. James, the head of the early church, was thrown from the Temple parapet and clubbed to death; he was then "buried on the spot, by the Sanctuary, and his headstone is still there by the Sanctuary" (as Eusebius reports in his *Church History*). So it is not quite clear how this first-century tomb became associated with him, unless we suppose that his body fell a long way, here into the Kidron Valley, and that "by the Sanctuary" means in the sight of the Temple Mount. The *nefesh* is also called the Tomb of Zechariah (whose death is recounted in Chronicles but has no obvious connection with this spot). But despite those religious stories, an inscription actually tells us who was really buried here: "This is the tomb and the *nefesh* of Eleazer, Haniah, Jo'azar. Iehudah, Shime'on, Iohannan, the sons of Joseph, son of Obed and also of Joseph and Eleazer the sons of Haniah, priests of

Figure 36. The Tomb of Bene Hezir, also known as the Tomb of St. James and the Tomb of Zechariah.

the family of the sons of Hezir." So this is the Tomb of Bene Hezir, the sons of Hezir. The name Hezir also appears in the Bible in the lists of the heads of priestly families, which probably means that this family looked back to the Bible for its genealogy and authority. It is a mild irony in this city of what one might call monumental falsehoods that the one monument which comes with a proper name attached has found it so hard to hold onto it.

In the Silwan Village on the other side of the valley there is a fascinating necropolis, largely dating from the eighth century B.C., with more than fifty graves in two rows cut into the rock face. Unfortunately, this is not a safe place for Western visitors to go, while the current political situation exists. Actually, it hasn't been an attractive prospect for a trip for a long while. In 1876 Charles Warren, who went on to fight the Boer and to become the commissioner of police in London when Jack the Ripper was at large, wrote: "The people of Siloam are a lawless set, credited with being the most unscrupulous ruffians in Palestine." J. L. Porter, the president of Queen's College, Belfast (a tough enough city), ten years later also called them "lawless, fanatical vagabonds," and another Victorian traveler called Kelly, who actually tried to enter a tomb, was terrified by the shriek of an old Arab woman which brought hundreds of swarming children and cursing men and women out of the tombs all around. He fled. Even the modern archaeologist who surveyed the site has little love for it: "Words cannot describe the filth we encountered. At that time there were no proper drains or sewers in the village and the sewage flowed in every direction . . . Piles of refuse and junk were heaped up everywhere." So now it is advisable to see the Tomb of Pharaoh's Daughter from a distance.

This square tomb (originally it had a pyramid on top) was cut out of the rock around it in the eighth century B.C. It looks much like a house without windows (Figure 37). The arch below was cut in the nineteenth century: the earliest photographs—we have Salzman's photographs from 1856, about as early as any photographs of Jerusalem—show the tomb without it. It was named the Tomb of Pharaoh's Daughter by Louis Félicien Joseph Caignart de Saulcy, the nineteenth-century French travel writer, social climber, and archaeologist who had an extremely Romantic view of the monuments he saw. "Mystery and danger sufficed to fix my resolution," he wrote of his first trip, "and I determined to proceed at once to Jerusalem." He imagined this to be the tomb of the Egyptian wife of Solomon, daughter of the pharaoh. (The wisest of men ended his days going against the word of God and making a politically ambitious marriage outside his own religion.) There was once a Hebrew inscription over the door, but a hermit who chose to make this grave his home in the medieval period cut through the inscription when widening the door, so that only two letters are now visible. (Memorial is easily erased.) Many of the graves were inhabited by hermits before becoming slum dwellings for the villagers.

Figure 37. The Tomb of Pharaoh's Daughter.

Another Hebrew inscription from a tomb on the main street of the village was removed by the French archaeologist Clermont-Ganneau and sent to the British Museum in the nineteenth century. It reads: "This is [the tomb] of . . . yahu who is over the house. There is no silver and gold here, but [his bones] and the bone of his slave-wife with him. Cursed be the man who will open this." The curse may have worked for all we know, but this is still all that is left of whoever built this grave for himself and his wife. Clermont-Ganneau could not decipher the inscription (and it took more than seventy years before a translation was made of the archaic and fading letters). But he could read one word, "the house," from which he rather brilliantly conjectured that this was the tomb of the steward "who is over the house." From this, and remembering Isaiah's outrage against Shebna, the steward of Hezekiah's palace, who "is hewing a tomb for himself high up, carving out a room for himself in the rock," Clermont-Ganneau called this "the tomb of the steward Shebna." In the absence of the name on the inscription, this can be no more than a guess—but it is another name that has stuck.

One of the least visited but most bewitching sites here is the little Monastery of St. Onophrios, just off the minor road through the Hinnom Valley, where it meets the Kidron Valley; it has only just been opened to visitors (Map 5). The monastery has only four Greek nuns tending it, and it was largely rebuilt in the twentieth century; but it has a beautiful, quiet, and shady terrace and gardens overlooking the valley. St. Onophrios is the prototype of the anchorite, the solitary and silent hermit. Onophrios moved from Thebes to Jerusalem to find total seclusion: angels will not speak to anyone who speaks to humans. (He finally retreated to Sinai: Jerusalem was an unlikely place for silence even then.) He is represented with long hair covering his nakedness. The chapel in his honor is built around his cell, which is actually an old tomb—burial places have provided the humblest dwellings over the centuries for hermits and the poor. And below in the lower courtyard, below the hostel, is a quite extraordinary set of Second Temple tombs, which give the best idea anywhere in Jerusalem of the burial customs of the period. For the six stone chambers, carved out of the rock, are still full of bones. One has a full skeleton laid out; another is piled high with collected bones from several bodies. It is rare and somewhat macabre to be so close to this traditional form of burial. But it provides a fascinating and intimate reminder of the privileged role of the dead in Jerusalem's imagination.

The most visited and most glittery tomb is further around the valley below Gethsemane—the Tomb of the Virgin. The Gospels do not mention her death, but as her cult became increasingly important, stories started to appear. The *Transitus Mariae* texts ("The passing of Mary") are extraordinary documents in Latin, Syriac, Coptic, Ethiopian, and Greek. They purport to be the story of the death and assumption of Mary. They tell how all the apostles (even the dead ones, who were raised from their tombs for the occasion) were transported in a shining cloud by the Holy Spirit from wherever they were spreading the good word all the way back to Jerusalem to witness the passing of the mother of Jesus. The story involves the killing of a good number of Jews in the process, and plenty of polemic. But one version, perhaps adapted to suit the site, does declare that Mary was buried "on the road that goes out to the head of the valley on this side of the Mount of Olives, where there are caves, a large outer cave, another within it, and a small inner cave with a raised bench on the east side." St. Juvenal, bishop of Jerusalem, at the Council of Chalcedon (451 A.D.) told the emperor that all the apostles had been there for the burial, but when the tomb was opened there was no body—thus proving the assumption to heaven. (He was also trying to disprove the claim of the city of Ephesus in Asia Minor to have the tomb: there was a strong market in such relics.) The *Transitus Mariae* was declared apocryphal already in the sixth century, but this hasn't stopped it from having a huge effect on the pious.

There was a church here in the sixth century, and Bishop Arculf from France, who, it will be remembered, was the first Westerner to describe the al-Aqsa mosque, described the church in 670 as "built at two levels, and the lower part, which is beneath a stone vault, has a remarkable round shape. At the east end there is an altar, on the right of which is the empty rock tomb in which for a time Mary remained entombed." What we have today is the Byzantine crypt with a crusader entrance way (the church itself was destroyed by Saladin for stones to repair the walls). There is a marvelous, monumental, vaulted stairway down into the dark, with ornate lamps hanging from the ceiling. On the right going down is the grave of Queen Melisande, daughter and wife of crusader royalty; on the left is the tomb of Baldwin II. In the crypt, the right section is run by the Greeks, the left by the Armenians (a typical division of space), and the mixture of icons and heavily bearded, black-clad priests in the incense-laden cavern offers an archetypal image of Eastern Christianity. The tomb (probably fourth century) looks suitably old and the rock bench has been chipped and worn away by the piety of the pilgrims of centuries. The *mihrab* in the wall behind Mary's Tomb marks the holiness of the site for Muslims, too, a holiness that comes because in one of the more elaborate versions of the Night Journey Mohammed was said to have seen a light "over the tomb of his sister Mary." The small tomb in the other wall opposite Mary's Tomb is actually first century, but it does not appear to have gathered any myths to itself.

Louis Félicien Joseph Caignart de Saulcy also excavated what he called with presumptive sexism the Tomb of the Kings. This site is on the other side of town, on the corner of Nablus and Salahedin Streets. The tombs are set in a deep courtyard (a quarry) and are an impressive complex with a fine façade. De Saulcy assumed that these were the graves of the kings of Judah. But this was where Queen Helena of Adiabene was buried, and, unlike many a robber over the centuries, de Saulcy actually found her sarcophagus, in a chamber reached through a secret passage under a grave: it had on it her Aramaic name, "Saddan" (which did not stop him from calling the complex the Tomb of the Kings), and it is now in the Louvre. Helena fascinated ancient writers and is a perplexing figure for the modern world, too. She was dowager queen of Adiabene in northern Mesopotamia and was converted to Judaism by Jewish merchants, along with her son, the king Izates. (They are one of the test cases for Jewish attitudes to proselytizing in this time period, and it has intrigued scholars to imagine how merchants converted the royal family of a Mesopotamian kingdom.) She came to Jerusalem on a pilgrimage during the great famine of 46–48 A.D., and she used her wealth to bring food for the city from abroad. She built a palace in Jerusalem and lived there for twenty years. She returned to Adiabene only when her son the king died, and when she died shortly afterward, the bones of both were transported to Jerusalem for burial in the magnificent monument she had already constructed (as Josephus writes), which was then outside the city walls, of course. Pausanias, the Greek travel writer of the second century A.D., adds the odd information that the stone door of her tomb is so contrived that it can only be opened on a certain day of the year, when it opens automatically; then, after a short while, the machinery closes it again. There is no sign that Pausanias had ever been to Jerusalem (which he called the city of Solomon), though he knew the Romans had by then razed it. But it does show that hers was a name to conjure with around the Mediterranean, even a century after her death.

De Saulcy wanted very much to find the graves of the kings of Judah—as have many others. The prize of prizes, however, is the grave of King David. The longest-running popular site is on Mount Zion, in the building that has the cenacle, the empty room above where Jesus is said to have held the last supper. There is, of course, no way that this is the grave of King David. (The only possible information is from the Bible, which places it in David's citadel—on the eastern hill, where we began this chapter, not here on the western hill.) The story really begins with Benjamin of Tudela—or fifteen years before his visit to Jerusalem. Then a wall of the church on Mount Zion fell in (as Benjamin narrates, in what is the longest tale in the *Itinerary*); two friends were working on the repairs and found a cave. When they investigated, looking for money, they found a "large chamber resting upon pillars of marble overlaid with silver and gold. In front was a table of gold and scepter and crown." They had found the tomb of David—and with it were the tombs of Solomon and the kings of Judah. But they could not enter. A wind knocked them down and they lay on the floor as if dead till evening. The patriarch called for Rabbi Abraham el Constantini, a pious recluse. He explained the significance of the find. But the next day the rabbi found the men lying on their beds in terror and declaring: "We will not enter there, for the Lord does not desire to show it to any man." So the place was bricked up. And, concludes Benjamin, he had this story from Rabbi Abraham himself.

This is a classic medieval story—a mixture of folktale, fairytale, and piety. Josephus, the Jewish historian, had planted the seed back in the first century. He says that Herod had heard that a previous king, Hyrcanus, had opened David's tomb and taken out a huge amount of silver but had left much more within. So Herod, with only his most trustworthy friends, entered the tomb. He found many gold ornaments and treasures, which he took away. He would have gone further in and opened the sarcophagi themselves, but two of his bodyguards were killed by flames as they entered. (Elsewhere Josephus says that they didn't actually find the coffins.) So they all fled. And Herod built a white marble monument by the tomb as a propitiation of his terror. Josephus doesn't say where the tomb is in the city, and this is the only story he knows about it, so historians worry how much of this tale is made up, too.

The treasure, as much as the luster of David, has proved a strong lure. Suleiman the Magnificent sent a *firman* on March 18, 1523, to the governor of Damascus demanding the expulsion of the Franciscans from their monastery there and taking over the site for Muslim worship; which is how it remained until 1948. In 1948, it took on a whole new guise. Because Jews were now prevented from visiting the Western Wall, many started to come here to pray—from where they could see over into the Old City. The Ministry of Religions, together with the Mount Zion Committee, began actively promoting the site as a sanctified shrine, with a heavy overlay of Zionist ideology. A link between the House of David and the present was cultivated with rituals, especially those commemorating the destruction of the Temple, and a site commemorating the Holocaust (which remains an impressively well-designed memorial). Bar Mitzvahs were celebrated here and the names of Bar Mitzvah boys from abroad were preserved on special documents ("Mount Cards"); pilgrims were given certificates with a new, specific logo as well as a picture of the Western Wall (pilgrim certificates are typical of the great Christian pilgrimages: the Ministry of Religions didn't seem to have any problem in imitating this custom). Shmuel Kahana, the director general of the Ministry of Religions, declared that Mount Zion was "the holiest place in the state . . . the organizational and spiritual center for all the country's holy and folkloristic sites"—a bizarre claim at every level, especially in retrospect, but one that he strove to make reality. Newspapers were more cynical: "a tourist tear-jerker," sniffed one; "the Hollywood of the religious lifestyle," another. But thousands visited. A massive menorah was erected—"the symbol of the state, and the symbol of the mountain, the symbol of the nation and its spirit," as Kahana trumpeted it—and stones from Mount Zion were sent around the world to be cornerstones for new synagogues.

But since 1967, when the Western Wall became available again, the status of David's Tomb and Mount Zion has steadily slumped, and it has again become a very minor site indeed, largely ignored by worshippers and politicians. In just a few years, it rose to prominence as a "holy site" through wholly invented traditions and because of the temporary exigencies of the political situation, and then slipped back into a more gentle obscurity, layered with memories and myths: in a brief compass, a model for so many sites in and around Jerusalem. It is a strange building to visit today, though the views from the roof at least make it worthwhile. Occasionally Orthodox Jews pray there (though the history of the place merits no such piety). The aggressive tour guides insist on the building's immense antiquity (it is their livelihood, after all). The Tomb of David embodies the desire of generations to reach back to the oldest city, and the fantasies this desire has generated. Perhaps that is enough to justify a visit.

THEM STONES

Jerusalem has a strange relation to stone. The rock of the Dome of the Rock, the stones of the Western Wall, the Stone of Unction, have the magnificence of stones that last: held down by the foot of Mohammed, still standing from the Roman destruction, much kissed in humility. The gravestones of generations line up against the hillsides, marking the spots where bodies turn back to dust and humans try to construct memorials against the destructiveness of time. Stones that would have cried out. For Western Victorian travelers in particular, Jerusalem's stones defined the city. John Lloyd Stephens was an American grandee who read *A Thousand and One Arabian Nights* and ventured abroad in 1830 to see the "splendor and opulence [that] once made the Prophet smile." He is best known today for his influential writing on ancient Mayan culture, but his travel books on the Middle East were best sellers. He found a myth to explain the stones:

> The boy next conducted us to a stony field, by which he said the Virgin once passed and asked for beans; the owner of the field told her there were none and to punish him for his falsehood and lack of charity, the beans were all changed into stones, and the country had remained barren ever since . . . "It was wonderful," said Paul as he picked up some little stones, as much like beans as anything else, "and see too," he said, "how barren the country is."

Herman Melville, dyspeptic as ever, finds stones everywhere—emotional as much as physical ones: "Stony mountains & stony plains; stony torrents & stony roads; stony walls & stony fields; stony houses & stony tombs; stony eyes & stony hearts. Before you and behind you are stones."

But it is Yehuda Amichai whose poetic stare most tellingly reveals the fragility of stones, as they slip from buildings into rubble and the wasteland, and as men strive to build them up again into houses to dwell in, memorials to stand:

> *The Mayor builds and builds and builds.*
> *At night the stones of the mountain crawl down*
> *And surround the stone houses*
> *Like wolves coming to howl at dogs*
> *Who have become the slaves of men.*

The oldest city of Jerusalem, the Canaanite or Jebusite town that David conquered and made his own, creeps out of the stones. Buried beneath later cities, the massive towers and tiny seals, the storerooms and toilets of houses and the tunnels cut out of the hard stone by wearied hands and blunt metal, are fragments of stone which the archaeologists try to make speak. Memorials and mundane objects, which we strive to comprehend. The image of the city that emerges is of a small hilltop town, walled with desperate and soaring defenses, hoarding its water supplies, dominated by a temple above it, and the wars around it. This the ground up from which Jerusalem grows. Can we see the powerful and enduring city of the historical imagination—royal David's city, the house of Zion, Solomon's palace—in the stones and holes of the excavation site? This hope is the lure of the hunt, the discovery, the revelation, which drives the archaeologist; but it also brings the inevitable disappointment of the lost, the fragmentary, the unknowable and shattered past. Jerusalem, more than any other city, lives in this space of mingled hope and disappointment in what has gone before.

Map 6

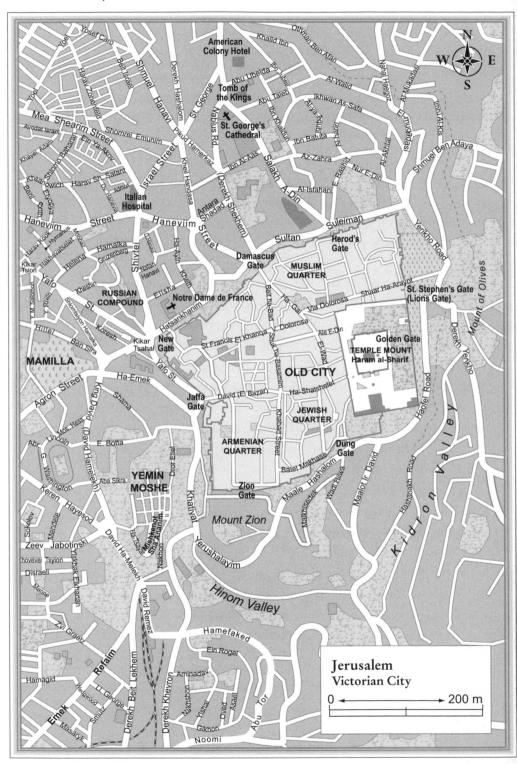

Jerusalem
Victorian City

0 ◀————————▶ 200 m

STEPHEN GRAHAM WAS AN ODD chap by any account. He believed in tramping and zigzag walking. That is, he spent most of his life on the road with a backpack traveling the world, meeting strangers, sleeping in barns or storerooms. He was very keen to distinguish between his traveling, on which he set out to learn from the world, and the wandering of hobos and bums, who were quite a different class of tramp. He particularly loved Russia and Central Asia, which he visited repeatedly through the interesting times of the first quarter of the twentieth century. But he also went to New York in the 1920s, where he invented zigzag walking: turn the first left and then the first right, and so on, and just keep going—it was, he said, amazing what you would find in the city, walking all night like this. He wandered in and out of speakeasies and hung out with the huddled masses of American immigrants. From these trips he turned out a string of books, which are as much about himself as about the places and people he encountered. He was born in 1884, at the height of the British Victorian Empire, and it is strange to think that he did not die until 1975, when so many of the places he wrote about had changed beyond recognition.

One trip he took gives us a unique insight into the world of Jerusalem before the First World War. This was a journey he made to Jerusalem with a boatload of Russian pilgrims at the beginning of the twentieth century. His book, *With the Russian Pilgrims to Jerusalem,* gives us an insider's picture of a phenomenon that has now completely disappeared, but that changed the face of Jerusalem. Every year from the middle of the nineteenth century through to the Russian Revolution, thousands of poor Russian peasants made the pilgrimage to Jerusalem, gathering in the city from Christmas onward and aiming to leave after Holy Week. They were hungry, ill-educated, and desperately pious. They far outnumbered the richer and well-fleshed nobles who made the same trip. But the presence of the Russians every year was part of the Jerusalem calendar, and their demand for trinkets was part of the Jerusalem economy, just as buildings were constructed around the city to cater to them.

Graham describes how his boat set out with 560 pilgrims on board, and only three toilets for all of them (which made the conditions in the hold unbearable, especially when the rolling seas brought on mass nausea). It took a fortnight for the aged boat to make the trip, which even in those days usually took only four days. Most of the peasants had little to eat but *sukharee*—rye bread, turned green with age, which was soaked in warm water with salt. Graham traveled as a peasant. He was deeply committed to the honesty and nobility of the downtrodden poor—and was very sniffy about the English tourists in Jerusalem whose conversations he could overhear unrecognized, and whose reactions to the peasants as well as to their religious zeal seemed so trivial and snobbish. Anthony Trollope, an exemplary Englishman, visited Jerusalem in 1858, many years before Graham, and in his novel *The Bertrams* he wrote of the Russian pilgrims in exactly the tones Graham despised: "cut-throat looking wretches, with close shaven heads, dirty beards, and angry eyes; men clothed in skins, or huge skin-like-looking cloaks, filthy, foul, alive with vermin, reeking with garlic—abominable to an Englishman."

The poorer Russians walked from Jaffa to Jerusalem, the better-off took the train (which by now was running up from the coast). Their aim was to bathe in the Jordan—"thousands of starved, illiterate, ragged men" processed to the river, stripped down to white shrouds, and threw themselves into the water. They also went to the ceremony of Holy Fire, where they would take the fire and extinguish it with their caps, in which they intended to be buried. Pilgrimage was fundamentally about dying in a particular way in Russia. "When I announced my intention of going to Jerusalem," wrote Graham, "friends told me I was sure to be disappointed, that everyone going there nursed high hopes which were destined to remain unfulfilled . . . the banality and sordidness of the everyday scenes would be a great shock to me." His friends were obviously well versed in the clichés of Victorian travel literature, which rehearsed the disappointments of the holy city so often. But with the Russian pilgrims, Graham found a different perspective, a different way of seeing Jerusalem. He was sickened, thrilled, and constantly engaged with his fellow pilgrims' experience. And he was certainly not disappointed.

When Graham visited Jerusalem, the skyline between the Mount of Olives and Mount Scopus had just been changed by the Victorian towers that still dominate the vista. The slender square tower was built by the Russians between 1870 and 1877 for pilgrims who wanted to visit the Jordan but were not strong enough for the trip. From the tower they could at least see the river. It has in it a twelve-thousand-pound bell, which was carried in the winter of 1884 from Jaffa on the coast to the top of the Mount of Olives by Russian pilgrims, women mainly. It took three weeks to complete the task, and they sang and chanted all the way, with ranks of women replacing each other every few minutes as each became tired. The bell passed beneath the house of the American Colony (then just inside the walls of the Old City). Bertha Spafford, sixty-five years later in 1950, remembered how the cheerful pilgrims waved to her as she watched them from her roof. Christian bells could not be rung in Jerusalem from the time of the Muslim capture of the city until 1831, when the brief rule of Ibrahim Pasha from Egypt relaxed the restrictions. Although the Ottomans took over again in 1840, thanks to support from the European superpowers, bells from then on have competed with the muezzins' call for prayers in the public display of calling the faithful to worship.

The other great tower on the ridge between Mount Scopus and the Mount of Olives is the Augusta Victoria (Figure 38). On Kaiser Wilhelm's politically charged visit to Jerusalem, a private prayer service was arranged for the royal couple at the top of the Mount of Olives (a carpet and chairs were placed on a cistern in the Russian area). The empress expressed a wish to own some property on the Mount. When empresses speak in this way, events follow: a collection was raised in Germany and abroad, and the land was purchased for a convent, church, and hospice for travelers. It was built in 1910—with all the building materials, except for the cement, stone, and water, brought from Germany, symbolically enough— and at that time it was the most modern building in the city: the first to have electricity, produced by its own diesel generator. The four bells in the 150-foot tower are huge—the biggest weighs six tons. The cost of repairing the roads damaged by transporting their weight from Jaffa was higher than the cost of the bells themselves. The church, with a massive organ, is strikingly built in the "modern orientalist" style, light and spacious inside. The deeds to the building were presented to the kaiserin on her silver wedding anniversary, and when the building was opened the happy couple were represented as crusaders in statues in the open courtyard (where they still stand in niches on the wall), and there was the image of a

Figure 38. The Augusta Victoria Hospital. The tower dominates the skyline of Jerusalem between Mount Scopus and the Mount of Olives.

crusader on the front of the menu for the grand opening dinner. An echo of Wilhelm's entrance into Jerusalem twelve years earlier . . . Neither saw the completed project, however, and in the war it was used first as the Turkish headquarters for Jamal Pasha and then after 1917 as the headquarters for the British command. In this guise in 1921 it hosted one of the most consequential meetings in Middle Eastern history. Sir Winston Churchill, fresh from the Cairo Conference, met Abdullah, the son of the emir of Mecca. On the advice of T. E. Lawrence (Lawrence of Arabia), and somewhat to the contrary of the discussions at Cairo, Churchill offered to make Abdullah first emir and then king of Transjordan—a new country and a new dynasty (which still rules in Jordan, as Transjordan is now known). Abdullah himself ruled until he was assassinated in the al-Aqsa. The negotiations, power plays, and decision making of these few weeks have been raked over by historians, but no one can doubt the importance of Churchill's four days in Jerusalem at the

Augusta Victoria—and the wry suitability of this German imperial
monument as the place where countries were made by the fiat of
the victorious power.

The Augusta Victoria is now a modern hospital, catering largely
to Palestinians, while the Russian tower is closed for long-term repairs. Tourists visit neither in general, but both are instantly recognizable landmarks, visible across the city, signs of imperial majesty,
as they were intended to be.

Further down the Mount of Olives in Gethsemane is one of the
most conspicuous buildings in Jerusalem, with its golden, onion-
shaped domes and shimmering white façade, set amid the green of
the hillside (Figure 39). This is the second great Russian building of
the late Victorian period, the Church of St. Mary Magdalene. It
was built by Alexander III in 1888 and dedicated to his mother,
Maria (and hence named after her name-saint). The bulbous cupolas with their Orthodox crosses would be standard enough in Moscow, but they stand out distinctively amid the crusader domes and
Muslim minarets of the Jerusalem skyline. The five domes on their
bell towers (four small at the corners, the largest in the middle)
symbolize Christ and the four Evangelists; the Orthodox crosses,
unlike Catholic crosses, have a slanted footboard, aimed upward on
the right toward the thief who repented, and downward on the left
toward the thief who railed at Jesus. (They also say the footboard is
historically accurate.) The façade is sculpted white sandstone with
Roman arches, rising to a gabled roof and a third floor with scal-
loped windows and light, elegant arches. The arches at the ground
level on either side of the door contain raised tombs, the one on
the left, for Alice, the mother of Prince Philip, husband of Queen
Elizabeth II of England. His royal standard is draped over the coffin.
He is often called "Phil the Greek" by his loving subjects: it is not
usually with any recognition of his family's long connection with
the Orthodox Church.

Inside, the church is without pews (as with all Orthodox churches

Figure 39. The Russian Church of St. Mary Magdalene.

in which the congregation stands for services), and the sanctuary is dominated by a huge canvas painted by the Russian artist Alexander Ivanov, and set above the iconostasis. It is in a rather severe realist mode, but unlike the art of the Soviet workers, this is a picture of a religious miracle. The story goes that Mary Magdalene went to Rome to complain to the emperor Tiberius that Jesus' trial had been unfair (she gained access to one of the emperor's parties by virtue of her former profession). She carried an egg with her to symbolize the life and resurrection of Jesus. The emperor Tiberius laughed at her and said that Jesus was no more likely to have arisen from the dead than her egg would turn red. Whereupon the egg did indeed change color, and Mary preached the Gospel in the palace of the emperor. Hence Christians paint eggs at Easter. It is not the sort of picture or story you would expect to find in an English parish church, and certainly not on so massive a scale. The iconostasis itself is made of beautifully carved marble with painted bronze screens that pick up the striking ochre colors of the interior of the building. The treasure of the church, however, is the icon of the Virgin Mary, set to the right of the iconostasis in a carved wooden frame.

This icon came to the church from Lebanon in 1939. Metropolitan Elias, the priest in charge of the icon in Lebanon, dreamed that two great martyrs, Katherine and Barbara, told him that Mary herself instructed him to give the icon to Abbess Mary in Palestine. He had never heard of anyone by such a name, but when he had the dream three times, he made inquiries, found out about Abbess Mary at the convent attached to the Church of St. Mary Magdalene, and made her the offer of the icon. The icon was blackened with age. It was called "Hodigitria" ("the path") or "the unburned bush," because it alone survived when its church burned down in 1555, or "the healer" and "quick to hear" because plague had been cured by processing the icon around the local Lebanese village. When Abbess Mary drove it back to the church, it had an immediate effect. Father Seraphim, who had incurable stomach cancer, declared himself to feel the power emanating from the icon and survived for ten more years. ("Feeling the power of the icon" is a standard expression in such miracle stories.) The icon itself became lighter and clearly visible, and one day the astonished nuns saw tears fall from the eyes of the image. When Metropolitan Elias finally visited the new home of his beloved icon, he burst into tears and blessed the nuns: "I now understand why the Most Holy Lady desired to be with you, sisters. She sees your love towards her, your faith, your prayers and your sighs." The piety of the old pilgrims, along with the love of miraculous stories, has survived the revolution's purge of the opium of the people and lives on here in the Orthodox church.

At the foot of the iconostasis are two glass cases. Each holds a saint of the Orthodox Church; the feet of the skeletons—in slippers—stick out from under the shrouds. On the right is Elizabeth. She was the wife of Grand Duke Sergei Alexandrovitch, the brother of Alexander III (they came to Jerusalem on a royal tour, as we saw in Chapter 3, to start the Alexander Hospice project). When she saw the Church of St. Mary Magdalene, she asked to be buried there, as now she is. Her husband was assassinated in 1905 by a bomb thrown by an anarchist (she visited the revolutionary in prison to ask him to repent: he did not repent and in fact said that he would have killed the grand duke earlier if *she* had not so often been by his side—her saintliness was recognized even by bomb-throwing revolutionaries). She withdrew to become a nun in Moscow and spent the rest of her life doing good deeds for the poor—assisted by Barbara, her noble companion, who was the abbess of the convent. The grand duchess was murdered along with the rest of the royal family in 1918. Her body was taken up by the White Army and brought to Jerusalem finally in 1921, where it was buried in the crypt. The two bodies were brought up to their current resting place in 1981, when they were declared saints. Neither seems to have done any miracles, alive or dead (which is a bar to becoming a saint for the Catholics but not for the Orthodox); but here they are, beatified, a remarkable final twist to a story of Russian imperial ambition in the holy city.

Both the tower on the Mount of Olives and the Church of St. Mary Magdalene belong to the White Russians. After the revolution of 1917, both the White Russians from their exile in New York and the Red Russians in power in Moscow claimed authority over the former czarist property in Jerusalem. The British recognized the White Russian claims (though there is some evidence that they continued to deal with the communists, too). But in 1948, when Israel came into being, it gave up the convent in Ein Kerem and the Russian Compound (the two Russian sites in Israel's territory, which we will look at next) to the Red Russians because the Soviet Union had supported Israel's creation in the United Nations. In 1964 the compound, excluding the cathedral, was sold to Israel for four and a half million dollars, three million of which was paid in oranges. But Jordan, which still held the Old City and the Mount of Olives in 1948, continued to recognize the White Russians. In 1964, when the abbess of the Convent of the Ascension was the octogenarian princess Bagration, a former grand duchess, the young king Hussein, Abdullah's son, visited her there and had tea under portraits of the last czar and czarina, and they commiserated with each other on the burdens of royalty. This power share between different Russian groups has continued under the current Israeli control, though the White Russians are dying out, and the Red Russians (if they can still be called that) are less red. Both sides remain deeply suspicious of each other—and arguments about the Russian property continue, as we will see. All cities have property disputes, and Jerusalem has more rows over ownership than most, but in Jerusalem, somehow, these disputes seem to get caught up in world events with alarming ease.

The Russian Compound was Russia's grandest project for Jerusalem, one of the earliest developments outside the city walls, and it had a major effect on the city and its history. The Crimean War, it is always said, started from a dispute over who had the rights to the keys of the Church of the Nativity in Bethlehem, just outside Jerusalem. The keys had been in the hands of the Orthodox Church, but the Ottomans ceded them to France, as the one true protector of Catholic interests in the Holy Land. There had already been a row—a fight, indeed—when the Greek Orthodox monks had pried loose and stolen a silver star that the French had set in the floor of the chapel at Bethlehem (for cleaning, the Greek Orthodox unconvincingly claimed)—and locked the French out of the chapel. Russia weighed in on the side of the bereaved Orthodox Church, and Britain and France joined with the Ottomans in opposition. There are grander causes for the brutal three-year war: Russian imperial expansion, which challenged the equilibrium in Europe after the treaty of Vienna, and the struggle for the financial profits to be made as the Ottoman Empire weakened. But that an argument over a key should turn into a major international conflict seems archetypal of Jerusalem's place in history. (Rabbi Soloveichick used to joke: "Crucifixion was a normal and frequent form of punishment in the Roman Empire. But you do one crucifixion in Jerusalem and look what happens . . .") The Crimean War ended with victory for Britain, France, and the Ottomans. The Ottomans were fully aware that they had survived solely because of help from Europe, and one *quid pro quo* was the relaxing of rules against foreigners owning property in the Holy Land. It is still a surprise that one of the first countries to benefit from this change was the Ottomans' defeated enemy, Russia. Three years is a long time in politics, but not only did the Turks sell to the Russians what had been the military parade ground outside the city walls to the north of the Jaffa Gate, but the sultan added a part of the land himself as a gift to the czar. (It is hard to imagine Britain welcoming a German national architectural project in London in 1948 and donating land in the process.) The Russians proceeded to build an imposing compound for the 20,000 pilgrims who visited each year. The imperialist overtones of this project were not lost on the other countries. The British ambassador wrote home to suggest that the pilgrims were actually former soldiers, and that the boast on the streets was that Jerusalem would be in Russian hands before the year was up. His fears were unfounded, but they indicate as sharply as possible the constant mutual scrutiny and testing of the European powers in Jerusalem in the years after the Crimean War.

The compound is still in place (Map 6), but with the exception of the cathedral it was taken over and converted into government buildings by the British Mandate and then inherited in this form by the Israeli authorities. It was once a walled and self-contained "city within a city," but now it has also been built all around and the walls have not been maintained. This makes it hard to view, and it is actually rather shocking that seven Victorian buildings of considerable architectural beauty along with their plazas should have been allowed to become so run down, and reused with so little regard for their original form—especially when there is so much earnest reconstruction of any building with the smallest touch of religious significance. Charlie Ashbee, despite his campaigning passion for preservation of the buildings of London, was interested only in the medieval and "traditional" Jerusalem, and he showed no interest in this complex, which he called "bastard Moscow." The buildings were turned over to the civic authorities without regard. The worst irony is that this is where the Israeli Authority for the Preservation of Historic Buildings is housed.

The compound was funded by a collection of private and public funds—more than a million rubles, which was a huge sum, enough to run the delegation for a hundred years. The "Committee on Palestine" chose the Russian architect Martin Eppinger to design the project, and under his care the six main buildings were started between 1860 and 1864. Eppinger placed the cathedral central to the design, and it was built first. This building—the Church of the Holy Trinity—is the easiest of the whole compound to view today, and the only one whose vista has not been ruined by later buildings, though the cars do not help. The elegant frontage has two corner towers with cupolas topped by tall crosses (without the footboards: these are Pravoslavic crosses), which flank a triangular pediment above two floors of Roman arches. The large central dome has four smaller cupolas around it, and at both sides and at the rear of the church are six-sided bays, with inset arches, columns, and fine wrought-iron windows, which form the apse inside. The triangular pediments on the arches of the central dome give a rather frilly feel to its roofscape (Figure 40). Inside, the church has a restrained baroque splendor, with a particularly fine, round, candle-lit chandelier in front of the iconostasis. The pillars are decorated with icons, and the south apse has large portraits of Constantine and Helena, founders of the Christian architecture of Jerusalem, while the north has the Russian saints Olga and Vladimir. Vladimir, Olga's grandson, was the first ruler of Russia in the tenth century to embrace Christianity: she had failed to persuade her son to convert. The services are beautiful, with lavishly coped monks in green and gold, the swinging of incense, and excellent male singing: the iconostasis opens dramatically to reveal the priests at the altar and the glitter of gold and silver of the ritual vessels. But at other times, it is a quiet, reflective place, surrounded by hectic political life in the other buildings of the Russian Compound. (It is against protocol here to put your hands in your pocket or to cross your legs, let alone to talk in a loud voice.) Back in the 1970s when the politics of the Cold War were particularly tense, Rostropovich, the great cellist, was allowed out on a visa from Russia to play in a concert in Jerusalem. He disappeared and was frantically sought by his minders, as the threat of an international incident grew more insistent.

Figure 40. The façade of the Church of the Holy Trinity—the center of the Russian Compound—rising above the traffic.

He was finally located, sitting in the church here in the Russian Compound, which he had wandered into: day-dreaming quietly, lost in the echoes of his homeland in Jerusalem.

On either side of the cathedral, Eppinger placed two square buildings of equal dimensions and similar design. Each had a string of rooms around the outside of small courtyards, one with a small dome in the middle (Figure 41). The building to the north was the men's hostel, where the pilgrims stayed; to the south was the building for the Russian delegation (the Dochovania), whose delegates expected to live in a certain style too. There is a grim fulfillment of the symmetry of this design in that the delegation building is now a courthouse, the men's hostel a prison—the two arms of the law. The long corridors with strings of small rooms suit the needs of the lawyers and the innumerable officials of the court; the same small rooms are used for prisoners on the other side of the cathedral. The gardens viewed through the long corridor windows add a pleasing touch of calm greenery to the tense focus and bustle of the lawyers going about their business. But the prison is a particularly strident and squalid place. Although you can still see the ambition of the Russian builders on the outside wall at the side of the prison block, where the frontage reflects the nineteenth-century design and the craftsmanship in its construction, the rest of the building is covered with air conditioners, barbed wire, and pipe-work; and it is heaving with vans and cars and a mass of unhappy relatives and stressed policemen. The building was turned into a prison by the British, and it shows every bit of its shoddy make-shift adaptation. It is now the holding prison where many Palestinians in particular first come into contact with the Israeli legal system. The combination of slow desperation, anger, and the explosiveness of arguments, along with the bustle and macho swagger of the police (much as anywhere in the world), is as far from the world of the humble pilgrims as can be imagined.

The e-shaped women's hostel was also a prison where several

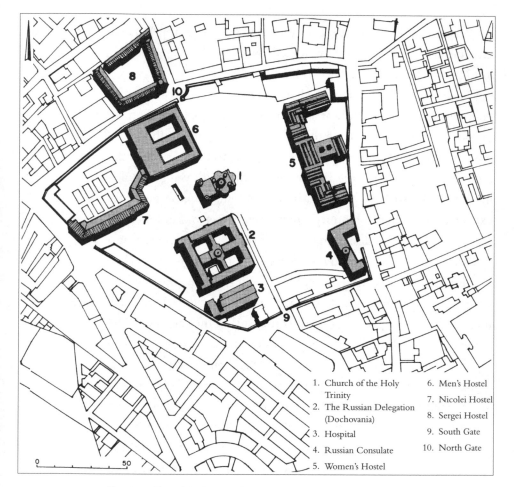

1. Church of the Holy Trinity
2. The Russian Delegation (Dochovania)
3. Hospital
4. Russian Consulate
5. Women's Hostel
6. Men's Hostel
7. Nicolei Hostel
8. Sergei Hostel
9. South Gate
10. North Gate

Figure 41. Plan of the Russian Compound.

Jewish fighters were held and executed by the British in the build-up to the War of Independence. Zionists remember it as the place where Barazani and Feinstein, two prisoners who had been condemned to death, committed suicide with a hand grenade that had been concealed in a basket of oranges, rather than face the death penalty at the hands of the British, their enemies. The building, which is now a quiet and often empty museum dedicated to these dead fighters, is the only one that gives a real impression of how the pilgrim cells would have looked in their heyday. Neither the courts nor the prison are easy or much fun to visit.

The hospital, further to the south, is now the government building that deals with traffic offenses and fines. There is still a surprisingly grand staircase there, with its Russian wrought-iron work, and
some lovely original windows. Around the outside of the building
at the first-floor level is a corridor with stone floors, a wood roof,
and a balcony where the recovering patients could take the sun.
But these small hints of the original design are swamped by the
poor-quality open-plan office space that has been constructed inside the shell of the old building. In any city, there is nowhere quite
as sour and measly as the traffic-fine administration. The pity is not
that the compound should have become government buildings but
that the buildings should have been so shoddily reused.

The Sergei Hostel, which was constructed in 1890 after the rest
of the compound and is just outside its northern gate, is the only
one of the seven buildings, apart from the cathedral, where a real
sense of the pilgrims' lives can still be felt. This building, also designed by Eppinger, was for the wealthier nobles, who clearly didn't
appreciate sharing space too closely with the humble pilgrims. The
upper storey, around the inner courtyard, had twenty bedrooms,
with decorated ceilings, silk-lined walls, Persian carpets, and heavy,
ornate furniture. Below are the public rooms, including stables,
chicken coop, and a laundry. The courtyard, once for carriages and
the general business of servicing the comfort of the nobility, now
has a little collection of old agricultural instruments and has been
planted out with greenery, which makes it a very pleasant place to
stop. (It was, surprisingly, a pet project of the volatile and celebrated
general Moshe Dayan.) The two towers, connected to the upper
floor by a covered wooden walkway (Figure 42), are the toilet
blocks: the nobleman or woman could walk out of the bedrooms
into a separate area, which could be serviced from below by the
staff. The eastern wing of the building is shut up and empty, as it
has been since 1948. (You can see some of the mouldering decorations through the dusty glass and appreciate the style of the Russian
upper classes.) The ownership is still under dispute. Because it was

Figure 42. The toilet block of the Sergei Hostel in the Russian Compound.

not part of the original Russian Compound, it was not ceded to Russia in 1948 nor sold back to Israel for oranges; but because it is in Israeli territory it is not part of the White Russian portfolio. So it sits empty. Vladimir Putin, the Russian premier, is said to have remained desperate to get it back for Russia. Whereas most of the compound has been destroyed through appropriation by the administrative system, here is one beautifully proportioned set of rooms left to decay because the administration cannot resolve what to do with them.

The watchtower of the compound still stands on the corner of Mounbaz and Helena haMalka (the street named for Helena of Adiabene, whose tomb we saw in Chapter 5). There are Russian inscriptions on the walls, and the old gateposts, where the compound was locked at night, still stand. But these are only the ghosts of this huge Russian project, which has been absorbed back into the city, as the city has spread around and through it. It once stood as a grand statement of the Russian Empire and its interest in the Holy Land.

JEWISH IDEALS AND GENTILE KNOW-HOW

The first development outside the city walls was a housing project directed by the wealthy English Jew Moses Montefiore. The first house outside the walls—it is still standing—had been the summer house of the British consul James Finn, in Talbieh, about a mile from the city: a one-storey building with just a dining room and a living room, and a balcony facing east (the consulate in those days was a very modest affair, where business was conducted from the front room of Finn's family house); and Bishop Gobat, the second bishop of the Anglican cathedral, had opened a Protestant school on Mount Zion. But it is Montefiore's construction of Mishkanot Sha'ananim that signals a sea-change in attitude to the urban development of Jerusalem. It is today a familiar sight on the hill across from the Old City and Mount Zion, its austere terrace of houses with an incongruous windmill above it, where many Israelis walk, and picnic in the gardens around it.

The money for this project actually came from an American Jewish millionaire, Judah Touro. Touro had fought in the defense of New Orleans in the War of 1812 under Andrew Jackson, the future president of the United States; wounded and left for dead, he had been helped from the battlefield by his friend, Rezin Shepherd, who nursed him back to health. The two became millionaires in the import and export business. Touro was a shy and retiring man who never married, but he was sufficiently honored in the New Orleans community that all the churches rang bells on the day of his funeral and a public holiday was declared. He left his money to charitable causes, including $50,000 to be managed by Montefiore—"it being my earnest wish to cooperate with the said Moses Montefiore of London, Great Britain, in endeavouring to ameliorate the condition of our unfortunate Jewish Brethren in the Holy Land, and to secure to them the inestimable privilege of worshipping the Almighty according to our religion, without molestation." Montefiore had first visited Palestine in 1827, and he had been engaged in a long, drawn-out campaign to persuade the sultan to let him buy land and help the poor Jews. Montefiore's status as one of the richest men in Europe, combined with his diplomatic roles on behalf of the British government at the time of the Crimean War, when the sultan was so dependent on British support, finally gave him a strong negotiating hand, and in 1855 he was granted the *firman* that enabled him to purchase land outside the city walls. Not only were foreigners generally not allowed to own land in Palestine, but also a specific rule forbade building anywhere close to the walls of Jerusalem "for security reasons." Montefiore bought 38,250 square meters west of the Pool of the Sultan for the sum of £1,000. (This might look like a bargain today for what is Mishkanot Sha'ananim and Yemin Moshe, two of the most exclusive areas of the city, but it was regarded as an exorbitantly high price at the time, explained at least in part by the unwillingness of the Turkish owner to sell, coupled with his apparently decent and respectful response to Montefiore.) In 1857, consequently, a windmill and two houses were built, followed by twenty more houses in 1860, in a walled compound with cisterns and areas for gardens (Figure 43).

The idea was to create a space outside the cramped and disease-ridden Old City where poor Jews could live healthily and earn a living. As was so often the case in Victorian culture, a rulebook was produced for the community. The rules were particularly strict on cleanliness (again a typical product of the new fascination with sanitation in London and Paris, where political debates on the disposal of sewage, new sewer systems, and the health of the working classes were hot political topics). Rule 5 specified that each resident had to clean his home every day and spray the floor with water every day. Rule 6 required residents to use the refuse containers. Rule 7 guaranteed that the cisterns would be kept covered. Rule 9 insisted that the synagogue would be cleaned twice a day and water poured on the floor at least once a day. Rule 8—with the proper gesture of memorial—declared that a chapter of the *mishnah* (Talmudic law) should be read every day and the *kaddish derabbanan* (mourning prayer) should be said after it "for the soul of the departed benefactor Judah Touro." The Book of Regulations ended: "Take heed not to transgress the fraternal covenant, so that no conflict and discord shall break out amongst you. Seek the welfare of your brethren

Figure 43. An early photograph of the first development of Mishkanot Sha'ananim.

wherever you go and in whatever you do, and you shall dwell safely in your domiciles." Mishkanot Sha'ananim was modeled on the idealist communities that were such a feature of Victorian philanthropy and industry, such as Robert Owen's factory housing project at New Lanark, or Bournville, the new town for Cadbury's workers, where cleanliness, godliness, hard work, and rigorously maintained social order were the principles enforced by the earnest social reformers who founded them.

The only trouble was that no one wanted to live outside the walls. There were robbers, a Muslim graveyard nearby, and all the threats of the open countryside. Eventually twenty families were persuaded to take up residence in the simple two-room houses, but they insisted on running back to the city at night before the gates were locked. In 1865 a cholera epidemic killed 15 percent of the Jewish population of the Old City, but no one in Mishhkanot Sha'ananim was infected. This was well noted, and, as fears of being outside the city disappeared, Jews were asking Montefiore for more such housing by 1875. It is less clear that the Jews who lived there became model workers. Many subsisted still on charity. The windmill worked for a few years, though never very well, as the winds there are light and irregular; indeed, steam mills made it unnecessary soon enough, but it has remained as the most visible landmark of Mishhkanot Sha'ananim. The British blew off the top of the windmill to prevent it from being used by Hagganah forces under the Mandate, but it was restored. The housing was far too close to No-Man's-Land between 1948 and 1967, and the property was used only by the genuinely poor. Since 1967, it has all been restored again. The Jerusalem Municipality has used it to house visiting artists, musicians, and academics—the photographs of guests on the walls are a gallery of the most celebrated names in literature, music, theater, and intellectual life—and it is still restricted in its guest list. The simple houses for Montefiore's poor are atmospheric duplexes for the great and good of the cultural world. (It is a fabulous place to stay, and much of this book was gratefully researched from it . . .)

The tension between the rich and the poor in this housing complex has erupted several times since its inception. The adjoining area of Yemin Moshe was not developed by Montefiore himself. Squatters, who thought that the land was intended for the poor, quickly took over—171 families eventually—and built shacks out of old oil drums, boxes, and random planks. (The shanty village was called Shekhunat Khap—*khap* is the Yiddish for "grab"—or, by the Christians, "the Box Colony.") The heirs of Montefiore were forced to have the squatters evicted through the offices of one Mr. Valero, a banker. (The squatters went to the Western Wall and cursed him, and also tried their luck with the pasha. Neither recourse worked.) The heirs decided to build more small houses for the deserving and industrious poor. But by now the project could attract a different sort of protest. The newspaper *Ha-Or* in 1892 complained that land prices had risen in this area because of the railway, and given that this was the first property travelers would see as they approached the Jaffa Gate, shouldn't the land be used to make houses for the wealthy? Nonetheless, by 1896, 130 small houses had been built in a similar style to Mishkanot Sha'ananim.

In 1967, the same story played itself out with a different conclusion. The houses had been occupied by very poor people since 1948 because this area was so dangerous to live in thanks to the Jordanian snipers. In 1963 the government decided to expropriate the land and restore the area for public purposes. At first, the rate of expropriation was slow and the residents moved on willingly. In 1967, in the space of less than a week, the area became the center of the city instead of a borderline, and the houses became extremely attractive prospects. Some residents were happy to leave what were still then ruined and depressing houses with some financial compensation. But it became clear that many did not wish to leave and felt disenfranchised by the government's decision. A full-scale political row broke out, with debates in the Knesset, public protests, and a growing anger among the residents. The aim of the government had been to create an artists' quarter; and some artists did move in—but mostly only those who could afford to contribute extensively to the restoration process. There is a nice and—for once—true story of an American woman buying a house in Yemin Moshe: a price of "thirty thousand" was agreed on. The American wrote out a check for $30,000—when the owner thought she was agreeing to a price of L30,000—not quite $10,000. Such inflation has continued. It is now a particularly beautiful area through which many people wander happily, up the famous steps, and through the stone streets with their hanging baskets of flowers. But there is also here a buried—and largely forgotten—history of the confusion of public interest, financial pressure, and sheer opportunism in the question of landownership in Jerusalem.

Me'a She'arim turned out to be the largest of the new burst of Jewish developments outside the walls of the Old City which fol-

lowed Montefiore's lead, and it has become the most familiar at
least by name because its strictly Orthodox communities have become a byword for the extreme religious ideologies that so distort
the Israeli social and political world. Like Mishkanot Sha'ananim,
Me'a She'arim was constructed as an idealist community—by a society that took its name from the portion of the Torah being read
the week the society was founded in 1873: "And Isaac sowed in
that land, and found in the same year a hundred-fold [*me'a she'arim*]
and the Lord blessed him" (Genesis 26.12—*parsha Toledot*). The society was a housing association, founded by five Old City Jews
from different countries, which enabled its members to buy houses
on easy terms spread over a long period. But the conditions on
which a purchaser could join the community were laid down in a
book of regulations, which originally had eleven clauses, but which
by 1889 had expanded to more than sixty rules. At first, like the
rules of Mishkanot Sha'ananim, these emphasized cleanliness and
the appearance of the neighborhood: one regulation called for the
planting of decorative trees and bushes; another restricted the raising of livestock in the area. But quickly the rules became more focused on religious matters. Regulation 1.10 reads: "It is forbidden
for anyone to make over his property, or part of it, not only to a
non-Jew but even to a Jew belonging to a sect of those violating
the Words of Our Sages," just as 2.7 stresses: "It is forbidden to lease
an apartment to one who is not held to be a good Jew." Notice that
it is "one who is not held to be a good Jew" which is the criterion
for ownership: there is a very strong sense of agreed group values
and the exclusivity of the group here. From the beginning, this
walled and gated compound was intended to keep out anyone and
anything but the strictly religious (and to keep out especially anything that smacked of modernity and change, the threat of what is
known as the *haskallah,* the Jewish enlightenment). The gates were
removed in 1915, as other neighborhoods grew up around Me'a
She'arim, but the conscious self-isolation and fierce protection of
the values of the group have certainly been maintained.

Ironically enough, the buildings were designed by Conrad Schick, a German evangelical Christian. The first 10 houses were finished in 1874; by 1881 the project of 140 houses, arranged in a square so that the backs of the houses form a wall against the outside world, was finished. The purchase of the property and the building contracts were arranged by the British consulate. The residents could not do without the help of outsiders to get their project going. Indeed, they were largely dependent on foreign charity, as much of the ultra-Orthodox community still is. In Victorian Jerusalem, there was a centralized system known as *halukkah,* which channeled European gifts to the "poor Jews," as the collectors of charity always called them. Many Jews came to Jerusalem when they could no longer work; many others came to spend their lives in religious study and prayer. Montefiore, like many a Victorian, wanted to wean the poor off their dependence on charity. The residents of Me'a She'arim still see their role as preservers of the faith: men make the world a better place by constant study, while women bring up the children, with perhaps a small job on the side. Financial handouts—from the government as much as from Europe and America—are the only reason the community is economically viable at all. The clash of worldviews between Montefiore together with his conceptual heirs and the generations of Me'a She'arim is one of the defining tensions for Jewish Jerusalem.

Many different sects live in this neighborhood, distinguished externally by their clothes and internally by small but fiercely patrolled items of dogma. Some sects hate each other as much as they hate the secular, outside world. The Toldos Aharon sect comes from Hungary, and, thanks to inbreeding, many have red hair and blue eyes and pale white skin. They wear luxurious gold silk robes on the Sabbath, stitched in patterns of mystical import. Their clocks run on a different hour from official Israeli time, as they do not recognize the State of Israel. The Gerer *hassidim* are so strict about not displaying any public connection between men and women that a man will walk five yards ahead of his wife and children. They wear a *spodik,* a fur hat that is taller and thinner than the broad, flatter *streimel* of the Satmer (also a Hungarian sect, from Szatmar, a village now in Rumania: other *hassidim* told me gleefully that Szatmar is a corruption of Santa Maria; this may not be true, but truth rarely spoils a good story in Jerusalem). Before Sabbath, when each sect is dressed in its finery and is getting ready for the holy day and on the way from the ritual baths or going toward synagogue or finishing last-minute shopping, the combination of public modesty—averted gazes, covered heads, stooped bodies—with the excitement and color and bustle of preparation marks out the religious community fixed on its own course.

The streets themselves are narrow, with small shops and a little market in front of the courtyards around which each group lives. This is one of the densest areas of population in Jerusalem; every small and airless house is crowded. Privacy is difficult (though the sexes are kept separate), which enforces the obsessive and paranoid concern for boundaries and the observation of minute differences in rules and behavior. The scholar of medieval life Huizinga captures the tone brilliantly when he refers to the "proud or cruel publicity" of this life constantly in the gaze of others. There are more than fifty synagogues here, and more than two hundred schools or study houses, though most are difficult to spot as there are no signs, and certainly no grand buildings in the style of modern American synagogues. Unlike most of Jerusalem, here you do not see many people hanging out, chatting, or watching the world go by. This is an area on a mission.

The different sects are united by their resistance to the secular state and by any infringement on their enclave. The famous signs by the entrance to Me'a She'arim (Figure 44) demand that women dress modestly and all behave with respect: "groups passing through our neighborhoods severely offend the residents: please stop this." (No one likes being the object of tourists' gawking. The adverb "severely," like the use of "strictly," which always appears before

Figure 44. A sign above one of the passageways in Me'a She'arim.

"forbidden," is typical of the level of rhetoric here.) These rules are enforced, with physical violence on occasion. Women should not visit this area in trousers or shorts or without a top that properly covers their arms and is fully closed. Head covering is advisable. "Mini dresses are the epitome of moral deprivation," as one poster shrieks. Men should not wear shorts, either. Taking photographs may result in protest. No radios or video cameras are tolerated. (But if you walk the streets in neighborhoods outside Me'a She'arim late at night and find a shop with a television on, you may well find a bunch of young *hassidic* Jews discovering forbidden fruit.)

The walls are pasted with signs. Rabbi Teitelbaum, the late head of the Satmers, quipped that the decrepit walls of Me'a She'arim "would have collapsed long ago were it not for the posters that hold together the crumbling stones." These posters reveal the aggression and barely controlled violence that goes into patrolling the boundaries of these extremist sects. When the archaeologist Yigael Shilo died young of stomach cancer, posters immediately appeared triumphantly celebrating "with joy" God's punishment of a man who had desecrated graves by virtue of his archaeological digs—the death of an "evil, wicked, abominable apostate, the archaeologist, Yigael Shilo, who is now a dead corpse, after suffering great and deserved pain while he was alive. Hell and perdition will now complete his punishment." This level of unabashed rhetorical hostility is also thrown at rival sects, at political figures, at television—"this unmitigated abomination which causes so much disorder and suffering throughout the world . . . Cursed is the man who rents a flat or shop to anyone possessing this destructive instrument. It is strictly outlawed by authority of the learned and saintly rabbis." The saintly rabbis also, of course, condone stone-throwing at cars that drive through the area on the Sabbath, the physical assault of those who do not observe their authority, and massive political rallies against soccer on the Sabbath (the chief rabbi in the 1920s had already banned it) and against homosexuality under any circumstances. The head of the rabbinical religious court solemnly stated that the Israeli failures in Lebanon in the war of 2006 were directly caused by the Israeli government's willingness to condone a gay pride march in Jerusalem that very week. The humble walk and intense commitment to holy study are constantly on the edge of the eruption of rage.

This conflict with modernity and its visible signs all around Me'a She'arim means that you cannot ever really feel like you are in the dismal medieval ghettos of Poland or in some museum of the *shtetl*, however alienating or nostalgic a trip through these streets can be. But behind the doors things are different again. There are three hot steam baths attached to the ritual bath on the first floor of an anonymous building in an alley off an alley off Even Yisrael Street. Each is hotter than the next, and the first is scalding. Naked *hassids*—only men, of course—crowd in from the lockers: there is whipping with branches to stimulate the blood; water is called for and poured over pink and steaming bodies; men soap each other; and relaxed conversation grunts and swoops as bodies slither across each other with no apparent regard for decorum. Young boys help older men and wash them; there are no signs of sect or status. In middle Europe and Russia this was known (in Yiddish) as a *schwitz,* and before the Sabbath, the baths are packed. The Turks have their Turkish baths, but here a piece of old Europe has been transplanted into the Mediterranean climate. After the ritual bath and the *schwitz,* the *hassids* put on their Sabbath clothes and return to the paraded piety of the street.

A *tisch* is an occasion when the rabbi of the group speaks, and drinking and singing take place. *Tisch* is German for "table," but that bland word doesn't capture the extraordinary atmosphere of religious exposition, mixed with the ecstasy of group singing, fueled by a drunkenness that feels like more than the effect of alcohol. At Toldos Aharon, many hundreds of men (and a few women in a gallery above, who can look down through narrow slits in the wall on the men below) gather to hear the rabbi's words and to sing and drink into the night. The Gerer have a hangar of a building where 14,000 men gather to hear the rebbe speak: packed in, identically dressed, every man and the galleries of over-excited boys intently receive a sip of wine passed in cups from the rebbe's table and a sliver of food. The congregants respond in unison to the rebbe's blessing and sing in harmony. This occasion has all the signs of a cult: but here, away from the eyes of others, the room drags everyone into its embrace, and the emotional power of the religious experience is palpable.

Me'a She'arim polarizes Jerusalem. Gershom Scholem, perhaps the greatest scholar of Jewish mysticism, called it "a dialectical paradise." For many, it is a backward, isolated, aggressive community that exists only on the misplaced charity of the state. For others, it is a vision of their grandparents' or great-grandparents' communities, which were destroyed in the Holocaust and deserve nostalgic support and a certain alienated distance. For others still, Me'a She'arim is the vanguard of Judaism, the one place where the old values are maintained and tradition fostered, without which true religious knowledge would fade away. It is certainly the product of a Victorian idealism, a conscious desire to create, architecturally and socially, an enclosed community formed on ideal principles. This could be described as a trendy, state-of-the-art project for the 1870s, full of Victorian longing for a lost past that never quite existed (Jews were forced into ghettos; they did not choose that life); or it could be described as a nostalgic and fearful reaction to the present and its threat (or promise) of change, as much as a positive choice of a way of life. But what was once a walled enclave outside a walled city is now a community hard and fast up against the modern city and fully intertwined with it. This exacerbates all the tensions. Now it is a tourist destination, another, unwilling living museum in Jerusalem; at the same time, there are no more walls around Me'a She'arim, and the fight to preserve its imagined boundaries has become ever fiercer and more aggressive. Consequently, Me'a She'arim has become an icon for contemporary concerns about the role of religion in modern political society, and for the role of the ultra-Orthodox in Judaism. It is yet another story of how history, religion, and politics combine in such emotionally complex and exhausting ways in Jerusalem.

THE INVASION FROM THE WEST

THE ENGLISH ARE COMING (AND SO ARE THE FRENCH AND ITALIANS)

Right on the edge of Me'a She'arim is the Ministry of Education. This was once the Italian Hospital, with attached church; the building is topped by a tower, which is a replica of the Palazzo Vecchio in Florence, and which instantly draws the eye when you are on the rampart walk. The Vatican has inevitably had a long influence in Jerusalem, for many centuries through the Franciscans, but the Italian nation itself had only a late and brief imperial strut in Jerusalem. (Like the British, the Italians had a fondness for building in imitation of their own domestic architecture.) The hospital was constructed in the late nineteenth century and is one of a series of medical establishments that changed the healthcare of Jerusalem significantly: the British eye hospital, the French hospital, and a series of smaller clinics brought Western medicine to the city, which suffered greatly before both from a general low level of healthcare and from a high level of sickness, including periodic outbreaks of severe plague. In local Arabic, the word "ticho" came to mean "ophthalmologist" after Albert Ticho, the doctor who helped alleviate the endemic eye disease in the Arab population. Jerusalem was filthy, backward, and disease-ridden, even for those who visited from the newly industrialized Western cities, who might be thought to be used to squalid urban conditions. In 1807, Chateaubriand, the viscount after whom the steak is named, was disgusted in a very Parisian way: "In this heap of rubbish, denominated a city, the people of the country have thought fit to give the appellation of streets to certain desert passages." In the middle of the century, the English feminist writer Harriet Martineau regretted more genteelly that the streets were far worse even than those of her native Norwich. A 1901 guidebook warns: "The streets are not drained—few are wide enough for wheeled traffic. Attempts at sanitation are of the most primitive order. There is no water supply—no gas—no European shops—no postal delivery (except through the hotels)." (In fact, the Austrian and German post offices opened while the guide was in press. Travel guides are always out of date. . .) It smells foul, the book added, as the final touch. The streets were not paved till late, and there were almost no cars in the whole country, let alone Jerusalem, until the Mandate period. The Victorian traveler had to brave the street without the usual protection of carriage or broad sidewalks. The hospitals offered for the sick a brief respite of cleanliness and order and represent the best side of European imperialism.

The Italian Hospital has now been incorporated into the Ministry of Education, which has a large modern building nearby. But its closeness to Me'a She'arim is not only physical. In 1979, the minister of education and culture ordered the removal of all external crosses on the building—as Christian symbols that shouldn't be on a Jewish building. This meant hacking out the majolica coats of arms of Italian cities that decorated the friezes and arches. Hooliganism in the name of religious "sensitivities" comes from the top in Israeli society.

The Russian Compound prompted other countries to compete. In 1884 the French, ever keen to defend their role as the Protectors of Christian Pilgrims, decided to build a huge hospice for pilgrims adjoining the hospital of Saint Louis des Français, symbolically located in the area between the Russian Compound and the Old City walls, almost opposite the New Gate. Notre Dame (Map 6) was open for business by 1888, though the chapel was not finished until 1894, and it was only in 1904 that the last touch was added: the huge statue of the Virgin Mary on its roof, copied from Our Lady of Salvation in Paris. Notre Dame was founded by the Assumptionists, a Catholic order established in Nîmes in 1845 to counter the effects of the French Revolution in France. They published *La Croix,* still the most popular Catholic newspaper in France, and a publication notorious for its virulently anti-Semitic stance in the late nineteenth century. In 1900, the sect was suppressed in France because they were thought to be plotting against the Republic to restore a monarchy. They have since become a foreign mission. Notre Dame straddles their rise to prominence and removal from France. The building takes the grand scale of Parisian imperial spectacle, complete with a massive plaza, banks of windows, and classical echoes, and tempers it slightly with Eastern rows of crusader-style arches. It was severely damaged in the war of 1948; and, strapped for cash for repairs, the Assumptionists turned the building over to the Vatican. It is now an international pilgrimage center—and another of the landmarks to be seen from the rampart walk.

The British were not far behind. St. George's, the Anglican Cathedral (Map 6), feels like a piece of England transported to Jerusalem—as it was meant to do. The Cathedral Close and school look startlingly like a rural English cathedral or an Oxford College. The cathedral itself was built in 1899, and the bell tower slightly later in 1910 to mark the death of King Edward VII (who had visited the Old City in 1862 as a young man, where he had gotten a tattoo of a Jerusalem Cross on his arm. In 1882 George, his son, got a tattoo from the same artist on his own visit to the Arab quarter; it was removed when George unexpectedly became king. The British royal family seems less interested in body art these days). The cathedral is a classic example of Victorian revivalism, a hankering for an old England in an age of industrial progress, doubly estranged by its place in Arab West Jerusalem, not far from the Tomb of the Kings (as well as the Garden Tomb, with which Protestant evangelicals were so caught up). The bell tower was based on Tewkesbury Abbey, one of the most beautiful churches in the archetypically British countryside of the Cotswolds. But the history of this building gives an insight into far more than Victorian architectural nationalism. It goes to the very heart of the European politics of religion in the nineteenth century.

The Anglican bishopric of Jerusalem was founded in 1841. (The incumbent is officially known as the Anglican bishop *in* Jerusalem rather than "of" Jerusalem, so as not to offend the Greek Orthodox patriarchate or the Latin patriarchate, bishops of Jerusalem both, and chary of sharing the title.) It was, bizarrely enough, a joint project by Friedrich Wilhelm IV of Prussia and the English Anglican Church. The proposal was that the Prussians and the English would take turns nominating a bishop, with a power of veto for the archbishop of Canterbury; funding would come mainly from Friedrich Wilhelm. Friedrich Wilhelm's father, an ardent and bigoted Protestant, had forced the different Protestant sects of his kingdom into a union; Friedrich Wilhelm himself was influenced by the German theological scholarship of his day, and was more of a day-dreamer who hoped for a broader religious union between Protestants across the world. He sent Christian Bunsen to London as his agent to propose the joint project. Bunsen was an excellent ambassador. He was married to an English woman and had many friends in England, including Dr. Arnold, the headmaster of Rugby and the country's leading educationalist, the young Gladstone, already a political star and social reformer in the making, and Samuel Wilberforce, chaplain to Prince Albert and shortly to become bishop of Oxford, where he would famously debate against Darwin's theories. Bunsen met with the archbishop of Canterbury and Bishop Blomfield, classical scholar and head of Anglican congregations abroad, who were both fired with enthusiasm for the proposal. Within a few months, a bill had been rushed through Parliament to allow foreigners to become Anglican bishops, and by Christmas of the same year the first bishop was consecrated and on his way to Jerusalem—slightly delayed because he declined to take the first ship available, the inauspiciously named *HMS Infernal.*

Evangelical Christians were thrilled. The London Society for Promoting Christianity among the Jews celebrated Friedrich Wilhelm as raised up "like Cyrus, for the accomplishment of prophecy." But Bunsen indicates that the politics of this project were actually rather more complicated than they might at first seem from the speedy completion of the plan. He wrote to Gladstone, who was expressing doubts, that "it is surely impossible not to see the finger of God in the foundation of an English church and a congregation of Christian proselytes on the sacred hill of Jerusalem. And would you do nothing to avail yourselves of practical conjunctives which it is not presumptuous to term providential in their coincidence with those symptoms of Zion's revival?" His first sentence is clear and to the point: this is a chance for English, Christian expansion into Jerusalem, with an evangelical and national agenda. God must be supporting such a move. The second sentence needs more than one reading and is typical of extremely careful diplomatic talk in a complex situation. He is encouraging the politician Gladstone to see the possibilities for taking practical action in the current situation (which he is happy to see as heaven-sent: "providential"); this practical action is to be understood as relating to "Zion's revival," that is, to the possibility of a new rule in Palestine, where the Jewish nation's return will hasten a Christian evangelical hope of a new world. Bunsen is testing the water for Gladstone's approval for a very early type of Christian evangelical Zionism—in which the British would indeed play a major practical and ideological role in the later nineteenth and early twentieth century. This is the so-called Restoration movement that actively campaigned from the 1840s onward for the return of the scattered Jews of the world to Palestine, to rebuild Jerusalem, as a prelude to their conversion to Christianity, which would in turn herald the Second Coming of Christ. The bishopric was conceived as a first and crucial step in this project. "The restoration of the Jews is in a great part to be accomplished by human agency," declared the reverend Alexander McCaul at the London Jewish Society, celebrating their active role in hastening this end.

The project rushed through. But there were soon heated protests. How could the archbishop propose a joint project with a church that had such a different make-up and ideology from the English Anglican church? What did such a union mean? Would it draw the church too close to Rome? Did it mean that English bishops could start to gain authority in the German-speaking Protestant world, or was that just a pipe-dream? Could the English and German churches be true partners? And so forth. As so often, the controversy focused not just on abstract issues but also on individuals. The first bishop of Jerusalem was Michael Alexander, professor of Hebrew at King's College, London, who had been born a Jew in Poland and was a subject of Prussia; he had converted to Christianity at age twenty-six at St. Andrew's, Plymouth, after coming of age in Ireland. He was what we now call a multicultural figure for a multicultural job. He was largely supported in his new role, and, though constantly struggling with his health in Palestine's climate, he fought on in what proved difficult political circumstances. Alexander's appointed chaplain, however, was George Williams, a fellow of King's College, Cambridge. He was certainly a Christian with strong moral principles. In 1859, he resigned from his position in the university because he felt the authorities did not support him when he tried to summon the highest university court to try a student seen entering a prostitute's house: he wrote a public letter decrying the fact that the vice-chancellor appeared to think that "fornication is a light offence." But he was objected to as chaplain for Jerusalem because he was "tainted by Puseyism"—that is, because he was associated with the theologians of the Oxford Movement (the intellectually anguished Christians around Newman, many of whom indeed ended up converting to Catholicism). Williams was thus not properly evangelical enough for the evangelicals, and not sound enough for those who worried that the new bishopric was dragging the Anglican Church toward Anglo-Catholicism. The fierceness of the debate about the appointment indicates what strong feelings were engaged by the expansion of Anglicanism into Jerusalem.

Alexander arrived in Jerusalem as a bishop without a church or a congregation. His party included his wife and six children, two governesses, a butler, George Williams, Dr. Edward McGown (a physician), Dr. Ewald (another clergyman), his wife and child, and an Italian nurse called Palmera. He quickly founded Christ Church, a Protestant church inside Jaffa Gate, opposite the entrance to David's Citadel, a church that has almost no signs of its Christianity, to such an extent that a cross was finally fitted to a wall only in 1948 in order to convince the Jordanians that it was actually a church and not a synagogue and ripe for plunder—and it was taken down shortly afterward. The stained-glass windows are topped with the Star of David and have inscriptions in Hebrew, as do the altar and the floor. There are no images of humans, let alone a crucifix, here, even over the altar, where there is no more than a tree, swathed in flowers, with a cross of branches (Figure 45). The church was designed to attract Jews, and its services were in Hebrew. It is easy to see why the Jordanians could think it a synagogue. Although in its simplicity it is quite unlike most of the grand imperial gestures of foreign building in this period, it has a clear missionary agenda.

The disputes over the correct form of Anglican evangelicalism continued over the next twenty years in Jerusalem itself, as the second bishop, Gobat, argued repeatedly with the British consul James Finn about the correct methods of proselytizing the Jews. Finn, a sparky and intense character, was also an active evangelical who was eventually fired as consul after complaints by Montefiore about his proselytizing (though the Jerusalem Jewish community countercomplained that he had actually helped them a great deal); the row is partly just the fuss caused by having too many large egos in a small town, competing for the same few souls. But it is also a symptom of the broad and intricate debate about the direction that Anglicanism should take that dominated the English intellectual classes in the middle and late nineteenth century. And the row quickly became intermeshed with nationalist politics. With Bismarck as the guide of Prussian foreign policy, and with the financial and military antagonism between England and Prussia growing, the close ties with England in Jerusalem could not last. As Charles Warren huffed in 1876: "The connection with the German Church

Figure 45. The altar and window in Christ Church, Jerusalem.

is most embarrassing." In 1881, when a fourth bishop was due to be appointed, both sides quietly agreed that the joint arrangement was over, and that Friedrich Wilhelm's plan had been "a midsummer night's dream" after all. It is then, with the resolutely and charmingly English George Blyth in charge as bishop, that the Anglican Church decided to build its cathedral in a wholly English style, a completely English Anglicanism for the Middle East—at around the same time that Kaiser Wilhelm built the Church of the Redeemer (with the funds that would have gone into the joint bishopric) and the Augusta Victoria with German materials.

Bishop Gobat and Consul Finn were also deeply involved with an incident that shows well how religion and politics intermeshed at a personal and international level in this period. A man called Diness, a Jew who was married to a *hassidic* woman, decided he wanted to convert to Christianity. He ended up seeking sanctuary at Finn's house in 1849, with a bunch of Jews rioting outside and trying to force entrance. Diness claimed to be an Austrian subject but had no passport and could not prove it. By default, as a Jew, he would come under the jurisdiction of the Russians, who provided consular protection for Jews, as the French did for Catholics. But he chose to flee to Finn for protection. As a rare convert, he was a real prize. Constantin Basily, the Russian consul, took the opportunity to lecture Finn (and anyone else) on British religious intolerance, and asserted his rights to protect the Jew. Count Joseph Pizzamano, the Austrian consul, wanted to protect his consular privileges. Letters flew between the consuls and between the consuls and their governments at home. A full-scale international incident was brewing. The Ashkenazi chief rabbi tried to spirit Diness' wife and newborn child away and to get them into Russian protection. Finn stopped them from boarding a boat to Beirut and brought them back to Jerusalem. The wife's father burst into Finn's house during a consular dinner party and demanded his daughter back, convinced that she had been kidnapped for forcible baptism. In August,

Gobat baptized Diness, and things quietened down briefly. In 1851, Diness divorced his wife (the pressure from the Jewish community was too great for the mixed marriage to survive). He wished to remarry, but a piqued Gobat refused. So Diness went off and joined the American Christian Missionary Society, where he was re-baptized as a different sort of Christian. Up to this point, he had been supported by the Anglican Church; now he took up the job of dragoman (guide and general factotum) for Dr. James Barclay, the head of the American Missionaries. When he was left in the lurch by Barclay, who returned to America, Diness after a period of some financial distress eventually returned to the Finn household, where he became the first professional photographer in Jerusalem. After a long, messy life he ended his days in Dayton, Ohio, claiming with mendacious grandiosity that he had been educated at Oxford and Heidelberg.

The competition between the consuls of different empires over a religious convert in an evangelical hothouse, a dispute that threatened to explode into an issue of major diplomatic difficulty, was conducted at a highly personal level. Finn, Pizzamano, and the others saw one another regularly; they write formally, but about and to individuals who live a few streets apart. Victorian Jerusalem is a city that is part of the major cultural, religious, and political wars of the period, but it remains a small town with small-town fusses and small-town egos. Christ Church and the Anglican Cathedral of St. George's were part of that small-town politics.

It is a sign of the changing times that for over twenty-five years now the Anglican bishop of St. George's has been a Palestinian—who serves a largely Palestinian Christian community, which makes up the small congregation. The worshippers at St. George's are no longer the expatriates, exiles, and explorers of the empire that built the church, but the small group of Arab Christians who experience more prejudice than most in the Middle East, as Arabs in the eyes of the Jews, and as Christians in the eyes of the Muslim Arabs. Conversion of the Jews, it need hardly be emphasized, is not the main agenda any longer. It is perplexing to think what these Christian Arabs make of the Cotswolds architecture of their cathedral or its place in the history of Jerusalem. It certainly stands out in east Jerusalem, and the contrast when you step off the streets into the cool and spacious nave of the cathedral, or wander in the close after the *suk,* is one of those disjunctions to the senses that make Jerusalem what it is. The school attached to the cathedral, St. George's School, was where many of the Arab upper-class children, both Christian and Muslim, were educated along with British children, and they remember it as a place of rare tolerance and fairness—a "hint of paradise," as Sari Nusseibeh, now head of al-Quds University, then son of the Jordanian governor of Jerusalem, recalls: St. George's "was surrounded by gardens full of flowering bushes and bougain-villea. In spring the sweet smells of jasmine and honeysuckle wafted through the classrooms." Like paradise, those school days are lost.

AND SO ARE THE AMERICANS . . .

The United States of America had only the smallest official representation in Jerusalem in the nineteenth century. America was certainly expanding as a trading power through the Mediterranean; its growing navy was engaged in gun-boat diplomacy with the north African coastal kingdoms to protect its business, though the government adopted a more diplomatic manner with the Ottomans. At first, only a few hardy American tourists or pilgrims made it to Jerusalem. As travel became easier, more Americans visited the Holy Land, but they were still a rare sight in contrast to the Europeans, and in Jerusalem a single consul regularly had only a handful of visitors to concern himself with. But one group of Americans did became very well known and dominated all the discussion about American life in Jerusalem from 1881 until the arrival of Allenby—the American Colony. The American Colony

Hotel (Map 6) is now one of the most luxurious hotels in Jerusalem and a super place to stay or to have a drink—it has been a regular neutral meeting place for foreign journalists as well as Arab and Israeli figures since 1948, and it was here that the Israelis and the PLO secretly negotiated in 1992. The house was a palace originally owned by Rabbah Effendi, who had it built for himself and his four wives, in what was then an open site outside the city. It was sold to the colony in 1894. It still shows its original structure of luxurious, heated upstairs winter apartments for the wives, connected by a long balcony, around a courtyard (where the trees were planted by Count Ustinov, the actor Peter Ustinov's grandfather, who first encouraged the colony to take in guests as a hotel), and cool summer apartments downstairs. The hotel is still owned by the descendants of the original colony members.

Anna and Horatio Spafford, the founders of the colony, were a remarkable couple. They lived in Chicago, and after the traumas of the Great Fire, when the family's investments were destroyed, Anna and her four daughters set off on the steamship *Ville du Havre* for Europe. The ship sank and all four daughters were drowned, the baby violently torn from Anna's arms by the waves. Anna, one of only forty-seven survivors, was found unconscious on a floating spar. "Saved alone. What shall I do?" she telegrammed home when she recovered consciousness. She returned to America, with the belief that God had saved her for a greater purpose. They had three more children, two girls and a boy. The boy died of scarlet fever at age four. At this point, the family decided to go to Jerusalem with some members of their congregation. It is hard to imagine the strength of character or faith that enabled the family to stay together and go on with such purpose after such terrible events. They arrived in Jerusalem in 1881 to live a simple Christian life. They were not missionaries but taught and cared for the sick and tried to make ends meet by small holding and making things to sell.

It was a precarious existence. In 1894 they were joined by seventy Swedes, followed by fifty more in 1896.

For eighteen years the group was pursued by the American consul, Merrill, who accused them of sexual misconduct with an aggression and obsessiveness which is hard to find motivation for. British and American missionaries, too, upset at the arrival of an unofficial group in their crowded and fervid space, spread rumors and attacked them. When the Swedish novelist Selma Lagerlöf arrived in Jerusalem, she was told by Merrill of the terrible evils of Mrs. Spafford and the moral danger to her fellow country-folk under her spell. She decided to visit the colony to see if she could save them. After nervously meeting Mrs. Spafford and then repeatedly visiting the colony, Lagerlöf ended up writing her Nobel Prize–winning novel, which so praises their work. Eventually, the Anna Spafford Baby Hospital was established to care for young babies and mothers, and the colony was instrumental in the provision of aid in 1917 and 1948, when its location put it in the front-line of fighting. When Mrs. Spafford died in 1924 at age eighty-one, she was widely acknowledged as one of the most impressive figures in Jerusalem whose dignified and selfless care for others in the face of such personal suffering was an exemplar of the religious life.

The American Colony is threaded through Jerusalem life of the period: it was a member of the colony who set the sails of the windmill in Mishkanot Sha'ananim, as no one else knew how to do it; it was from here that the white flag of surrender, now in the Imperial War Museum in London, was taken by the Arab mayor in 1917; it was Bertha, Anna's daughter, on a picnic, who joined Kaiser Wilhelm and Augusta when they prayed on the Mount of Olives; it was from the colony's first house that General Gordon had seen the site of the Garden Tomb; it was young Jacob from the colony who discovered the inscription in Hezekiah's Tunnel. Ronald Storrs and Lawrence of Arabia were frequent visitors. Jerusalem was a small town, and the American Colony became one of the hubs around which it revolved.

AND THE GERMANS, TOO . . .

The Germans complete the ring of new national settlements around the Old City. The Templers were a Protestant sect that rejected the ritual of the German Church. They had, as such cults usually do, a charismatic leader, Christoff Hoffman (1815–1885), who established Templer settlements elsewhere in Palestine, before they came to Jerusalem in the 1860s and 1870s. They left Germany in part to avoid religious persecution as a dissenting group, in part lured by the Holy Land itself. A foundation stone for a new community was laid in the Valley of Refa'im outside the walls in 1873. In 1878 the community from Jaffa moved to Jerusalem, and the German Colony was developed. "Few buildings stood between it and the Jaffa Gate," wrote Bertha Spafford, "so it stood out conspicuous and alone." The houses were distinctively German, *Strassendorf* style: a street in the center, with two-storied houses on either side, with red-tiled roofs, cellars, distinctive green iron-work, green shutters, and well-built stone facing—often with a biblical inscription in Gothic writing over the door. It was the only street in Jerusalem to be tree-lined. There was a low stone wall around the development. They made good wine and white bread with flour from their own mill. Unlike the poor of Mishkanot Sha'ananim, these were hard-working and well-trained Europeans, doctors, bankers, craftsmen, as well as the required bakers, shoemakers, inn-keepers, and so forth. (When Fast, of Fast Hotel fame, bought his plot there and started to build, two ancient sarcophagoi and some graves were found. They rapidly disappeared, as Fast was terrified his house would be reclaimed for archaeology.) Mrs. Goodrich-Freer, visiting in the first years of the twentieth century, knew exactly what she was seeing in the German Colony: an "admirable example of cleanliness and order."

But the railway came soon, and near to the German Colony; with it came an Arab neighborhood, which, complained the settlers, disturbed the peace with calls to prayer. The borders of the colony were gradually and irrevocably sucked into the broader urban growth. Unlike Me'a She'arim, which has struggled to preserve itself over the years, the little German village with its pious industry has long passed. The last Templers themselves were deported by the British to Australia during the Second World War, since they had become, as a community, strong supporters of Hitler and had started a Nazi youth movement that exercised aggressively in public. Not long ago, a cache of Nazi paraphernalia was found in an attic as one of the old houses was sold. Emek Refa'im, however, is still the main street of the German Colony, and the original German houses are readily recognizable at its top end. Usually people rush past them, eyes fixed on the busier urban life ahead, for Emek Refa'im is now *the* street for trendy bars, restaurants, and boutiques in Jerusalem, where young people hang out of an evening and late into the night.

There is one last, unexpected legacy of the Templers. They were the first to use red-tiled roofs in Jerusalem. Red roofs have become a self-conscious sign and symbol of non-Arab—and therefore radical Zionist—building (though with the usual twist of power relations, they have also more recently been adopted for more affluent Palestinian housing as a sign of distinction). As early as 1908, Arthur Ruppin, the Zionist who spearheaded land purchases in Palestine and was instrumental in the construction of Tel Aviv, wrote: "In contrast with the pitiful Arab villages, with their huts of baked clay, the Jewish colonies, with their wide streets, their strong stone houses, and their red tiled roofs, look like veritable oases of culture." Ruhi Khalidi, too, the Arab politician and writer who spoke in the

Ottoman assembly against the Zionists, visited many Jewish settlements and noted specifically "the beautiful houses whose red roofs shine with the rays of the hot sun." In the current political climate, where "color coding" has become a fevered part of the gestural politics of the region—the orange of the radical Zionist settlers was aggressively sported during the pull-out of Jewish settlers from Gaza in 2005–2006—red roofs have become a badge of political affiliation for the new settlements in the Occupied Territories. It is a nasty little irony that this architectural flag-waving should unconsciously signal its inheritance from German Christian idealists who became Nazis.

Several other Victorian developments sprang up outside the Old City. By 1880 perhaps as many as 2,000 Jews lived outside the city walls in what had become nine new settlements: in addition to Mishkanot Sha'ananim and Me'a She'arim, there were Mahaneh Yisrael, Nahalt Shivah, Beit David, Even Yisrael, Mishkenot Yisrael, Kiryah Ne'emenhah, and Beit Ya'akov, each with between 20 and 70 houses. (The land for Nahalt Shivah was bought by one Mrs. Hurvitz, who dressed up as an Arab woman to make the purchase to conceal the fact that seven rabbis' sons wanted to settle there.) By 1897 there were 46 such settlements, some with as few as 6 houses (Shevet Ahim), some as large as 209 (Shevet Tzedek). This new city changed Jerusalem forever. Jerusalem is not often thought of as a Victorian city, but the modern city came into being between 1850 and 1914. It is not just that this was when the city spread beyond the walls for the first time; nor just that the railway, the telegraph, and other modern technologies arrived then. It is rather that the city spread beyond its walls as a direct response to specifically Victorian principles: the construction of small, self-contained communities dedicated to cleanliness, order, religious law, and social rules. These idealist communities were themselves developed by philanthropists in Europe in response to the urban sprawl and misery of industrialization. In Jerusalem, with its own religious and social pressures, these new communities took on their own particular form. But this was in a profound sense a Victorian civic development.

Jerusalem in the nineteenth century was a peculiarly fascinating place, as the real city, as opposed to the city as an image of hope, longing, and idealism, became the focus of European interest again, after centuries of disregard since the Crusades. The tourist trade started up with the invention of the steamship and the loosening of the control of the Ottomans over their empire, and the city's grim realities entered the imagination and prose of countless travelers. Cook's Travel company made the trip easy and affordable, and, as one disgruntled member of the British upper class, Lord Russell, noted, this now meant that in Palestine you might "meet people you don't know." At the same time, Europe was undergoing a revival of evangelical Christianity, in part in reaction to the new doubts raised by Darwin and scientific advances in general, in part in response to the internal divisions and doubts in the church itself. Again, in the aftermath of the Crimean War, it became possible for pilgrims and missionaries to come to Jerusalem and Palestine, and many did. The different sects and countries competed to establish missions, to work for the poor, to convert the Jews, and to assert the dominance of their liturgy and rights over the holy sites. Jerusalem became a cacophony of religious competition in the name of humility and bringing people to the love of God.

But beyond the stream of European visitors, pilgrims, missionaries, and tourists, Jerusalem and Palestine became the focus of the imperial and nationalistic forces that defined the political world of Victorian Europe. In modern scholarship, it has become common to talk about "the imperialist" and "the subaltern," "the conqueror and the conquered"; and "post-colonial studies" has become a booming field. Nineteenth-century Jerusalem shows how the model used in this burgeoning area is too dependent on a simple model of victor and victim, colonizer and colonized. Jerusalem was a city in a collapsing Ottoman Empire—"the sick man of Europe." The city was ruled by Turks from Istanbul. Its population was predominantly Jewish: Jews were an absolute majority by 1880. But the land was worked predominantly by Arabs. The Greek Orthodox Church was a major landowner and was backed by the Russian Empire, which was still seeking to expand into the Middle East. The British and French Empires, which barely trusted each other, were both opposed to the Russian advance and both keen to profit from the collapse of the Ottoman Empire, which seemed inevitable. The German expansion was also marked, and the connection between the Germans and the Ottomans caused a good deal of suspicion to all the other sides. At the same time, the Austrians and the Italians were making their presence felt. What was at stake was not just the control of the religious sites, however big a role such interests played in the rhetoric of the day. The prime motivation was the economic power that was promised by control of trade routes to the east, just as oil is today a crucial factor in the conflict in the Middle East. All these empires were struggling to be in prime position as the Ottomans collapsed. At the same time, Jewish nationalism in the form of Zionism began to develop in Europe, and there was constant arguing in Palestine and Europe about the proper amount of Jewish immigration to Palestine. Arab nationalism was starting in Muslim countries. The spread of the Egyptian Ibrahim Pasha's control over Palestine and even parts of Syria—the first signs of Arab nationalism—was rebuffed by the European powers rather than by the Ottomans. The liberalizing Egyptian ruler moved into Palestine in 1831 but was removed by the European powers in 1840. Jerusalem was the place where *all* these imperial forces were in dynamic tension with one another. The simple model of victor and victim just won't do.

Jerusalem was still a small city in the nineteenth century, however. The form the battles took here was partly in competitive building, as we have seen; but it was also and more stridently at a personal level. The British consul wrote to London worrying about a remark of the Italian consul; the French consul accused the Russian authorities of misconduct; the French attacked the British consul, who cut him in the street. When one consul flew a flag it caused an Arab riot; then another consul demanded a heightened protocol of welcome. And so on, for pages of bitchy, formal complaint and counter-complaint in the consular records and diaries of the time. All the major players met in the small social circle of Europeans, observing one another, reading and over-reading each other's reactions. They competed to have authority over groups of pilgrims. These conflicts would be nothing but petty rows, if they were not the tip of vast imperial movements. The First World War and the British Mandate come as the climax of this passage of history.

Victorian Jerusalem is fundamental to the development of the Jerusalem we see today. Monumental and imposing buildings all around the city come from this period, as do many of the most familiar neighborhoods just outside the city walls. And Jerusalem was fundamental to the development of European ambitions at a political and religious level throughout the nineteenth century. Jerusalem, more than any other city in the Middle East, is part of the imagination and policies of the international community. The nineteenth century was an absolutely crucial period in the development of Jerusalem, not just as a physical site, but as a city in people's minds.

Map 7

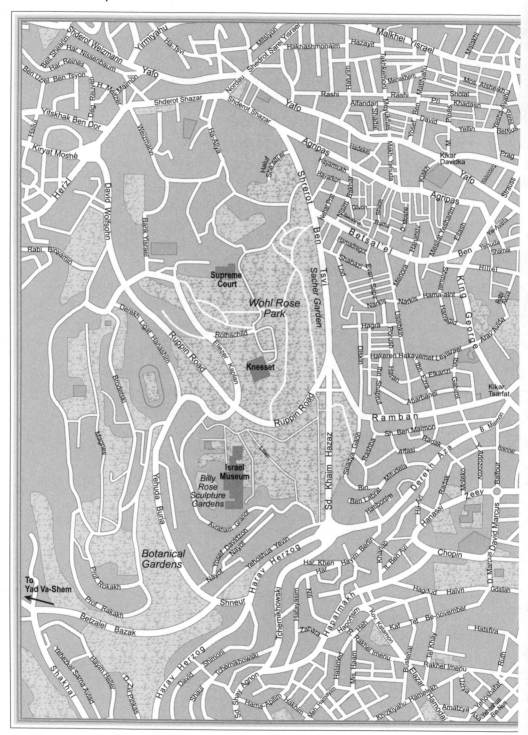

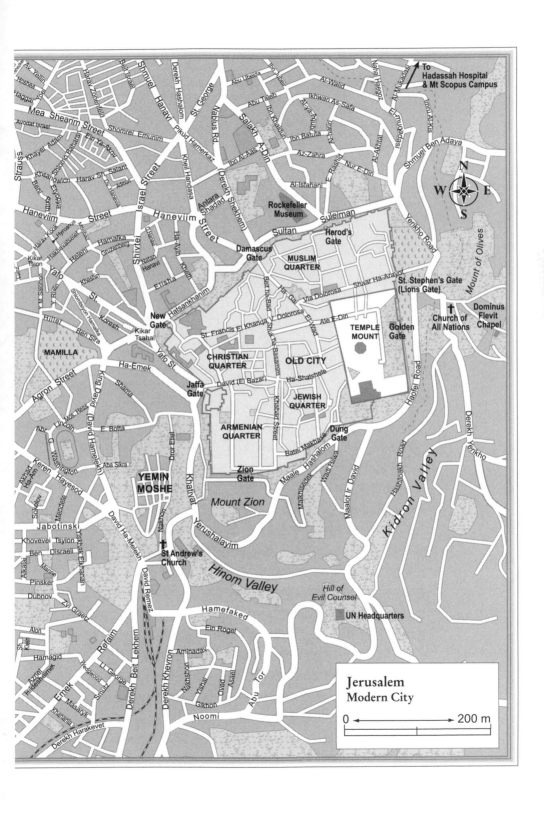

Jerusalem
Modern City

0 ———— 200 m

7   The Modern City

CHARLES WARREN, archaeologist, police chief, freemason, and
boy's own hero, was typical of the Victorian British interest in Jerusalem in that he believed unshakably in three things: his imperial
right to explore and dominate the East, his Christian religious duty
toward Palestine, and his British practical ability to find a political
solution to Palestine's problems. In 1841 Christian Bunsen, it will
be remembered, hinted privately to Gladstone about the politics of
change in Ottoman Palestine and the potential role of the British
Empire. In 1876, Warren spoke out in the most explicit terms in
his well-received book *Underground Jerusalem,* which chronicled his
Palestine adventures: "Will not those who love Palestine, love freedom, justice, the Bible, learn to look upon the country as one
which may shortly be in the market? Will not they look about and
make preparations and discuss the question?" The idea of a country
being "in the market" will strike most modern readers as a shockingly blunt account of the economics of imperialism—the sort of

thing kept behind the closed doors of power these days. Warren, what's more, had a specific agenda that such colonization should be "with the avowed intention of gradually introducing the Jew, pure and simple, who is eventually to occupy and govern the country." William Thompson, the archbishop of York, was equally stark in his statement of principle when addressing the Palestine Exploration Fund in 1875: "Our reason for turning to Palestine is that Palestine is our country."

From the 1840s to the 1890s the Restoration of the Jews was a banner under which many British evangelical Christians and politicians marched. As early as 1841, the year of the Jerusalem bishopric's foundation, the London *Times* understood the Protestant mission to Jerusalem precisely in these terms and thundered out the Restorationist credo: "Let the four Allied Powers now publish to the four quarters of the world their determination to restore the Jews from all nations to the Holy Land, and to assist them in rebuilding the walls and Temple of Jerusalem." When Allenby finally marched into Jerusalem in 1917, a point usually taken as the beginning of the modern city of Jerusalem, there had been seventy-five years of political and cultural preparation in Europe for this moment.

The history of modern Jerusalem, like Caesar's ancient Gaul, is divided into three parts. First is the period of the British Mandate, which ran from 1919 to 1948: Jerusalem was ruled through these years by the British authorities. Second is the State of Israel from its inception in 1948 until the Six Day War in 1967, a period when Jerusalem was divided into two with a physical barrier, where west Jerusalem was ruled by Israel, east Jerusalem by the Jordanians. Third, from 1967 onward, has been the unified city of Jerusalem under the State of Israel, or under the occupation, as the Palestinians say.

The basic outlines of the three periods can be told in a few paragraphs. The First World War resulted in the long-anticipated dismemberment of the Ottoman Empire. The British, along with the allied powers, divided up the territory, making the new countries of Iran, Iraq, Transjordan, and Lebanon, and defining their boundaries with Syria, Egypt, and Arabia. These new countries obtained independence under the guidance of the Western imperial authorities. The area known as Palestine was made a Mandate territory ruled by Britain. From the turn of the century onward, Zionism, the political movement aimed at creating a Jewish homeland in Palestine, had been growing: Jewish immigration to Palestine and the purchase of property there was also increasing over this period. This development was resisted first by some Arab activists and, gradually, by more of the population, who also came to resent the British administration, not least for initially supporting the proposal of a Jewish homeland as enshrined in the Balfour Declaration, itself the political embodiment of the aims of the Restorationist movement. There was repeated, sporadic violence against Jewish farmers and against the Jewish urban population. In 1936, Arab resistance to the British swelled into open revolt, starting with a general strike. The upheavals lasted until 1939, but the revolt was crushed with military action and with exile or imprisonment for its ringleaders.

In 1939, the British also turned away from their initial support for a Jewish homeland in Palestine. After the Second World War, and with full knowledge of the Holocaust, Jewish activists increased pressure for a Jewish homeland. Some of these activists formed violent, underground groups that assaulted the British administration. Arab terrorist groups also turned to violence against the British, in opposition, not only to British colonial rule and to Jewish immigration, but also to increased Jewish influence in the region. By 1948 the British had had enough, and they turned the whole problem over to the United Nations. The United Nations voted to partition the country, to create two states, a Jewish and an Arab state, with Jerusalem as a *corpus separatum,* an international city, not owned by any one people. This plan was rejected by the Arab nations as a block, and when Israel's independence was declared in 1948, all the Arab countries attacked the new state. They were defeated, and in the process Israel gained more land than the U.N. had originally offered. Most Arabs resident in the new Israel fled as refugees. The Arabs refer to the events of 1948 as *al-naqba,* "the catastrophe," and for many years they called Israel "the Zionist entity" to avoid recognizing its existence. Jordan appropriated the land intended for a Palestinian Arab state, including the West Bank.

In 1967, Arab countries, fired up by Gamal Abdel Nasser, the ruler of Egypt, again prepared to destroy Israel. Again they were crushingly defeated, when Israel launched a preemptive attack in the Six Day War. Israel conquered the Sinai, the West Bank, the Golan Heights—and East Jerusalem. Immediately after the war, Israel offered to return all the lands in exchange for recognition and peace: the Arab states notoriously said no three times: no to recognition; no to the return of lands; and no to peace treaties. In 1973, the Arabs again tried—and nearly succeeded—to destroy Israel (the Yom Kippur War). But again they were defeated. Since then, Sinai has been returned to Egypt, and a peace deal has been signed between Israel and Egypt; a peace treaty has been signed between Israel and Jordan. But wars in Lebanon, and a constant pattern of reciprocal violence culminating in the two Intifadas, have kept the Middle East and Jerusalem at the center of international conflict.

I have tried to tell this story in as simple and as neutral a way as possible. But it is not really possible to be wholly neutral when the subject is so contentious, and it would be easy to complain about this or that emphasis, this or that omission, even in so bare an account. It would also be easy to rewrite the story in a strongly one-sided fashion, as many have done, either as the story of the Palestinians' tragedy as victims of colonial expansion, or as the story of the miraculous and heroic return of the Jews to their homeland in the face of overwhelming odds. Of course, there have been very few moments in the history of Jerusalem that have not been contentious: the earliest days are a consistent source of ideological claim and counter-claim about who was there first; Herod's Temple attracts the extremists of historiography on all sides; even the dull years from the late seventeenth to the early nineteenth century, when in religious and political terms Jerusalem was little more than an isolated Ottoman-ruled backwater—even this apparently sleepy calm has become the focus of a heated discussion about religious and political tolerance, with an all-too-obvious contemporary agenda. But all these arguments pale into insignificance in comparison with the history of modern Jerusalem. There are few topics quite like this in any period in any part of the world, where *every* step of any historical account is so argued over, and where so much of the historiography reeks of rhetorical posturing, self-serving apologetics, and downright lies. The story of the foundation of the State of Israel has been told innumerable times with a whole range of different biases, prejudices, and purposes. There is no fact, it seems, that remains self-evident and that does not get sucked into a welter of competing narratives.

Take the fact that a large number of indigenous Palestinian Arabs were forced to leave their homes in 1948–1949. That may seem like a neutral description, and, as far as I am concerned, it is a true enough assertion. But each and every element of this statement has been challenged—except for the date itself. First, there is a fuss about the numbers. Some people deny that the numbers are as large as has often been claimed. Golda Meir famously and scandalously called Palestine "a land without a people for a people without a land"; but Arab claims that "nearly a million" Palestinians were expelled are certainly far too high, though they are often used for cheap rhetorical effect. Scholars now agree that at least 650,000 Arabs did become refugees. But in this sphere of constant argument and counter-argument, it is misleading just to mention the Arab refugees. More than 650,000 Jews were also forced to leave *their* homes in Arab countries when the thriving communities of Cairo,

Damascus, Baghdad, Yemen, and so forth all disappeared in the years after the Second World War. The different histories of the Jewish and the Palestinian refugees of this period, where all the Jewish refugees were absorbed into Israel or other foreign communities, while so many Palestinians remain in refugee camps sixty years on, is a fundamental and festering aspect of the political landscape of the region. Nor is Palestine the only place where such dramatic redistributions of population took place in the twentieth century. In Salonika, the Greeks expelled the Turks, and in Smyrna the Turks expelled the Greeks, thus destroying centuries of multicultural civic life in two of the most vibrant communities of the Mediterranean. The swift and bloody partition of India at the end of British rule, with the foundation of the Muslim state of Pakistan, resulted in the deaths of up to 1,000,000 people in sectarian fighting, and many millions—perhaps as high as 12,000,000 people— crossed the borders in one or the other direction as refugees. The consequences of all these politically and religiously motivated shifts of population are still being worked through, often violently. So to mention the Jewish refugees and not the Palestinian refugees, or the Palestinian refugees and not the Jewish refugees, will always look like a rhetorically loaded attempt to claim the moral high ground as the sole victim of injustice.

Within this battle over what the authorized version of history will be, some extremist Jewish historians have even outrageously denied that Palestinians should be called indigenous, on the grounds that they were temporary conquerors of a territory originally and rightly held by Jews, as if 1,300 years of possession were somehow discountable. This is an argument that will persuade only the ideologues of fundamentalist religion or nationalism.

The debate around the term "Palestinian" is more complex. The title "Palestinian" has been denied to the inhabitants of the region, on the grounds that no country called Palestine has ever existed there (unless you count the short-lived Roman province Syria-

Palestina, an administrative area of the Roman Empire from the second century A.D.), and that there was no distinctive Palestinian cultural or national identity until the formation of Israel. Golda Meir again: "It was not as though there was a Palestinian people in Palestine considering itself as a Palestinian people and we came and threw them out and took their country away from them. They did not exist." Earlier, British officers had expressed views that echoed this sentiment in a less polemical manner: Stewart Perowne, aide to the high commissioner Sir Arthur Wauchope, wrote home to his father about what a British education—St. George's School— meant for its Arab students: "By giving them a British education . . . one is not really de-nationalizing them, because for the most part they have not the remotest idea of what their nationality implies; they have no traditions." But even he was embarrassed enough by this to add: "That is a generalization, but there is truth in it." (Interestingly, after 1948 Perowne stayed on in Jordan and worked to build and establish villages for Palestinian refugees on behalf of St. George's Church, helping to create the nationality he had earlier denied.)

In 1948, before he was assassinated by Jewish terrorists, Count Folke Bernadotte, the Swedish United Nations mediator in Jerusalem, wrote: "The Palestinian Arabs had at present no will of their own. Neither have they ever developed any specifically Palestinian nationalism. The demand for a separate Arab state in Palestine is correspondingly weak. It would seem as though in existing circumstances most of the Palestinian Arabs would be quite content to be incorporated into Transjordan." The Mandate was set up over an area the British called Palestine, as the region had been known for many years in the West; but there has indeed never been an Arab-ruled country called Palestine: there are no agreed borders of a country called Palestine. The slogan on banners all over Europe at present, "Free Palestine," reveals a deep ignorance of history at the very least. When an American survey in the 1920s attempted to find out how the local population thought of themselves, the vast majority of residents in what was then known as Palestine said that they regarded themselves as part of a Syrian kingdom, a result that embarrasses everyone but the Syrians and is consequently usually forgotten (or explained away as a temporary aberration because of the excitement of the new kingdom of Syria, shortly to be dismantled by France). From 1948 to 1967, east Jerusalem and the West Bank were part of the Hashemite kingdom of Jordan; its inhabitants were citizens of Jordan and had Jordanian passports: well into the 1960s, King Hussein of Jordan could declare: "Palestine is Jordan, Jordan is Palestine." But the relationship between the Jordanians and the Palestinians has also often been a violent one: the Jordanian army slaughtered thousands of Palestinians in 1970 ("Black September") and exiled more.

There is indeed a very strong case to be made that a Palestinian national and cultural identity was significantly strengthened and, in its modern political aspiration, created by the coming of Israel. "Pan-Arabism" was the political watchword of the early part of the twentieth century. This was an attempt to link all the Arabs together and to throw off the Ottoman Turkish yoke. The movement was led by Sharif Hussein, the ruler of Mecca, who was an eager negotiator with Britain, and who received the promise of Arab freedom from the British, looking as they were for his support against the Ottomans and their allies, the Germans. It was this movement, rather than any specific Palestinian concerns, that attracted most political radicals in the earlier part of the twentieth century. Very few Arabs, and then only from the elite, wished to oppose Zionism and did so in the name of *Falestin* (Palestine): but they were largely ignored prophets. The attachment of the poorer population was focused primarily on their own farms, their families, their tribes; the richer families focused on Jerusalem, or whichever city they dominated, and on a more general Arab culture: for all the love of the land, any appeals to a shared Palestinian identity are few and weak before the coming of Zionism and the State of Israel. Nonetheless, whatever historical nuance and contextualization should be given to the gradual development of the word "Palestinian," it is at best mischievous to deny that it is an important and relevant form of self-identification today, especially for the refugees in the camps.

And were they forced to leave? ask some Zionist historians tendentiously. The old story for Israeli schoolrooms was that the inhabitants of Palestine were told to leave by their fellow Arabs in the happy expectation of returning in triumph to their homes after the destruction of Israel. Revisionist historians have shown that the actual circumstances were less palatable. While many did become refugees without direct force being applied, fear of violence affected others and military action forced out others still. It would be foolish to suggest that the refugees did not experience their flight as the result of the force of circumstances and, in most cases, fear or experience of the force of Israeli arms.

Every element of my attempt at a simple, neutral statement is subject to such quibbling over terms—some of which is merely fractious, some of which is proper historical care. But beyond this skirmishing looms the wider and more pressing question of how such a sentence fits into the big picture. We can ask how many refugees fled and what made them flee—but we also have to explore the significance and consequences of their flight for the region. There are several competing ways of telling this story, and this is really where the problem lies.

The extremes are easiest to rehearse because they are often screamed most loudly. An extremist Arab historiography explains that the *naqba* was forced on a peaceful region whose inhabitants had lived in harmony for centuries, by a Zionist plot to steal land, backed by support from Europeans, who were trying to make up for the horrors of anti-Semitism during the Second World War. This story makes an icon of the village of Deir Yassin, where more than a hundred Arabs died—massacred by Israelis, including the future prime minister of Israel, Menachem Begin. The village is now destroyed, and a mental hospital has been built where once it stood. (Even here a baroque irony . . . This hospital houses the ward reserved for patients with Jerusalem Syndrome—the psychiatric disorder, special to Jerusalem, where sufferers believe themselves to be the Messiah.) The existence of a State of Israel is an injustice, formed in blood and violence, to be resisted with blood and violence. In its most extreme form, such historiography ends up in a blanket refusal to recognize Israel, a policy of aiming to destroy Israel, and a support of suicide bombers as heroes and martyrs.

An extremist Zionist version, on the other hand, talks of the peaceful attempt to buy land to settle, resisted with Arab violence from the start; the need for a homeland, a proposal supported by the world, in the traditional place where Jews have always lived, a haven for the poor, dispossessed, and abused. Jews made the desert bloom. This small, fledgling state of pioneers was viciously and unjustly assaulted by the massive Arab countries around them, and it was only a miracle, embodied in acts of extraordinary bravery by the young heroes of the new state, that enabled Israel to survive. This story makes an icon of the 1936 Arab massacre of the Jews of Hebron, a peaceful religious community that had lived in Hebron for centuries, and that was indiscriminately slaughtered, its members' bodies mutilated by an anti-Semitic mob fired up by the Nazi-supporting mufti of Jerusalem. In its most extreme form, this historiography justifies the possession of land as a divinely led mission and aims to expel all Arab presence from the area, a policy it supports with violence and administrative oppression.

Both of these bare accounts, which can of course be expanded into more detailed histories, have recognizable elements of truth in them: Arabs did die in Deir Yassin, Jews did die in Hebron, in both cases miserably and with shocking violence. But both of these commonly heard versions of events are extremist precisely because they fail to recognize any aspect of the other side's position, and each tells merely part of a story—and an exaggerated and unbalanced part at that. If these extremist accounts were countered by a strong central, agreed version, they could be marginalized. Unfortunately, even the more moderate accounts are drawn toward the extremes by the very polarization of the political situation these days. People shout at each other a lot in the Middle East. This affects the kinds of stories that get heard. The general level of rhetoric is now so heated and uncontrolled that language itself is under threat: "Words had to change their ordinary meaning and to take on those which were now given to them. Reckless audacity came to be considered the courage of a loyal ally; prudent hesitation, specious cowardice; moderation, a cloak for unmanliness; ability to see all sides of the question, inability to act. Frantic violence became the attribute of manliness." Those chilling words were written by Thucydides, the ancient Greek historian, describing the effect of civil strife and its pattern of violent reprisal in fifth-century B.C. Athens. But they are perfect for today, too—as, rather depressingly, Thucydides himself predicted. And, what's even more upsetting for a historian, many histories, histories written by scholars and not just the arguments of street-brawling men and women, are full of mealy-mouthed avoidance of issues or, equally dispiritingly, a ready willingness to offer half-truths or shoddy versions of events. It is very hard, after reading dozens of histories of this period, along with dozens of autobiographies, biographies, and diaries, not to become angry at what is happening to Jerusalem, the city of peace, through the circulation of such aggressively distorted versions of events, which contribute to the problems of violence in the city rather than analyze or alleviate them.

If our aim is a lasting and just peace, it looks today—with the hindsight of history—as if things have simply gotten worse and worse over the last forty years: a history of missed opportunities, fantasies of power, and failure of the imagination. The levels of extremism and hatred have risen on both sides to such a degree that it will take more than one generation of fragile agreement and education and contact before an acceptable working arrangement may be possible—and even that seems a distant political reality, for all the personal decencies and friendships even now across the divides.

But perhaps there are some small gestures that might help. It would, for example, be good to try to avoid the grand national stereotypes that have become such a feature of the current debate: "the British," "the Jews," "the Arabs," "the Israelis," "the Palestinians," "the Muslims." These blanket terms inevitably lower any debate to the swapping of slogans and certainly make for poor history. The casual use of the term "the British," for example, ignores the distinguishing elements of class, religious inclination, and education that radically affected responses to Jerusalem under the Mandate. (It is fascinating to see how little consciousness of Britain's involvement in the history of the Middle East the contemporary debate in Britain shows, but that is another question.) As we have already seen, Britain did have a long tradition of "restorationism"—the proposal to return the Jews to Palestine for Christian religious motivations—but this was mainly among the educated, religious, upper-class English (including, for example, Sir Winston Churchill). But many people from the same background took a radically opposed view and actively countered any indications of Zionism, sometimes from anti-Jewish feeling, sometimes, like Lawrence of Arabia, from strong pro-Arab nationalist feeling, sometimes because they were unattracted by the intellectual case for restorationism and became sucked into a vibrant opposition by the strident arguments around them. So whereas Storrs could declare that "there was in the world no aspiration more nobly idealistic than the return of the Jews to the land immortalized by the sprit of Israel," E. T. Richmond, the director of the Antiquities Department, could set out to change policy from within, a policy which—with a strength of rhetoric characteristic of disagreement even in the British camp—he stated was "dominated and inspired by a spirit which I can only regard as evil." The issue of the Jewish return to Palestine was debated ferociously in government circles, in private discussions, and in the places where Jews, Arabs, and British met. Arguments shifted in those different contexts. It was not an issue on which one could easily remain neutral.

The soldiers on the ground who had to enforce British policy were less likely to follow a restorationist line. Many autobiographies and diaries of rank-and-file soldiers and police are supportive (in a rather patronizing way) of the local Arabs, the *fellahin,* whom they saw as simple and rather exotic farmers, much put upon by the Turks and living in distressing poverty. From experiences in India and Egypt they felt comfortable with and superior to "the natives." But they did not trust or feel comfortable with the Jews—neither the Jews from the East, who were like Arabs but somehow other, nor certainly the Western Jews, who seemed to them to be intelligent, argumentative, educated, aggressive, and consequently far more difficult to deal with. Anti-Jewish stereotypes were a familiar part of the world in which they had grown up in Britain, and they proved a resource for response to the new and confusing culture of Palestine. Stewart Perowne again: "And there are always the Jews waiting to get hold of anything they can." As Jewish and Arab terrorism developed and became more unpleasant, British policy became brutal to Arab and Jew alike; the penalty for possession of arms, for example, was death. The rank-and-file soldiers, frightened, attacked, and confused by their enemies' hatred of them, responded with aggression. The Arabs who had welcomed the British as their liberators from the Turks became terrified of what are still remembered as atrocities in their villages around Palestine. Many British soldiers came to hate Palestine.

British gentlemen like Keith-Roach, Storrs, and Ashbee wrote sharply sophisticated, self-interested books about their time in Jerusalem, but so too did the English Jew Sir Herbert Samuel. He was the first non-baptized Jew to hold Cabinet office and was acutely conscious of any decision that might affect the social progress of Jews in European countries such as England. But he was in broad support of the Balfour Declaration. When he found himself high commissioner of Mandate Palestine, he bent over backward to appear fair to both sides—and became an object of deep mistrust and even hatred from the Jews, as British policy failed to satisfy their growing demands. His sense of the English treatment of Jews was quite different from that of Storrs, a committed restorationist, or Keith-Roach, a career administrator, who worried, like many of his class and background, that the Jews were all too closely connected to a socialist or communist agenda. Norman Bentwich, first attorney general of Mandate Palestine, also a prominent Jew, had a different experience, too, of how Jews fit into Mandate Palestine. Helen Bentwich, his wife, recalls that when she played tennis at the club, a woman would clap every time she lost a point, and was heard to mutter "bloody Jews" as she left the court.

British policy, a collective responsibility, was made and enacted by individuals with complicated personal investments. The policy itself, however, was, at its deepest level, inconsistent. It maintained its support for the Balfour Declaration, which promised a Jewish homeland in Palestine; it offered its support for Pan-Arab nationalism against the Ottoman oppressors with a vaguely worded promise of freedom for Arabs. Behind the scenes, the Sykes-Picot Agreement laid out an imperial carve-up of the Ottoman Arab colonies among France, England, and Russia. Palestine was in this way "thrice promised." As even one ordinary soldier noted: "Our British attitudes towards both Arabs and Jews were confused." The enactment of this conflicted policy was unsurprisingly conflicted.

So the final evaluation of the Mandate will need to be more careful than it often has been. When the British high command left, they felt the Mandate had been a failure because they had not prevented the coming war, itself the result of years of internal strife and violence. Law and order, the pride of the British Empire, was crumbling. Many commentators since have also been highly critical of the motives and behavior of the British regime in Palestine, with its mixture of self-interest and conflicting promises to different groups. But when they arrived, illiteracy in the Arab villages was at around 80 percent for men and nearly 100 percent for women, as it had been for many decades; when they left, 65 percent of Arab boys attended school, as did 35 percent of girls—which is a considerable improvement, if not a complete endorsement of an educational policy. Healthcare facilities increased exponentially, and the endemic malaria, eye disease, and other serious plagues became a thing of the past. For the first time the legal system functioned without bribery and corruption. The tax system was completely revised, from the crushing extortion of the Ottomans to a fair and reasonable order. Above all, for the first time there was an adequate water supply in Jerusalem. The pumps, piping, and unified water system improved the quality of life in Jerusalem beyond measure. This was an achievement of the British Mandate. The building of roads and trains also enabled people to circulate more freely and, most pertinently, prevented the famine that had devastated Jerusalem in the years immediately before the British took over. As so often with the history of this period, the Mandate leaves us with a strong sense of an opportunity lost, and even a responsibility shirked. But there were also many decent officials who struggled to do a good job under difficult conditions, and the resultant development of the fabric of life in Jerusalem changed the city significantly and for the better. With the classic cognitive dissonance of empire, many British officials found the hostility they experienced irksome and baffling in the face of what they saw as their civilizing presence.

In the same way that the phrase "the British" conceals a complex history of different responses to Palestine and different engagements in the business of the Mandate, the Palestinians, too, are not an easily generalizable group—hard though this is to appreciate from the rhetoric of the Palestinian as much as the Israeli activists. The Palestinians' sense of themselves as a group has fundamentally changed over the twentieth century, and consequently a sense of cultural or national identity has grown at different rates for different groups. The rich, educated, elite families of Jerusalem have had a quite different experience from the poor farmers who have not yet escaped the refugee camps, and many of this elite class are profoundly alienated by what Sari Nusseibeh, for example, calls "the demons" of Hezbollah and Hamas. The Palestinian who became a second-class citizen in Damascus or Amman has another view of Pan-Arab unity, and another motive for a national homeland. Whereas the PLO under Arafat was aligned with no one Arab regime (and was often hated by them all for that reason), other groups such as Hamas are happy to be strongly affiliated with particular Arab regimes. Attitudes to Islamic fundamentalism vary hugely, on both religious and political grounds. A founding clause in the charter of Hamas declares *all* Palestine, including, say, Tel Aviv, to be *waqf* property, which would make it illegal on penalty of death to transfer it from its status as a trust to non-Muslim owners: such a declaration is factually untrue, indeed both historical and theological nonsense: it is a commitment not just to destroy Israel as a state but also to bar any Jew from owning any property in Palestine. The charter also rejects *any* peaceful, negotiated solution, including a two-state model, in the name of jihad. Many, even those who voted for Hamas, do not share this vision. Many Palestinians, including the Palestinian Christians, do not wish to live under extreme *sharia* law. A shared dislike for Israeli policy is one link between almost all Palestinians, but that veils a vast range of social and intellectual differences. The collective responsibility for policy or another citizen's actions can only emerge in a system with proper institutions for justice, authoritative government, education, and so forth. This changes the moral claims on the collective—and thus changes what can be meant by "the Palestinians," who remain a politically, institutionally, and socially fractured collective.

The Jews, in turn, stretch from the extremist religious groups such as the Satmer *hassidim,* who do not recognize the State of Israel, to the totally secular, socialist kibbutz workers, across a range of political opinions, a range of educations, and a range of national backgrounds: many of the new immigrants from Russia are further culturally from Sephardic Israelis than are the Palestinians. It is a deeply riven society, with tensions between Eastern Jews from North Africa and the Arab countries and Western Jews from Europe and the United States, major social problems connected to poverty, and unbridgeable disjunctions between secular and religious Jews, *helonim* and *haredim.* Opposition to government policy is strongly expressed, though not always strongly enough to result in change. Hundreds of thousands can gather to protest against what they see as an unjust war, but it is still fought. Israel is a democracy with strong institutions, so it makes sense to talk of Israeli policy and to engage with a country's politicians and citizens at such a level.

Wars, like racism, need to enforce a strong sense of the undifferentiated enemy. Strident yelling about "the Jews" and "the Palestinians" helps maintain the conditions of war. It is morally bankrupt to attack any and every Jew or any and every Israeli because of the government's policies, just as it is wrong to attack any and every Palestinian because of the actions of Hamas—or any and every American because of the Republican Party's policies, or any and every English person because of the Labour Party's decisions. Nations are imagined communities, but that doesn't mean that the imagination needs to be impoverished. A little more self-conscious care before bandying generalizations about "the Israelis," "the British," or "the Palestinians" might help make discussion of the contemporary situation a little less fevered and a little more productive. What starts as a casual dismissiveness or lazy aggression leads to set-

tlers chanting "Death to the Arabs!" and radical Palestinians chanting "Death to the Jews!"—and the justification of the wholly unacceptable suicide bombing or the wholly unacceptable violence
toward Arab villages by settlers.

Jerusalem is and will continue to be the epicenter of the storm.
It remains the most problematic sticking point in the attempted,
imagined, rejected, and hoped-for negotiations between Israelis and
Palestinians. The return to 1967 borders, one of the phrases central
to all recent peace initiatives, if followed to the letter would mean
redividing the city and returning the Old City, including the *Kotel*
and the Jewish quarter, to Arab and, presumably, now Palestinian
sovereignty. It is a sign of the extraordinary vigor of Israeli public
debate that some Israelis have contemplated this as an acceptable
conclusion to a secure peace, though the majority balk even at the
thought of giving up the Western Wall again. More likely—though
difficult to work out in detail—is the less provocative phrase "with
a capital in East Jerusalem" as part of the establishment of a Palestinian state.

For their side, Palestinian Jerusalemites complain bitterly of what
they term the ongoing "Judaization" of Jerusalem. By this they
mean two things. First and most evidently they object to the growth
of Israeli building in what were previously Arab neighborhoods,
sometimes by compulsory expropriation. Coupled with the huge
number of new developments in the hills around Jerusalem, this
has changed the small Ottoman town into a large, modern, urban
sprawl (though far less rapid and extensive than the growth of
Amman in Jordan). It has made the Arab residents of Jerusalem feel
squeezed out, hemmed in, and challenged in their own homes and
streets. New roads service Israeli settlements but divide Palestinian
communities. As one of the Israeli planners has noted, there is a
fundamental disjunction of views even among the most gentle of
Jerusalemites: whereas Israelis can think that Jewish-Arab coexis-
tence will end up in reconciliation and peace, in the eyes of the

Arab community the unification of Jerusalem is seen as conquest, and consequently they cling to their struggle to establish a separate identity against any attempts at unification.

Second, there is a less tangible but equally strongly felt sense of a radical shift of atmosphere. Those with long memories recall when many of the Jews of Jerusalem spoke Arabic; when there was a shared and less aggressively confrontational culture of the streets. The new immigrants to Jerusalem have little sense of this old feeling and less desire to recover it. Sari Nusseibeh captures well the nostalgia, idealism, and despair when he describes his early life in Jerusalem as "living in a fairy tale invaded by Detroit." Teddy Kollek, the celebrated mayor of Jerusalem, recalls how in the first days after the Six Day War, "Arabs were astonished at what they saw and heard as they walked around and looked at the houses they had lived in. They knocked on the door, were invited in for a cup of tea and sat down to discuss with their Jewish hosts whether they would have their property returned or what compensation would satisfy them. Jews did the same in the Jewish Quarter." This now may sound like a fantasy on the part of Kollek, who always believed that the city could be unified in peace. But the same story is found in the Arab press at the same time: Nabil Khoury wrote: "Hundreds of former friendships were brought back to life. On June 29th, in Jaffa Road, the main street of Jerusalem, the Hebrew tongue disappeared. On that day, along the entire length of the street, only Palestinian Arabic, in all its different dialects, was heard." There is always some selective memory and some nostalgia for an imagined paradise in Jerusalem: the Palestinians do not care to recall that already in 1948 there were 100,000 Jews and 40,000 Arabs (many of whom were Christian) in the population of 165,000; no one cares to remember the depredations and humiliations of living under the Ottoman regime; nor the barbed wire and drastic reduction of civic liberties under the last years of the Mandate; nor the sporadic outbreaks of urban violence, which would regularly shut the *suk,* from the 1920s onward. But if there was cause for some hope back in 1967, it has been systematically and slowly undermined since, by violence and policy decisions on both sides, from politicians and terrorists alike.

While the Arabs have their understandable complaints about the building and housing programs of the city, the planning of the urban development of Jerusalem is a scandal for everyone. There have been several master plans since the British schemes of Ashbee (1920–1923) and Kendall (1944). No one plan has been completed. The mishmash of overlapping and uncompleted master plans has created an underlying chaos. Different departments of local and national government have responsibilities for different aspects of planning, and the lack of coordination further adds to the problems. The skyline around Jerusalem has become a mess of huge projects, where financial motives appear to have outweighed any aesthetic or social concerns. "The multitudinous windows of the new Hilton look to me like the heavy-lidded eyes of insomnia sufferers, aching for rest," wrote a grumpy Saul Bellow (who published his diary of a trip to Israel in 1976, the year he was awarded the Nobel Prize for literature: there are many more such buildings now). The elegant Victorian developments and pleasing streets of Arab villas have been encroached on and around by major roads and infill developments of undistinguished architectural merit. The development of the central area of the former No-Man's-Land between Jaffa Gate and Damascus Gate has been slow and incoherent, while opposite Jaffa Gate a large development of modern luxury houses, designed by Moshe Safdie, has been purchased largely by foreign visitors, who use them only for visits, which has created a luxury desert in the middle of town. And, of course, the traffic is terrible. Political motives always lurk behind planning decisions: land-use laws have greatly restricted Arab building and encouraged Jewish building. A quota system on building permissions has functioned for many years. (The Supreme Court also upheld a ban on any

Arab ownership in the Jewish quarter of the Old City.) Planning
has become part of the problem of Jerusalem. There is a huge
model of Jerusalem, which the planners use, in the basement of the
modern town hall. It is the best way to see the city whole—and to
appreciate how uncontrolled and shoddily motivated its development has been.

THE CITY OF THE MANDATE

GOVERNMENT HOUSE: THE DISPLAY OF POWER

Things seemed more promising when the Mandate began, with
Storrs and Ashbee in charge, and with a serious commitment to the
development of the city with aesthetic, social, and planning principles in place. Some of the finest planners and architects of the period worked in Jerusalem, including the planner Patrick Geddes
and the architects St. Austen Barbe Harrison and Clifford Holliday.
Two of the finest buildings of this era are Government House and
the Rockefeller Museum, both designed by Harrison (who also designed the central post office and the Government Printing Office,
as well as the British representative's residence in Amman). Government House, the British high commissioner's residence, is built
on the hill opposite Talpiot usually known as the Hill of Offence
(because it was the scene of Solomon's idolatry) or the Hill of Evil
Counsel—neither especially optimistic names for the location of a
governor's house. It provides a stunning view of the city, and there
is now a garden and promenade along the escarpment that is a very
pleasant place to walk or run. The building (Map 7) has been the
center of the United Nations' operation in Jerusalem since 1948,
and it is difficult to arrange a visit, but Harrison's vision is worth
trying to see.

Harrison had lived in Athens and studied Byzantine and Islamic
architecture. He was deeply fond of the Eastern Mediterranean and

did not return to England for any significant time after he joined the Colonial Service: he died in Greece in 1976. He was, surprisingly for an architect who worked in the glare of the most public and civic of commissions, a deeply private man, who loved the desert and silence and avoided social life. True to the tradition of Ashbee, he was a "regionalist" who believed in using local materials and craftsmen; his principle was to "avoid flouting local tradition." He also followed the fashion of adopting a medieval form for non-religious public buildings, in a monumental style that drew on Byzantine and Romanesque simple grandeur, which was particularly suitable for

Figure 46. Government House, designed by Harrison, as seen from the sunken garden.

Jerusalem, where the crusader influence is so strong. Harrison was especially concerned to meld Eastern and Western influences together and to link Mediterranean regional architecture with this medieval authority. The glaring white limestone façade of the building (Figure 46) shows its modernist roots in its non-symmetrical stacking of rectangular blocks, broken by two small flat domes on either side of the arched entrance to the central tower. The windows are narrow and rectangular above and arched below. It looks like a modernist take on a crusader fort, bringing together medieval revival elements with the local Oriental architecture. The building was reviewed in *Country Life* for 1931 under the heading "A Crusader Castle of Today," and Harrison's abstract Orientalist style was christened "Near-Eastern Modernism."

The design inside is centered on a cruciform public area, with a drawing room with arched alcoves looking out through large arched windows onto the garden and the view of Jerusalem beyond (Figure 47). The Oriental influence is obvious and is actually based on the standard design for look-out pavilions in Islamic architecture—which suits the position of Government House with its prospect out over the Old City. No expense was spared (the project embarrassingly went several thousand pounds over budget). This was the third site that had been tried (the first two had been turned down in London with a bureaucratic fussing that vexed the quiet Harrison), and Harrison was keen that every detail, from the fireplaces to the paving in the garden, should be precisely designed and carefully constructed—a typical Arts and Crafts credo. The splendid ballroom, with its whitewashed arched alcoves and modern square-vaulted ceiling, ends with a cylindrical fireplace set in a niche reminiscent of a *mihrab,* an Islamic prayer niche. The fireplace and the niche are decorated with fine tiles by David Ohanessian, the Armenian master potter who was brought over by the British to repair the façade of the Dome of the Rock. The Oriental influence continues in the garden, where a semicircular terrace is laid out in an arabesque pattern. From the upper walk of the terrace, you can look down into a sunken garden designed to provide shelter from the winds on the hillside. It provided also a more private space during garden parties.

Government House was the center of the Mandate, not just because the administration was led from here but also because so much of colonial life revolved around formal occasions for which Government House provided the hub. On the king's birthday a parade in the city ended with a reception at the governor's house. Visiting dignitaries were entertained here, and there were dances and other more informal tea parties and social events. (Before Government House was built, Storrs and Ashbee put on *The Merchant of Venice*—of all plays—with Storrs as Shylock and Ashbee as Antonio.) But social life was dominated, as elsewhere in the empire, by a strong expression of decorum, propriety, and form. The public

Figure 47. The interior of the sitting room in Government House, now the head-quarters of the U.N. in Jerusalem. This view captures well the Oriental elements of the interior design. (Courtesy Israel Antiquities Authority. Photograph © The Israel Museum, Jerusalem.)

spectacles of the empire were an essential element in displaying power, maintaining social distinction, and creating an image of imperial civilization. The Mandate authorities also organized horse races just outside Jerusalem; The Club, where the niceties of propriety and gossip were exercised to the full; Gilbert and Sullivan concerts; and even a hunt, nicknamed the Ramle Vale, where pink-clad huntsmen chased jackals across the scrub. As the Scottish regiment marched through the town, kilts swinging and bagpipes blaring, the empire was strutting its stuff.

Each high commissioner, however, was faced with an increasingly intractable task. Government House was the site for a constant round of separate meetings with the Zionist and the Arab lobbies. It was impossible to satisfy both. Sir Herbert Samuel, acutely conscious of his status as a Jew in such a position, struggled to be seen as scrupulously fair to both sides. Sir Arthur Wauchope gained a reputation for being too easy on both sides and was replaced. Sir Harold MacMichael was appointed to establish a stronger sense of law and order in Palestine. But each was greeted by escalating violence and increasingly bitter argumentation. The Jews wished to increase immigration; the Arabs wished to stop it entirely. A series of royal commissions toured the country and made resolutions that were turned down by both sides—or accepted by one side and therefore turned down by the other. The Commission on the Western Wall is the best known and is still cited today in arguments about the Temple Mount Plaza. Both sides increasingly turned to violence to make their points. Herbert Samuel's ceremonial progress from Jaffa to Jerusalem was marred by the series of death threats he had received. Sir Harold MacMichael survived an assassination attempt by the Irgun-Stern gang (he was especially disliked by the Jews for his strict observance of government policies). Arab riots were put down by the army with the loss of many lives. A general strike by the Arabs in 1936 increased tensions all around, and the

British response to these years of Arab disturbances had a long-term effect on the politics of the region. A large proportion of the adult male Arab population, maybe as high as 10 percent, was killed, wounded, or imprisoned, and the traditional leadership of the few great families of Jerusalem, the Nusseibehs, the Nashashibis, the Khalidis, the Husseinis, was severely undermined in its authority and reach.

The outbreak of the Second World War raised the stakes even higher. Jews were desperate for a place to escape the killing fields of Europe; the English were terrified that the Arabs would follow the mufti and become aligned with Hitler. Palestine was a crucial base between the African theater and the war in the eastern Mediterranean. After the war, when the consequences of the British restrictions on immigration had become all too evident—in 1939 the English had backed away from their support of the Zionists under the terms of the Balfour Declaration in order to shore up their position in Palestine—the violence reached unprecedented levels. The center of the city was barred off with barbed wire and anti-car devices—the heavily defended British area in the Russian Compound was known scornfully as Bevingrad, after the hated British foreign minister, Ernest Bevin. ("Congratulations," the young Teddy Kollek joked, "you have succeeded in rounding yourselves up.") Finally, the toll of British lives in Palestine was so great that the government in London was forced to retreat from the Mandate. The officials in Palestine at one level were relieved to escape such a distressing and dangerous environment, but at another level some at least were shocked and depressed by the failure it represented. W. Fitzgerald, the chief justice, wrote privately to Sir Harold MacMichael: "I confess to a feeling which does not appear to be shared by other officials, of sadness at the end of this Palestine journey. All that we did or tried to do seems to have gone for naught."

Government House still stands in its dominant position above the city. It is now occupied by the U.N. peace-keeping force, whose hard-pressed officials may have somewhat similar feelings to the British officials about their task as outsiders deputed to maintain order in a strife-ridden city.

ROCKEFELLER MUSEUM: THE POWER OF DISPLAY

The opening of the Rockefeller Museum was delayed by two days in 1938 because the British archaeologist G. Starkey was murdered by Arab villagers on his way to the ceremony, a brutal and random killing painfully typical of the troubles of this era. The plan for the museum had been prompted by the Chicago archaeologist James Henry Breasted, who visited Jerusalem in 1925 (though Geddes had already proposed a museum back in 1919, a plan that went nowhere for lack of funds). Breasted was surprised to discover that there was no major museum to display the results of the last decades of intense European archaeology in the Holy Land. He approached the high commissioner, Field Marshal Lord Herbert Plumer (the Etonian general who had won the battles of Ypres and Messines in the First World War, inasmuch as any First World War battle was a victory; he was much liked in Palestine for his robust common sense, though he, too, could not stop the tide of violence here, for all his success as a military leader). Plumer approached Rockefeller, who offered the immense sum of $2,000,000. The hill of Karm-el-Sheik in East Jerusalem was purchased from the al-Halili family: the mufti of Jerusalem in the seventeenth century was an al-Halili, and he had built his summer house here, one of the first buildings outside the walls. Harrison was chosen to design the museum.

It is his finest building, showing a brilliant fusion of East and West (Map 7). It has a plan in the shape of a butterfly (Figure 48). The central axis of the white limestone building runs from the

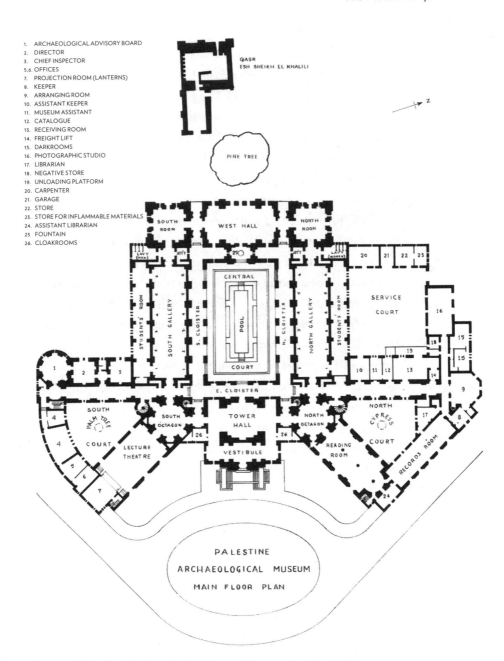

1. ARCHAEOLOGICAL ADVISORY BOARD
2. DIRECTOR
3. CHIEF INSPECTOR
5,6. OFFICES
7. PROJECTION ROOM (LANTERNS)
8. KEEPER
9. ARRANGING ROOM
10. ASSISTANT KEEPER
11. MUSEUM ASSISTANT
12. CATALOGUE
13. RECEIVING ROOM
14. FREIGHT LIFT
15. DARKROOMS
16. PHOTOGRAPHIC STUDIO
17. LIBRARIAN
18. NEGATIVE STORE
19. UNLOADING PLATFORM
20. CARPENTER
21. GARAGE
22. STORE
23. STORE FOR INFLAMMABLE MATERIALS
24. ASSISTANT LIBRARIAN
25. FOUNTAIN
26. CLOAKROOMS

QASR
ESH SHEIKH EL KHALILI

PINE TREE

WEST HALL

SOUTH ROOM

NORTH ROOM

CENTRAL

POOL

COURT

SERVICE COURT

STUDENTS' ROOM

SOUTH GALLERY

S. CLOISTER

N. CLOISTER

NORTH GALLERY

STUDENTS' ROOM

E. CLOISTER

SOUTH PALM TREE COURT

SOUTH OCTAGON

TOWER HALL

NORTH OCTAGON

NORTH CYPRESS COURT

LECTURE THEATRE

VESTIBULE

READING ROOM

RECORDS ROOM

PALESTINE
ARCHAEOLOGICAL MUSEUM
MAIN FLOOR PLAN

Figure 48. The plan of the Rockefeller Museum. (Courtesy Israel Antiquities Authority.)

monumental entrance, with its octagonal tower, through a court-yard to an old pine tree behind the building. (The ancient pine tree finally collapsed in the 1990s.) The tower was the part of the design that proved to be most controversial. E. T. Richmond, the stri-dently pro-Arab official, complained that it was too "dominating" and was a "breach of architectural good manners" in that it threat-ened to overlook the Arab city with an imperial monument: "Jeru-salem has enough towers already." Breasted replied with praise for the building's "reserved and austere lines," and the tower stayed as a sign of the "reverence felt by western civilization for the past of Palestine." Architecture always has its politics in Jerusalem.

The two rectangular wings are the main display areas: they are long, with high ceilings and natural light from the high-set win-dows. The "butterfly wings" lead the visitor around from the en-trance hall into each wing. The display cases are rare surviving ex-amples of the museum style of the early twentieth century: most museums threw theirs out many years ago. Although there has re-cently been some updating of the written materials, it feels like stepping back seventy-five years to wander through the lines of square glass cases. In fact, when the Israeli archaeologists took over the museum in 1967, they were amazed to find that the Jordani-ans had touched almost nothing during their curatorship since 1948. The same yellowing temporary handwritten signs were still in place in the cases. Only the Hebrew inscriptions on the wall had been plastered over, and when the plaster was removed, the mu-seum looked exactly as it had decades earlier.

The central courtyard is magnificent (Figure 49). It is flanked by rows of wide arches that form cross-vaulted arcades. In the middle is a long, sunken ornamental pool. Above the arches are ten bas-reliefs that were carved by the celebrated English Arts and Craft sculptor Eric Gill (working in full Arab costume, according to the pictures of his stay), which portray the ten major cultures repre-

sented in the museum. Canaanite culture is represented by a man collecting
sheaves of corn; the Phoenician by
three men in a boat. Ashbee would
have approved. At the far end of the
pool is a niche decorated with the
richly colored tiles made, of course, by
David Ohanessian. The low pool, the
arches, the tiled niche, all show Harrison's love of Eastern architecture and
echo the beauty of the courts of the
Al-Hambra in particular, though in
Harrison's own, more severe artisanal
style.

This combination of cultural models
(signaled by Gill's thematic reliefs) is
also evident in the library and meeting
room. The library is vaulted, austere,

Figure 49. The central courtyard of the
Rockefeller Museum.

and thoroughly like a crusader crypt. The meeting room is circular
and domed, surrounded by curtained arches. A frieze of ancient
Greek lettering runs around below the dome with an inscription
from Plato, which includes the first use of the word "archaeology"
(in quite a different sense from its modern use, but no matter). The
ceiling is also decorated by Ohanessian. It feels like a room from
Constantinople or Alexandria.

The Rockefeller Museum is never crowded because it is in East
Jerusalem, albeit only a few yards from the walls of the Old City;
but it has a fascinating exhibition and is worth seeing in its own
right as a building and as a monument of the role of museums as a
spectacle of culture. Museums so often are the product not just of
nationalist pride but also of the imperial urge to explore, conquer,
and put on display the fruits of empire (which is one reason there is

such a fuss in these post-colonial days about returning objects to the lands from which they came). No surprise that the British and the Americans wanted a grand building to show off what their explorers and scientists had uncovered from the Holy Land.

REACHING OUT TO THE LORD

The British officers of the Mandate were expected to attend religious services, not just as regular Sunday worshippers at St. George's, but also as a formal presence at the major occasions of the other churches' calendars. This was also a period of building new churches, though in a quite different style from the imperial grandeur of the Victorian period. The losses of the First World War overshadowed all ecclesiastical architecture of the period. Clifford Holliday was another of the Arts and Crafts clique working in Jerusalem. He designed St. Andrew's Scottish Church, which stands on the hill overlooking the Valley of Hinnom (Map 7), an easy walk from Mishkanot Sha'ananim. The foundation stone was laid by Allenby (who else?) in 1927, and the church and hospice were finished in 1930. It was dedicated as a memorial to the Scottish soldiers who had died in the First World War (and at first catered in particular to the Scottish regiments stationed in Jerusalem). Now the most crowded service is on Hogmanay, New Year's Eve, and it attracts plenty of non-Scottish celebrators. Although the site chosen gives the building an inevitable prominence on the skyline, it is beautifully blended into the mountain landscape and designed with a restrained simplicity, with a low tower and flat dome, combining local traditions. It is built in a porous stone that the moss loves, so that the building looks more aged than it is. It is promised that the heart of Robert the Bruce will be buried here in the near future—as was anticipated by Allenby. Robert, who fought for Scottish independence against the English oppressors, wanted his heart to be buried in Jerusalem. It got no further than Spain on its first attempt in the thirteenth century, and was buried in Melrose Abbey in Scotland. Another relic for Jerusalem, another story of a national liberation struggle and guerrilla warfare . . .

The grandest church of the period is the Church of All Nations, also known as the Basilica of the Agony, designed by the Italian ex- pressionist artist Antonio Barluzzi (Map 7). The church enshrines a piece of bedrock, said to be where Jesus prayed alone the night be- fore his arrest, and is set in the Garden of Gethsemane, the second holiest site in Jerusalem for Christians. Symbolically, the church that marks Jesus' soul-searching pain before betrayal was initiated in 1919, the year after the Great War, and was built with funds from many different countries, coming together in contrite prayer rather than in battle. It is one of the few buildings in Jerusalem that reveals an intelligent recognition of its place in history and consciously works with the physical and conceptual remains of former years on the site.

When the foundations for the Church of All Nations were being dug, the remains of a fourth-century basilica were found (it is men- tioned in Egeria, one of the earliest Christian pilgrims to have left an account of her travels in the Holy Land in the fourth century). This church was destroyed and abandoned in the earthquake of 746. A crusader church was also built here and then abandoned in 1345. The current rectangle of the basilica is laid at an angle over the first basilica. Outside and to the south (the right as you look at the façade) are the old foundations, which continue under the new church. In the floor of the church are small glass panels through which you can see the old Byzantine floor. This is a church that re- spects what it has been built on, and lets us see and appreciate its own history of discontinuous worship as it is embodied in the bricks, rather than just promoting a fantasy of unbroken continuity.

The impressive façade of the church consciously recalls both the Roman architecture of the time of Jesus and the Byzantine era of early Christianity (Figure 50). There are three Roman arches rising

Figure 50. The Church of All Nations at Gethsemane, designed by Antonio Barluzzi, with the Russian church of St. Mary Magdalene in the background.

on Corinthian columns. Each of the four column groups is topped by a statue of an Evangelist holding open an inscribed book. The triangular pediment has a marvelous mosaic that represents Jesus, the mediator between God and Man, offering his very heart to an angel, who takes it in two hands. Around Jesus, the poor and needy turn toward him in supplication. Both Jesus' final night of prayer before his condemnation and death and the church's prayer for all nations to turn in peace toward Jesus are powerfully evoked. At the apex of the pediment is a cross, flanked by two stags. The stag, in early and medieval Christian symbolism, is "the enemy of the serpent"—Satan. The stags here represent the triumph of Jesus over the grim world of sin and death.

The interior of the church is extraordinary. Barluzzi wanted to create an effect of oppression, despair, and darkness—the night of The Agony. The windows are paned with dark purples and blues and never let the light rise above the murky. (The colors and the themes are archetypical of the expressionist style.) The ceiling, too, is decorated with a dark-blue night sky. The ceiling is built as twelve small domes, which reduces any sense of soaring height. Yet each dome was dedicated, and funded, by a different country, and each has a flag or crest of that country. It is both lavish and lowering; both celebrating the possibility of a brotherhood of mankind and dedicated to solitary despair. In front of the altar is the rock itself—yet another rock in Jerusalem's religious landscape. It is surrounded by an iron sculpture of the crown of thorns, on which two silver doves are caught in agony on the snares of the brambles as they strive toward a chalice, the chalice of Christ's Passion: souls searching to share in the cup of sorrow. The back wall, too, incorporates the old, roughly dressed rock of the earliest building here. The contrast between the modern church, its three aisles each held up and divided by six slim columns of rose stone, its ornate decorations, its smoothness, and the harsh simplicity of the long-lost basilica of earliest Christianity makes for a striking and provocative juxtaposition—a question about continuity and change, about suffering and art, about cruelty and transcendence.

Next to the church is a small olive grove, carefully fenced around, which is said to be the remains of the olive grove into which Jesus and the disciples turned that last night. Olive trees grow new shoots out of their most gnarled and cracked barks, and are thus an easy symbol for resurrection or rebirth (as well as its other associations of peace). Amid the complex relics of Jerusalem, the unadorned grove of ancient trees, set here against the modern church, is curiously beautiful. The juxtaposition of the church, with its attempt through modern art to make sense of the violent conflict of people in the context of Jesus' Agony, and the old trees, such a different sort of memorial, makes for a poignant contrast between humans' political mess and the simplest religious hope for good in the world.

Barluzzi also designed in the 1950s the Dominus Flevit Chapel further up the Mount of Olives, which, strangely, fewer people visit: it is a memorable building with a great view—a church built in the shape of a teardrop ("Dominus flevit" means "The Lord Wept"), overlooking the whole city. The teardrop shape shows Barluzzi's modernism far more strikingly than the façade of the Church of All Nations. There are some attractive Byzantine mosaics in the peaceful garden, but the most amazing part of the church is the view from within it. It has a particularly beautiful, wrought-iron grill window above the altar, which provides from the dark interior a marvelously framed prospect of sunny Jerusalem (Figure 51). The altar here, unlike in most churches, faces west in order to create the view. But even here there is a political gesture. The cross of the altar and the cross-bars of the window are symbolically placed exactly across the Dome of the Rock—crossing out the Islamic monument, as it were, while letting you see it. A quiet but authoritative artistic gesture of supremacy . . .

Figure 51. The view through the iron window of the Dominus Flevit, designed by Antonio Barluzzi. The cross of the metal blocks out the golden Dome of the Rock almost completely.

INTO THE TWENTIETH CENTURY: HOTELS, MUSEUMS, HOSPITALS, AND UNIVERSITIES

It was in the Mandate that the basic institutions of the future State of Israel were put in place. The buildings reflect this. On King David Street, opposite each other, are the King David Hotel and the YMCA. The King David is Jerusalem's best-known grand hotel. It looks like a grand hotel from the interwar period (which is what it is), but more than most hotels it is part of the history of the city. Not only has many a statesman stayed here and many a political meeting been conducted in its rooms, but also during the Mandate, the British military police headquarters were housed here. The most famous terrorist bomb of the era was planted here on July 22,

1946. A team led by Menachem Begin, the future prime minister of Israel, from the Irgun, the Jewish terrorist organization, dressed as Arabs and gained entrance through the kitchen area with milk churns packed with explosives. Ninety-one people were killed as the wing collapsed. The Arab kitchen workers were told to flee (they did); a warning was sent, but either because the warning was too close to the explosion or because it was not believed or acted upon (one report later said that Sir John Shaw, the head of the secretariat, had sniffed: "I give orders here. I don't take orders from Jews"), there was no evacuation.

The attack was immediately condemned around the world: a "brutal and murderous crime," an "insane act of terrorism," declared Clement Atlee, the British prime minister, to Parliament. But the issue of the warning and the ultimate effect of the terrorism (not to mention the future career of its perpetrator) have made this a continuing source of controversy. In 2006 a group of right-wing politicians, including Benjamin Netanyahu, attended a celebration of the sixtieth anniversary of the attack, organized by the new Menachem Begin Center, a museum and conference center just down from Mishkanot Sha'ananim, built to honor the memory of Begin. The British made a diplomatic protest about the celebration of an act of terrorism that cost so many lives, and objected to the wording of the proposed plaque, which blamed the British for not evacuating the building. The history of the end of the Mandate—how the story is told—is still raw in Jerusalem, as is hardly surprising when moral sensitivity is crushed by such aggressive, nationalist acts of celebration.

The YMCA raises another tower to dominate the skyline (Figure 52). It was built by Arthur Harmon, the architect whose next project was the Empire State Building in New York (the YMCA was the tallest building in Jerusalem when built, so there is some continuity of purpose between the two projects). Harmon was a deeply committed Christian, and though the core of the building is a typical public building of the period, it is surrounded, not only by deliberate attempts to bring together the three Abrahamic faiths in architectural terms (the domed wings of the central building and the arched entrance hall are the most obvious features of this orientalizing gesture), but also by numerological hints of Harmon's religious convictions: the forty columns in the forecourt arcade are designed to represent the forty years of the Israelites in the desert and the forty days of Jesus' temptation; the twelve windows of the dome of the auditorium represent the twelve tribes of Israel, the twelve disciples, and the twelve followers of Mohammed. It is worth going up to the

Figure 52. The tower of the YMCA, designed by Arthur Harmon, one of the landmarks of the new city.

top of the tower not just for the view, which is awe-inspiring, but also to be up close to the sculptures around the turret, art deco–influenced symbolic portrayals of the four Evangelists. When Allenby opened it in 1933, he had, as usual, stirring words for the occasion. He was impressed by the monumentality of the building and declared that "under its shadow, jarring sectarians may cease from wrangling, fierce passions be tamed, and men's minds be drawn to loftier ideals."

The YMCA has been a marked success in its aims. The building housed the city's only swimming pool (until the 1960s), with single-sex swimming sessions to accommodate the more religious from all communities, and the sports facilities drew together Christians, Jews, and Muslims. Any initial concerns about a missionary agenda from the Christian organization were buried in shared sporting and, eventually, social and intellectual activities. The building has become another casualty of the current extremism. Fewer and fewer Muslims now use it. The Jerusalem International YMCA was nominated for the Nobel Peace Prize in 1993, and was awarded the first Jerusalem Marta Prize for Tolerance and Democratic Values in 1996. The days when young men from across Jerusalem could play ballgames against each other seem today like a lost era of innocence.

The skyline of the hills above the Mount of Olives, which is dominated by the Augusta Victoria and the Russian Church tower, spreads around to the Hebrew University on Mount Scopus and the Hadassah Hospital, both of which were also initiated under the Mandate. There were no Arab universities or hospitals in Palestine; the Europeans began by building smaller clinics and schools in the nineteenth century. The construction of a full-scale modern hospital and university on the hills above the city was a striking symbolic statement of the arrival of Western values and institutions in the old Ottoman environment. The Hadassah Hospital was designed by Erich Mendelsohn, one of the most successful expressionist architects in Germany. Although an ardent Zionist, he left Germany in 1933 and settled in England ("Judea is divine but too small for me," he commented). He brought a strict modern, Bauhaus aesthetic with him to Jerusalem (Figure 53). Two vast rectangular blocks, with standardized windows and industrially cut stone, emphatically assert the building's modernism. But the building is also carefully planted in the desert landscape (which, Mendelsohn laconically noted, "leads straight to eternity"). Mendelsohn's self-conscious commitment to the desert as an integral part of his architectural landscape had political overtones too in its transfer of a Bauhaus aesthetic away from its usual urban, Western environment, into a self-conscious Eastern frame: a statement about the new landscape for (his, German) Zionism. The flat domes and rectangles also recall the simplicity of local architecture, and the building is strikingly framed by the huge desert sky and the flat of the landscape.

Figure 53. Hadassah Hospital, on Mount Scopus.

The university was opened in 1925 at a ceremony attended by Allenby, Balfour, Einstein, Herbert Samuel, Chaim Weitzman, and many other dignitaries. For the Israelis—Jews traditionally have always been obsessed with education—this has remained an institution of deep pride: the Nobel Prize winners, the library facilities, the faculty and alumni . . . The campus at Mount Scopus, like the hospital, found itself cut off from west Jerusalem in 1948. It was still nominally an enclave of Israeli property but could only be reached by the winding road through Arab territory. In 1948 a convoy of medical staff and academics was attacked by Arab terrorists, ostensibly in revenge for the slaughter at Deir Yassin, and many were slaughtered in their buses—while, according to the Israelis, the observing British soldiers, without orders, did not intervene to prevent the murders. Since 1967 the campus has grown again, with a series of fortress-like buildings, and one more of those towers that ring the city. But here, too, fanaticism has sullied liberal ideals.

In 2002 the student café, incongruously named the Frank Sinatra Café, full of Arab and Israeli students, was blown up by a terrorist from the village on the slopes below the university. The fortress-like buildings are now matched by high-level security, as here, just as in al-Quds, the Arab university headed by Sari Nusseibeh, education has slipped into the mire of destructive political conflict.

THE DIVIDED AND UNITED CITY

Jerusalem was divided in 1948. In the face of the concerted Arab assault on the new State of Israel, the United Nations' plan for a two-state solution collapsed, partly because the U.N. did nothing concrete to make it happen—no peace-keeping troops were sent, not that the British would allow any forces in, and no prior agreements were established—partly, it has now emerged, because highly secret negotiations were held between the Jordanians and the Israelis. Golda Meir, in disguise, visited Jordan for talks with King Abdullah, who proposed that Jordan would annex the West Bank and that the crack forces of the Jordanian army, the Arab Legion commanded by Glubb Pasha, their English general, would not engage with the Israelis on the territory allowed them by the United Nations (the British were aware of the plan too, it seems). The United Nations' blueprint had declared Jerusalem a *corpus separatum,* an internationally recognized enclave, like the Vatican, to be ruled by no one nation. This, too, became impossible. The fighting for Jerusalem was particularly intense, and the Jordanian siege nearly starved the whole city into submission. But when the cease-fire came into action, the east city, including all of the Old City with its holy places, was in Jordanian hands, the west in Israeli.

The city was divided by a line on a 1:20,000 map, drawn by a rather thick pencil, with the result that the border was up to 60 meters wide on the ground (and any smudging on the map changed it further); it was often as wide as a street, turning neighbors into different nationalities, and putting some buildings into the dangerous limbo of No-Man's-Land. The only crossing point became the Mandelbaum Gate, a house owned by a Mr. Mandelbaum (and now in unified Jerusalem run as a Chabad house, an outreach center of the Lubavitch *hassidim*). No Jews could cross from the west, though the terms of the armistice had allowed for it, and only religious figures or worshippers at Christmas could cross from the east, except for the United Nations officials. The city became to all intents and purposes two cities. The wall was high and helped create for the citizens on both sides a fantasy of the other behind the wall. Snipers on the Jordanian side turned the area close to the wall into a dangerous, and hence poverty-stricken, area. In east Jerusalem, little work was done for the city. In the west, Jerusalem continued to grow at an extraordinary pace—it tripled its population between 1948 and 1967. East Jerusalem removed as many signs of Jewish life as it could: the Mount of Olives cemetery was desecrated and the gravestones used for building work; the synagogues of the Old City were destroyed. In west Jerusalem, the Mamilla Muslim cemetery became a park; villages were razed and renamed; Jews moved into Muslim and other deserted property. The sense of two separated and self-contained cities was aggressively expressed by both sides.

The border, inevitably, became the most contested area. A joint committee, "The Hashemite Kingdom of Jordan/Israel Mixed Armistice Committee," or MAC, consisting of two Israelis, two Jordanians, and a United Nations chairman (who usually had the casting vote), was established to deal with the day-to-day running of the border. It was not an easy task. There were two different maps with different armistice lines on them and no concerted effort was made to reconcile them; the map's thick line of division left plenty of room for argument, especially when it ran through a house and its garden or, in one case, left a house in Israel and its outside toilet in the forbidden No-Man's-Land. Nor did the Jordanians have any interest in agreeing on such lines: to do so would be tantamount to recognizing Israel's status, something they refused to do for many years in the hope of gaining for themselves land all the way to the Mediterranean. The stories are legion from this time about trying to keep the boundary secure—"The opportunities for inadvertent human mistakes and vicious mischief were rife," recalled the Israeli delegate to MAC. All too often they are shockingly arbitrary tales of the death of an Israeli who wandered too close to the boundary and was shot by an unknown sniper, followed by retaliatory raids—setting a pattern of repeated revenge and provocation that has continued to today. Escalation was already part of the problem: four members of an international archaeology seminar at Ramat Rachel were killed and sixteen wounded by Jordanian fire while they looked at excavations. In retaliation, Israeli troops raided a police fortress and army position, killing thirty-nine soldiers and policemen and wounding twelve. This, too, has become a familiar pattern.

There were exceptions. A child wandered into Jordanian territory and was clothed and fed by the officials into whose authority he was placed, before being returned safe and sound and better dressed two days later. A nun dropped her false teeth over the boundary into a bush, and they had to be recovered formally by a disgruntled United Nations peace-keeper. Colonel Dawud, the senior Jordanian delegate to MAC, who went on to become prime minister of Jordan in 1970, became good friends with Raphael Israeli, his junior counterpart from Israel (who helped replace Dawud's treasured electric razor when it needed a part available only in Tel Aviv). When his first son was born, Israeli was summoned from the celebration to an urgent meeting at MAC, only to be given a large gift-wrapped present by Dawud (who begged for secrecy). The story was leaked by a publicity-hungry United Nations officer to the press, and the Arab outrage at such behavior was cooled only when both men earnestly and publicly denied the event had taken place.

The most contentious area was the enclave on Mount Scopus, where the Hadassah Hospital and the Hebrew University were cut off from the rest of Israel. On the first and third Tuesday of each month, a convoy went from the Mandelbaum Gate. There were relief soldiers, whose kit was searched laboriously every time by the Jordanians; and United Nations officers, who went to Mount Scopus to test randomly the canned food to make sure no weapons were concealed. All the supplies were unloaded for inspection and reloaded. Israel provided military backup in case the convoy was attacked. The convoy of Arab Legion soldiers, U.N. cars, Israeli trucks, followed by U.N. cars, followed by further Arab Legion armored escorts, gradually made its way up the hill. Meanwhile, with access to the hospital and university blocked in this way, Israel built a new campus in west Jerusalem and a new hospital in Ein Kerem (Map 7). In 1962 a synagogue was added to the hospital with twelve magnificent stained-glass windows designed by Chagall which represent Jacob's blessings for his twelve sons, the founders of the twelve tribes of Israel. Chagall came from Vitebsk, a town whose Jewish population was destroyed in the Holocaust. "All the time I was working," he said, "I felt my father and my mother were looking over my shoulder, and behind them were Jews, millions of other vanished Jews of yesterday and a thousand years ago." The Israelis were clear that 1948 had been a fight for the life of the State of Israel, and the synagogue next to the hospital, forced away from its first site, is a richly symbolic place for this image of the blessings of Israel's children, and for this expression of inspiration from Chagall.

THE KNESSET: DEBATING ARCHITECTURE

The building of the Knesset, the assembly hall and legislative center of the government (Map 7), is a story from this era of the divided Jerusalem that captures all the confusion, grandeur, and disaster about Israeli planning—and seems to epitomize what makes Israeli society a uniquely frustrating and excitable place. As befitted the democratic principles to be enshrined in this of all buildings, a competition was held in 1956 to choose the design and the architect for the new building. The jury gave first prize to Joseph Klarwein, Polish by birth and German by architectural training. His design was a square neo-classical building with classical columns. The jury explained: "The use of classical insinuations in the architectural composition bestows on the building the attribute of inspiring awe in those approaching it." Almost immediately, the furor started. Uri Avnery published an article that pulled no punches: "There is a suspicion of 'favoritism,' suspicion of poor judgment, echoes of horse-trading, and manifestations of malignant sect-rule." The massed ranks of Israeli architects joined in with a rolling snowball of protest: the building was not modern, not Israeli, did not fit into its environment. It was a disastrous design. The committee was stumped. They had awarded the prize but could not ignore the tide of informed protest at their decision. They found a compromise: they sent Klarwein abroad to study modern civic architecture with the aim of getting him to adapt his plan.

While he was away, an engineer on the project, Shlomo Gur, became keen to get going and, with a new architect, Zvi Cohen, on board, started to dig foundations for a rectangular building with a greatly modified design. Klarwein returned and was understandably outraged at such plotting. Even the army got in on the act, vetoing a proposed move of the entrance to the north, as it would be too easily open to gunfire from the Jordanian border. After two years of committee haggling and increasingly bad tempers all around, a further compromise was found. A third architect, Dov Karmi, with his son Ram and a young British architect, Bill Gillitt, was brought in as consultant. The gentle Karmi was agreeable to all sides. His plan produced a new building. The classical columns disappeared, though square columns branching outward offer a trace of the original design. The engineer Gur and his chosen architect, Ratner, wrote a strident complaint that this was a new building, and there should be a new competition. When the committee dismissed their complaint, they resigned. But the rows continued. Ram argued with his father and left to design a parliament building in Sierra Leone. Dov Karmi died suddenly from a heart attack, and Klarwein, constantly humiliated by the chipping away at his prize-winning design, continued to fight a series of tetchy rear-guard actions against the new team brought in. Dora Gad, an interior designer, was hired to design the interior (much to the confusion of the older members of the Knesset who did not recognize the profession)—despite the fact that she hated Klarwein's design. Klarwein continued to fuss and dislike the art that now was decorating his building. The project limped toward its grand opening.

The building was not finished until 1966. It is hard to say who is the architect. The Knesset has been attacked—and still is—as a mishmash of a design, with too many hands to have any conceptual unity or strength. The fact that it is set alone on a hill as the centerpiece of a government compound has been criticized as an excessively monumental concept, the bombast of a dictator rather than the home of a democracy. The building has been called un-Israeli (whatever that means), influenced by Albert Speer (a deep insult in the Israeli context), Hellenizing (Talmudic abuse). The minister of the interior responded: "The shape of the building is Israeli, because it has a flat roof. In addition, the shape of the column is not Greek, but original. There is here both great and monumental simplicity. These are two things required for the Knesset building" (Figure 54). This has not stopped the debate. Even the gates of the compound have been attacked. They are modern iron-work designed by the sculptor David Palombo. Klarwein himself made it public that when he had taken the chief architect of New Delhi to see them, his visitor burst out: "What, you did that? It looks like

Figure 54. The Knesset, the building of the Israeli parliament.

Auschwitz!" Right to the end, it was not a happy and mutually supportive creative team.

The Chagall tapestries in the Chagall Hall at least have escaped
the attacks of the critics in general: a fine triptych of biblical figures
worked in bright, light colors to match the light and spacious.
But the modern ceiling of the hall, made of small brown squares,
prompted more of Klarwein's wrath: he described it as an "adver-
tisement for chocolate." The front wall of the plenary hall is also
impressive, a fine stone relief carved by Danny Karavan. But for
some—as the arguments rumble on—even the presence of such art
in the building is a contradiction of its aims of simplicity and
monumentality. The Knesset remains a building even whose supporters are forced into apologetics. The institution somehow reflects its building's architectural history: the Knesset has often been
a rancorous place, full of compromises, bitterness, unlikely alliances,

and judgments twisted by public opinion, misplaced ideals, and shoddy self-interest; and yet it still stands as an embodiment of democracy in action, "the worst form of government," as Churchill put it, "except for all the others."

THE SYMBOLS OF JUSTICE

The story of the Knesset is in striking contrast with the Supreme Court, which was built in 1992 and sits across the park from it, symbolically sited on a rise above the Knesset to mark the supremacy of law (Map 7). Here is a fine example of modern architecture, probably the best civic building in modern Israel, which has been a critical and popular success (and built without the crazy internal rows that dogged the Knesset). The architects are Ran Karmi, the son of Dov Karmi, who was so involved with the Knesset design, and his sister, Ada Karmi-Melamede: a family team. When she published the drawings, Ada Karmi-Melamede explained how the building was intended to become "the keystone between the city and the [administrative] complex," and, unlike the Knesset, the court is "relat[ed] to both its immediate environment and to its larger urban context." The building echoes local architecture: it has, for example, what she calls "a familiar 'Jerusalem stone alley,'" and the entrance hall is specifically "reminiscent of Absalom's Tomb." Certainly the arched colonnades, stepped paths, rough stone next to whitewashed walls, and changing vistas produced by jutting corners and angular pathways produce modern echoes of the Old City. She writes, too, of the decision to use Jerusalem stone and to have a single water channel through the central courtyard, for the symbolic representation of truth and justice: "'Justice reflects from the sky and truth grows out of the earth' [Psalms 85: 12]. The spirit of the Judaean desert and of Jerusalem is hewn in stone which is harsh and uncompromising in its stark beauty." That Jerusalem thing

Figure 55. The courtyard of the Supreme Court. Note how the sky is reflected in the window in the arch above the small round pool.

about stone again . . . As with the best buildings of the Mandate, the Supreme Court is acutely aware of the need to adapt traditional Jerusalem architectural features and materials into its modernism, and to fit the building conceptually as well as physically into the landscape of the city and its surrounding desert and mountains.

It is a very complex building to describe. There are three main parts: a square library wing with a round courtyard that contains a copper-clad pyramid; a rectangular administrative building that houses the judges' chambers and flanks a sequestered, arched courtyard; and a wing that holds the five courtrooms which extend like five fingers from the main hall. Much of the form of the building is established by a contrast between circular or rounded shapes and aggressively straight lines. Ada Karmi-Melamede quotes Judge Cardozo from the 1920s: "Law defines a relation not between fixed points, but often, most often, between points of varying position." She adds that in the Bible "Justice is figuratively described as a circle . . . By contrast, law and truth are described as a line," and thus the "circle and the line are conceptual design themes of this building." The half-circles of arches, round halls, and curved walls (even in the library) and the straight lines of pathways and channels are indeed beautifully balanced, particularly in the judges' courtyard (Figure 55), where the straight line of the water channel ends in a small rounded pool; the water and the windows reflect the sky and also the glaring white of the surrounding linear court, softened by its arched colonnades and doors.

MEMORIALS FOR THE MODERN STATE

The Knesset and the Supreme Court, built on either side of the Six Day War and the Israeli takeover of eastern Jerusalem, embody the power of the state. The Israel Museum and Yad Vashem, the two most extensive museums in the country, were also built on either side of the same divide, though both have their origins in earlier times (Map 7). Here is the story of the past, without which any regime cannot create its own sense of purpose or ideological universe. The Israel Museum was founded in 1965. It has rapidly become a world-class institution, and the early archaeological material in particular is spectacular and lies behind much of what we know as the earliest history of Jerusalem and the whole of the surrounding territory. The Shrine of the Book, where the Dead Sea Scrolls are displayed, is a remarkable construction and a milestone in museum architecture. The white museum roof is shaped like the top of one of the vases in which the scrolls were found. It looks strangely Eastern and rather sensuously curved. It is juxtaposed with a black basalt slab that rises above the museum. White versus black, the curve versus the slab—the architects explained that they were attempting to represent something of the oppositions that run through the scrolls—where the "sons of light" are frequently opposed to the "sons of darkness." The scrolls themselves are displayed in a dark, cave-like room (they were found in caves).

With the scrolls is also displayed the Aleppo Codex, the oldest known complete version of the Hebrew Bible from the early tenth century. It makes for an interesting juxtaposition. The Dead Sea Scrolls are the religious texts of a fundamentalist sect, the Essenes, who distanced themselves from mainstream Temple Judaism in the first two centuries B.C., and whose center at Qumran was destroyed by the Romans on their way to destroying the Temple in 70 A.D. The Essenes were fanatical about purity and about the strictest observance of their rules. Because it was forbidden to pollute inside their dwelling area, and it was forbidden to travel the necessary distance to get outside such an area on the Sabbath and forbidden to carry on the Sabbath, it was also forbidden to defecate on the Sabbath. (It is not recorded what the effect of such a rule was on the joy of Sabbath.) This sect insisted on sexual abstinence and therefore reproduced by converting others to their way of life. There is good reason to believe that the early Christians were influenced by their strict asceticism, and John the Baptist probably visited the community at Qumran. The Essenes avoided Jerusalem's Temple and its calendar and, like the fourth-century Christian ascetics of Egypt, took to the desert.

The Aleppo Codex, by contrast, is the carefully preserved authoritative text of normative Jerusalem, a sign of continuity and tradition in worship and study. Yet here they both are in the Shrine of the Book (for the people of the book): the texts of the transgressive extremists, who saw themselves, of course, as the "sons of light" and the holders of the one truth, next to the texts of what has become the standard Bible, saved by a community that lived for so many hundreds of years in Aleppo, before being forced into exile by the politics of the twentieth century. The poignancy and awe here come not just from the sight of these ancient artifacts, so precariously transmitted to us, but also from the long history of religious commitment and conflict each embodies. It is not easy to know what to feel about the historical irony that the cherished texts of these two ideological opponents should have ended up in the same museum space.

Yad Vashem takes its name, "a memorial and a name," from a verse in Isaiah: "I will give, in my house and within my walls, a memorial and a name better than sons and daughters; I will give them an everlasting name that shall never be effaced" (Isaiah 56: 5). A museum for the victims of the Holocaust was first built in the 1960s, but the current building, with a much larger exhibition space and a different display, was opened in 2005. It aims to hold a record—the name that shall never be effaced—of each and every victim. The central building is a long (140 meters), rising triangular prism, with ten galleries off a central tunnel. It hosts a permanent exhibition, and its collection of video testimonies, written records, and other memorabilia from the systematic Nazi destruction of European Jewry is an exceptional resource for historical research, for education, for bearing witness; and it is deeply moving. The building itself is part of the story the museum tells. The story of the Holocaust ends here with the rising of Israel from the ashes of the camps, and the exhibition ends by leading the visitor out onto a balcony that provides a stunning view across the landscape of Israel. It is one of the most powerful examples of how architecture can enforce an ideology. It is, like so much of Moshe Safdie's work, an undeniably impressive moment, and many find it overwhelming. I, too, was moved by its visionary power. But I was also nagged by doubts. The gesture is so strong, so emphatic. I began this chapter by lamenting the oversimplified stories that keep conflict in place in Jerusalem. So at Yad Vashem I started to wonder about the role of the building itself as a contribution to how the Holocaust functions in modern Israel.

The Holocaust plays a deeply important role in the history, the imagination, and the rhetoric of modern Israel. For those who fled Europe, or tried to flee Europe, the need for a home, a place of safety, was overwhelming: the systematic denial of rights, even the right to exist, across German-ruled Europe, together with the rejection by other countries of the Jews who did escape, formed the psychological life of a generation. The logic of "never again" is a powerful motivation in the concern for security and the very drive for a Jewish state. This is re-enforced by the rhetoric of Israel's enemies who threaten "to drive the Jews into the sea"—and who have tried to do this with military might in 1948, 1967, and 1973. (This rhetoric continues and is even exaggerated in the language of the documents and spokesmen of Hamas and Hezbollah.) Zionism started well before the Second World War, of course, and violent anti-Semitism long before Zionism, but there is a powerful sense in which the State of Israel is inconceivable without the impact of the Holocaust. When Eichmann was put on trial in Jerusalem in 1961, Israel staged more than a war-crime tribunal. It offered the image of due legal procedure as a response to a monster of the imagination (and in the process inaugurated the academic study of the Holocaust, which has become such an extensive field). And above all, it did it in Jerusalem, asserting Israel's continuing intense involvement in the past of the Holocaust.

Yet as time has gone on, the image of the Holocaust has been used in other ways, many of which are offensively trivializing. "Nazi," "worse than the Nazis," "completing what the Nazis started" are insults hurled, particularly by religious Jews, at anyone whose policies they disagree with—in disputes that can end in violence. Such language is also repeatedly turned against the Israelis with regard to their policies in Gaza or the West Bank—a rhetorical naiveté that not only is historically shameful but also, in its grotesque oversimplification, contributes to the violence it pretends to denounce. "Never again" in the mouths of politicians can be a mantra to justify any policy, however misguided or destructive. While there has been an increasingly sophisticated historical understanding of the Holocaust, and an increasingly sophisticated exploration of it in art, film, and literature, its role in political rhetoric seems to have become increasingly banal, manipulative, and bombastic.

When I stood at the end of Safdie's building with its magnificent view over the valley, I thought back to Liebeskind's Museum of Jewish Life in Berlin. The contrast seemed telling. Liebeskind's museum constantly throws the visitor off balance; it uses abstract shapes to disconcert perception, to explore feelings of darkness, alienation, and wandering, and to put the visitor into difficult and challenging relations to the physical environment. It is an engrossing, fascinating, and intellectually stimulating space to visit—and hundreds of thousands did even before any exhibition was mounted in it. Both Safdie's and Liebeskind's buildings are highly rhetorical modernist architectural constructions. But whereas Liebeskind is probing, questioning, disconcerting, Safdie demands assent, celebration, pride. My uncertainty at Yad Vashem stemmed from my worry that Safdie speaks too strident a political language—a language too easily assimilated to oversimplified and aggressive political agendas.

Such a worry is prompted often in Jerusalem today. Many Jerusamelites are moving away from the city. A growing number of absentee landlords, Jews mainly, live abroad but have property in the city. An increasing number of *haredi* (religiously extreme) Jews are moving in. The demography of the city is changing, and with it the echoes of the different communities that have made up the city's fabric are becoming more muted. Jerusalem is on the frontline between Israeli and Arab communities. The security fence is visible from many parts of the city—and there are many other barriers, visible and invisible, across the urban landscape. It is a city where tensions are constantly high, and where shouting seems often on the verge of breaking out. It is a city where the problems at all levels of civic planning and political conflict are tangible, and solutions seem intractable, except to the street philosophers and idealists of the cafés—or, worst of all, to the extremists, whose solutions, shouted and screamed daily, are part of the problem.

And yet, and yet . . . When the walls of the Old City drift into view, when the sun glints on the Dome of the Rock, when the twisting streets reveal a hidden vista, a beautiful balcony, a mix of faces and colors, it is still possible to see what all the fuss is about. "The slightest return of beauty makes you aware of how deep your social wounds are," wrote an anguished Saul Bellow. People fight over Jerusalem not just because of the religious ideals and history it encapsulates but also because of what it is like to be in the city. It is an unparalleled place because the edginess and passion of the reli-

gious and political life are set in these small streets with these buried memories, with these stones that live in men's fantasies, with
these buildings where men and women have made stories that have
changed our understanding of the world. To be in Jerusalem is always to wander in a city of longing, as one seeks to find one's own
place in the layers of history, imagination, belief, desire, and conflict
that make Jerusalem what it is.

Bibliography
Acknowledgments
Illustration Credits
Index

Bibliography

This bibliography contains only works quoted in the text and the studies in English I have found most useful in the preparation of this book. It could easily have been much longer, but to extend the list would make it less useful. Since there are no notes in the book, I would like to acknowledge here what will be obvious to scholars: how much I have learned from the books and articles listed below. I trust that those who recognize their own influence on my work will be satisfied with this bare acknowledgment.

Abu el-Haj, N. *Facts on the Ground: Archaeological Practice and Territorial Self-Fashioning in Israeli Society.* Chicago, 2001.

Agnon, S. Y. *Only Yesterday,* trans. B. Harshav. Princeton, 2002.

Al-Muqaddasi. *The Best Division for Knowledge of the Regions,* trans. B. Collins. Reading, England, 2001.

Ashbee, C. R., ed. *Jerusalem, 1918–1920, Being the Records of the Pro-Jerusalem Council during the Period of the British Military Administration.* London, 1921.

————. *Jerusalem, 1920–1922, Being the Records of the Pro-Jerusalem Council during the First Two Years of the Civil Administration.* London, 1921.

Avigad, N. *Discovering Jerusalem.* Jerusalem, 1980.

Bar, D. "Re-creating Jewish Sanctity in Jerusalem: Mount Zion and David's Tomb, 1948–67," *Journal of Israeli History* 23 (2004): 260–278.

Bar-Yosef, E. "The Last Crusade? British Propaganda and the Palestine Campaign, 1917–1918," *Journal of Contemporary History* 36 (2001): 87–109.

Bellow, S. *To Jerusalem and Back: A Personal Account.* New York, 1976.

Ben-Arieh, Y. *Jerusalem in the Nineteenth Century: The Old City.* New York, 1984.

———. *Jerusalem in the Nineteenth Century: Emergence of the New City.* Jerusalem and New York, 1986.

Ben-Arieh, Y., and M. Davis. *Jerusalem in the Minds of the Western World, 1800–1948.* Westport and London, 1997.

Ben-Dov, M. *In the Shadow of the Temple: The Discovery of Ancient Jerusalem.* Jerusalem and New York, 1985.

Bentwich, N., and H. Bentwich. *Mandate Memories, 1918–1948.* London, 1965.

Benvenisti, M. *City of Stone: The Hidden History of Jerusalem.* Berkeley, 1996.

Biddle, M., G. Avni, J. Seligman, and T. Winter. *The Church of the Holy Sepulchre.* New York, 2000.

Biger, G. *An Empire in the Holy Land: Historical Geography of the British Administration in Palestine, 1917–1929.* Jerusalem and New York, 1994.

Bliss, F. J. *The Development of Palestine Exploration.* New York, 1906.

Blumberg, A. *Zion before Zionism, 1838–1880.* Syracuse, N.Y., 1985.

Blyth, E. *When We Lived in Jerusalem.* London, 1927.

Breger, M., and O. Ahimeir, eds. *Jerusalem: A City and Its Future.* Syracuse, N.Y., 2002.

Burgoyne, M. *Mamluk Jerusalem: An Architectural Study.* Jerusalem, 1987.

Carswell, J. *Kutahya Tiles and Pottery from the Armenian Cathedral of St. James,* 2 vols. Oxford, 1971.

Cline, E. *Jerusalem Besieged: From Ancient Canaan to Modern Israel.* Ann Arbor, 2004.

Courtney, R. *A Palestinian Policeman.* London, 1939.

Creswell, K. *Early Islamic Architecture,* 2nd ed. Oxford, 1969.

Crombie, K. *A Jewish Bishop in Jerusalem: The Life Story of Michael Solomon Alexander.* Jerusalem, 2006.

Curtis, G. W. *The Wanderer in Syria.* London, 1852.

Dumper, M. *The Politics of Jerusalem since 1967.* New York, 1997.

Eliav, M. *Britain and the Holy Land, 1838–1914: Selected Documents from the British Consulate in Jerusalem.* Jerusalem, 1997.

Elon, A. *Jerusalem: City of Mirrors*. Boston, 1989.

Finn, J. *Stirring Times*, 2 vols. London, 1878.

Friedman, T. *From Beirut to Jerusalem*. New York, 1989.

Fuchs, R., and G. Herbert. "Representing Mandatory Palestine: Austen St. Barbe Harrison and the Representational Buildings of the British Mandate in Palestine, 1922–37," *Architectural History* 43 (2000): 281–333.

Gelvin, J. *The Israel-Palestine Conflict: One Hundred Years of War*. Cambridge, England, 2005.

Geva, H., ed. *Ancient Jerusalem Revealed*. Jerusalem, 2000.

Gibson, S. *Jerusalem in Original Photographs, 1850–1920*. London, 2003.

Gibson, S., and D. Jacobsen. *Below the Temple Mount in Jerusalem*. Oxford, 1996.

Gilbert, M. *Jerusalem in the Twentieth Century*. London, 1996.

Glubb, J. *A Soldier with the Arabs*. London, 1957.

Goldhill, S. *The Temple of Jerusalem*. Cambridge, Mass., 2005.

Goodrich-Freer, A. *Inner Jerusalem*. London, 1904.

Grabar, O. *The Shape of the Holy: Early Islamic Jerusalem*. Princeton, 1996.

————. *The Dome of the Rock*. Cambridge, Mass., 2006.

Graham, S. *With the Russian Pilgrims to Jerusalem*. London, 1913.

Greaves, R. W. "The Jerusalem Bishopric, 1841," *English Historical Review* 64 (1949): 328–352.

Hillenbrand, C. *Crusades: Islamic Perspectives*. New York, 1999.

Hillenbrand, R. *The Architecture of Ottoman Jerusalem*. London, 2002.

Israeli, R. *Jerusalem Divided: The Armistice Regime, 1947–1967*. London and Portland, 2002.

Jaffe, E. *Yemin Moshe: The Story of a Jerusalem Neighborhood*. New York, 1988.

Jeremias, J. *Jerusalem in the Time of Jesus*. London, 1969.

Kark, R. *Jerusalem Neighborhoods: Planning and By-Laws (1855–1930)*. Jerusalem, 1991.

Karmi-Melamede, A. "The Supreme Court Building, Israel," *Perspecta* 26 (1990): 83–96.

Keith-Roach, E. *Pasha of Jerusalem: Memoirs of a District Commissioner under the British Mandate*. London and New York, 1994.

Kendall, H. *Jerusalem City Plan*. London, 1948.

Kenyon, K. M. *Digging Up Jerusalem*. London, 1974.

Khalidi, R. *Palestinian Identity: The Construction of Modern National Consciousness*. New York, 1997.

———. *The Iron Cage: The Story of the Palestinian Struggle for Statehood.* New York, 2006.

Kinglake, A. W. *Eothen.* London, 1847.

Kretzmer, D. *The Occupation of Justice: The Supreme Court of Israel and the Occupied Territories.* Albany, 2002.

Kroyanker, D. *Jerusalem Planning and Development, 1979–1982.* Jerusalem, 1982.

———. *Jerusalem Architecture.* New York, 1994.

Lagerlöf, S. *Jerusalem,* trans. J. Bröchner. London, 1903.

Le Strange, G. *Palestine under the Moslems: A Description of Syrian and the Holy Land from A.D. 650–1500.* Beirut, 1965.

Levine, L. *Jerusalem: Portrait of the City in the Second Temple Period (538 B.C.E–70 C.E).* Philadelphia, 2002.

———, ed. *Jerusalem: Its Sanctity and Centrality to Judaism, Christianity, and Islam.* New York, 1999.

Marcus, A. D. *The View from Nebo: How Archaeology Is Rewriting the Bible and Reshaping the Middle East.* New York, 2000.

———. *Jerusalem 1913: The Origins of the Arab-Israeli Conflict.* New York, 2007.

Martineau, H. *Eastern Life, Past and Present,* 3 vols. London, 1848.

Melville, H. *Journals.* Chicago, 1989.

Monk, D. *An Aesthetic Occupation: The Immediacy of Architecture and the Palestine Conflict.* Durham and London, 2002.

Murphy-O'Connor, J. *Oxford Archaeological Guide: The Holy Land.* Oxford, 1998.

Narkiss, B., with M. Stone, eds. *Armenian Art Treasures of Jerusalem.* Jerusalem, 1979.

Nashabishi, N. E. *Jerusalem's Other Voices: Ragheb Nashabishi and Moderation in Palestinian Politics, 1920–1948.* Exeter, 1990.

Nusseibeh, S., and O. Grabar. *The Dome of the Rock.* New York, 1996.

Oren, M. *Six Days of War: June 1967 and the Making of the Modern Middle East.* New York, 2002.

———. *Power, Faith, and Fantasy: America in the Middle East, 1776 to the Present.* New York, 2007.

Parrot, A. *The Temple of Jerusalem.* London, 1957.

PASSIA (Palestinian Academic Society for the Study of International Affairs). *Documents on Jerusalem.* Jerusalem, 1996.

Perry, Y. *British Mission to the Jews in Nineteenth-Century Palestine.* London and Portland, 2004.

Peters, F. E. *Jerusalem: The Holy City in the Eyes of Chroniclers, Visitors, Pilgrims, and Prophets from the Days of Abraham to the Beginnings of Modern Times.* Princeton, 1985.

———. *The Distant Shrine: The Islamic Centuries in Jerusalem.* New York, 1993.

Prawer, J., and H. Shaminav. *The History of Jerusalem: The Early Muslim Period, 638–1099.* Jerusalem, 1996.

Reich, R., and E. Shukron. "Light at the End of the Tunnel: Warren's Shaft Theory of David's Conquests Shattered," *Biblical Archaeology Review* 25 (1999): 22–33, 72.

Reiter, Y. *Islamic Institutions in Jerusalem: Palestinian Muslim Organizations under Jordanian and Israeli Rule.* The Hague, London, Boston, 1997.

Richardson, R. *Travels along the Mediterranean and Parts Adjacent.* London, 1822.

Riley-Smith, J., ed. *The Oxford History of the Crusades.* Oxford, 1999.

Ritmeyer, L. *The Quest: Revealing the Temple Mount in Jerusalem.* Jerusalem, 2006.

Ritmeyer, L., and K. Ritmeyer. *Secrets of Jerusalem's Temple Mount.* Washington, 1988.

Robinson, E. *Biblical Researches in Palestine and Adjacent Regions,* 3rd ed. London, 1867.

Roitman, A. *Envisioning the Temple.* Jerusalem, 2003.

Rosenau, H. *Vision of the Temple: The Image of the Temple of Jerusalem in Judaism and Christianity.* London, 1979.

Rosovsky, N. *City of the Great King: Jerusalem from David to the Present.* Cambridge, Mass., 1996.

Schiller, E. *The First Photographs of Jerusalem: The Old City.* Jerusalem, 1978.

Schwartz, S. *Imperialism and Jewish Society, 200 B.C.E. to 640 C.E.* Princeton, 2001.

Shanks, H. *Jerusalem: An Archaeological Biography.* New York, 1995.

Shepherd, N. *The Mayor and the Citadel: Teddy Kollek and Jerusalem.* London, 1987.

———. *Ploughing Sand: British Rule in Palestine, 1917–1948.* London, 1999.

Sherman, A. J. *Mandate Days: British Lives in Palestine, 1918–1948.* Baltimore, 1997.

Shlaim, A. *The Politics of Partition: King Abdullah, the Zionists and Palestine, 1921–1951.* Oxford, 1998.

———. *The Iron Wall: Israel and the Arab World.* London, 2000.

Signer, M., M. Adler, and A. Asher, eds. *The Itinerary of Benjamin of Tudela: Travels in the Middle Ages.* Malibu, 1983.

Silberman, N. *Digging for God and Country: Exploration, Archaeology and the Secret Struggle for the Holy Land.* New York, 1982.

Stephens, J. L. *Incidents of Travel in Egypt, Arabia, Petraea, and the Holy Land.* New York, 1837.

Thubron, C. *Jerusalem.* London, 1969.

Ussishkin, D. *The Village of Siloam.* Jerusalem, 1993.

Van Paassen, P. *Days of Our Times.* New York, 1939.

Vermes, G. *The Dead Sea Scrolls: Qumran in Perspective.* London, 1994.

Vester, B. S. *Our Jerusalem: An American Family in the Holy City.* Garden City, N.Y., 1950.

Vincent, H., and F. Abel. *Jérusalem: Recherches de topographie, d'archéologie et d'histoire,* 4 vols. Paris, 1912–1922.

Wahrman, D., C. Gavin, and N. Rosovsky. *Capturing the Holy Land: M. J. Diness and the Beginnings of Photography in the Holy Land.* Cambridge, Mass., 1993.

Walker, P. *Holy City, Holy Places: Christian Attitudes to Jerusalem and the Holy Land in the Fourth Century.* Oxford, 1990.

Warren, C. *Underground Jerusalem.* London, 1876.

Wasserstein, B. *The British in Palestine: The Mandatory Government and the Arab-Jewish Conflict, 1917–29,* 2nd ed. Oxford, 1991.

Welch, P. J. "Anglican Churchmen and the Establishment of the Jerusalem Bishopric," *Journal of Ecclesiastical History* 8 (1957): 193–204.

Wharton, A. *Selling Jerusalem: Relics, Replicas and Theme Parks.* Chicago, 2006.

Wilkinson, J. *Jerusalem Pilgrims before the Crusades.* Warminster, 1977.

———. *Jerusalem as Jesus Knew It: Archaeology as Evidence.* London, 1978.

Wilson, C. W. *Golgotha and the Holy Sepulchre.* London, 1906.

Zander, W. *Israel and the Holy Places of Christendom.* London, 1971.

Acknowledgments

ONE OF THE PHRASES you hear a lot in Jerusalem is *ani yodea,* or *yodea, yodea,* "I know," "I know, I know." Jerusalemites certainly can't be told anything, and they hold a vibrant opinion even—or especially—when they don't actually know at all, as you will find to your cost if you ask a Jerusalemite for directions. I have to admit that there was a great deal I didn't know when I started researching this book, and many friends and colleagues have been extraordinarily generous with their time and knowledge, sharing visits to sites, walking the streets, suggesting books to read and people to meet. In Jerusalem I greatly benefited from the physical and conceptual doors opened by Jon Seligman, the head archaeologist of Jerusalem, by George Hinklian of the Armenian community, and especially by Mike Turner (Bezalel and UNESCO) and by Yussef Natsheh, the head archaeologist of the *waqf,* whose hospitality and help have always been generously offered to me. They prove that there is always hope when good people work together. Two friends in particular guided me around Jerusalem, read my chapters, and helped this book emerge: Carol-Ann Bernheim, whose enthusiasm for Jerusalem as a lived space is catching; and Avner Goren, archaeologist and guide, who seemed capable of getting in anywhere and finding what needed to be seen. They both love the stones and passed on that love.

The book was drafted in the spring of 2007 at Princeton, where I was a guest of the Council of Humanities and the Classics Department, which provided an intellectual environment perfect for writing and thinking. My thanks to all who made this sabbatical possible, and to those who had to put up with me writing while they had to teach and go to committees, especially Andy Ford, Constanze Guthenke, and, above all, my host and friend over many years, Froma Zeitlin. At Princeton, I benefited—more than they realized—from chats with Patricia Crone, Oleg Grabar, Dan Kurzer, and, as ever, Seth Schwartz.

In England, Julian Barnett put his unrivaled knowledge of Jerusalem's street life at my disposal. Diana Lipton took part in a long-running, hard-talking conversation on all things to do with Jerusalem. Shoshana Shira, still my flower and song, walked through many of the sites and was the manuscript's first reader and critic.

The book is dedicated to two dear friends, Daniel and Barbara Eilon, who first made me go to Jerusalem. Little did they think . . .

Illustration Credits

Project, Eran Laor Cartographic Collection and The Hebrew University of Jerusalem, Department of Geography, Historic Cities Project: 11

Joan Comay, *The Temple of Jerusalem* (1975): 12

Koninklijke Bibliotheek: 10

Library of Congress: LC-matpc-05009/LifeintheHolyLand.com: 3; LC-matpc-06552/LifeintheHolyLand.com: 24

Nahman Avigad, *Discovering Jerusalem* (Basil Blackwell, 1980): 27

Ritmeyer Archaeological Design: 13, 14

Said Nuseibeh (© 1992 Said Nuseibeh Photography): 19

SCPhotos / Alamy: 2, 50

Simon Goldhill: 1, 7, 16, 17, 18, 20, 21, 29, 30, 33, 35, 39, 40, 42, 44, 46, 49, 51, 52, 55

Todd Bolen / BiblePlaces.com: iii, 6, 37

Universitetsbiblioteket, Uppsala: 9

vario images GmbH & Co.KG / Alamy: 54

World Religions Photo Library / Alamy: 15

Index

Abd al-Malik, Caliph, 100, 102, 108,
118, 120, 125
Abdul Hamid II, 146
Abraham, 4, 5, 41, 46, 110, 116, 117,
139
Aelia Capitolina, 4, 17, 19, 24, 149, 179,
182
Agnon, S. Y., on Jerusalem, 133
Alami, Saida el-, house of, 1–3, 5–6
Al-Aqsa mosque, 24–25, 74, 94, 97–
106, 107, 112, 204; regarded as
Temple of Solomon, 55, 57; façade,
97–98; and Night Journey of Mo-
hammed, 98–100, 102–103; and
Caliph Omar, 100–102; and Saladin,
103; *Mihrab* of Zacharia, 103–104;
assassination of Abdullah I in, 104,
231; fire of 1969, 104–105; roof
beams from, 126, 127
Aleppo Codex, 327, 328
Alexander, Michael, 262
Alexander Hospice, 177, 178–179,
235
Alexandrovitch, Grand Duke Sergei,
178–179, 235
Al-Hambra, 112, 307
Alice, Princess, 232
Allenby, Edmund Henry Hynman,
308, 315, 317; entrance into Jerusa-
lem, 101, 140, 142–144, 145, 146,
174, 279
Allenby Square, 147
Al-Nasir, Muhammad, 122, 172
Al-Quds University, 147, 267, 318
American Christian Missionary Soci-
ety, 266
American Colony, 21, 45, 132, 142,
187, 212, 230, 267–270. *See also*
Spafford, Anna; Spafford, Bertha;
Spafford, Horatio
American Colony Hotel, 267–268
Amichai, Yehuda, 225
Anglican Church, 62; Anglican bish-
opric, 259–263, 265, 279
Anicia Juliana, 53
Antonia fortress, 125
Apocalypse of John, 52
Arab nationalism, 274, 284–286, 289,
291, 293
Arafat, Yasser, 81, 293
Arculf (French bishop), 101, 219
Armenians, 329; and Church of the
Holy Sepulchre, 10, 13, 26, 27, 29,
30–31, 35–36, 153, 154; relations
with Turks, 113–114, 152, 157;
Armenian quarter, 138, 152–158,
160, 162
Arnold, Dr. Thomas, 260

Arnulf, 54
Arts and Crafts movement, 134, 136, 300, 306, 308
Ashbee, Charles, 238, 290; and Dome of the Rock, 113; relationship with Storrs, 134, 136, 298, 300; policies regarding urban planning, 134–136, 139, 297, 298, 299; and the *suk al-Qatanin,* 135–136, 137; and Pro-Jerusalem Council, 136, 146, 146–147, 173; and walls of Old City, 139
Ashkenazi Jews, 90, 167–168, 169, 294
Ass and Colt, 11
Assumptionists, 258–259
Assyrians, 190–191, 194
Atlee, Clement, 314
Augusta Victoria, Empress, 140–141, 269
Augusta Victoria tower/hospital, 141, 230–232, 265, 316
Augustine, St., 51–52
Authenticity, historical, 5–6, 128–129, 200–204; regarding Church of the Holy Sepulchre, 18–19, 24, 71; regarding Via Dolorosa, 24–25, 182–183; regarding Temple of Solomon, 71; regarding al-Aqsa mosque, 102–103; regarding King David's palace, 209–211
Avnery, Uri, 322
Avodah Zarah, 86
Azariah son of Hilkiah, 200, 201–202

Babylonians, Jerusalem destroyed by, 4, 55, 69, 71, 166, 194, 200, 201, 202, 203
Baldric (bishop of Dol-de-Bretagne), 53–54
Baldwin I, 39
Baldwin II, 219
Baldwin V, 39
Balfour, Arthur James, 317
Balfour Declaration, 280, 291, 303
Barazani, Moshe, 242
Barbara, St., 235–236
Barclay, James, 151, 266
Barclay's Gate, 85, 151
Bar Kochba revolt, 4, 19, 149
Barluzzi, Antonio, 309, 310, 311–312, 313
Baruch (friend of Jeremiah), 201, 202

Basil, St., 40
Basil I, 53
Basilica of the Agony, 309, 310, 311–312
Basilica of the pool of Siloam, 156
Basily, Constantin, 265
Bassa, 156
Bathsheba, 210
Bauhaus aesthetic, 316
Begin, Menachem, 287, 314
Beit David, 272
Beit Ya'akov, 272
Bellow, Saul, on Jerusalem, 133, 297, 331
Bell towers, 229–231
Ben-Dov, Meir, 90–91
Benedictines, 180
Benjamin of Tudela, *Itinerary* of, 74–75, 213–214, 221–222
Benoit, Père Pierre, 149
Bentwich, Norman, 291
Ben-Yehuda, Eliezer, 194–195
Bernadotte, Folke, 284
Bernard of Clairvaux, 54–55
Bethlehem, Church of the Nativity, 237
Beth She'an, 156
Bevin, Ernest, 303
Bismarck, Otto von, 263
Bliss, Frederick J., 20, 56, 126, 207
Blomfield, Bishop Charles James, 260
Blyth, George, 265
Boniface of Ragusa, 16
Breasted, James Henry, 304, 306
British Empire, 274, 278–279, 285; Sykes-Picot Agreement, 142–143, 291; Balfour Declaration, 280, 291, 303
British Mandate, 4, 77, 126, 275, 279, 284–285, 296–297; policies regarding Church of the Holy Sepulchre, 10–11, 12; policies regarding Western Wall, 78–80; and city walls, 133, 134–139, 146–147; policies regarding water, 198–199, 292; and Zionism, 241–242, 248, 280, 289–292, 302, 303, 313–314; policies regarding social welfare, 292; urban planning under, 298–299; Government House, 298–300, 301, 302–304. *See*

also Ashbee, Charles; Keith-Roach, Edward; Storrs, Ronald

British Post Office, 147

Bunsen, Christian, 260–261, 278

Burâq, al-, 77, 97, 99

Burnt House, 170–171

Byzantine architecture, 298, 299, 309

Byzantine Empire, 15, 40; Heraclius, 15, 40, 125–126

Cairo Conference, 231

Cairo Genizah, 75

Cardozo, Benjamin N., 326

Cathedral of St. James, 35, 153–158, 160, 175; Kutahya tiles in, 157–158, 159

Catholicism, 52–53, 62, 141, 236, 262; and Church of the Holy Sepulchre, 10, 19–20, 23, 27, 28, 29, 33–34, 38, 174; Urban II, 53; and France, 142, 237, 258–259; Latin patriarchate, 174–175, 259. *See also* Crusaders

Cave of Zedakiah, 150–152

Chagall, Marc, 321, 324

Chanukah, 62

Chapel of St. Polyeuctus, 160, 161

Chateaubriand, François-Auguste-René, vicomte de, on Jerusalem, 257

Chesterton, G. K., 140

Christ Church, 263, 264, 266

Christian martyrs, 49, 156

Christian proselytizing of Jews, 263, 265–266, 273

Christian Quarter Road, 7

Chronicles, Book of, 64, 66, 165, 190, 198, 214

Churchill, Sir Winston, 231–232, 289, 325

Church of All Nations, 309, 310, 311–312

Church of Mary Magdalene, 232, 233, 234–236; icon of the Virgin Mary, 234–235

Church of St. Anne's, 180–181

Church of St. Mary of the Latins, 178

Church of St. Stephen, 156

Church of the Flagellation, 182

Church of the Holy Redeemer, 177–178

Church of the Holy Sepulchre, 1, 2, 7–43, 46–47, 71; vs. Chartres and Notre Dame, 7; Chapel of the Franks/St. Mary of Egypt, 8; façade, 8, 9, 10–13, 16; courtyard/parvis, 8, 9, 13–14; and crusaders, 8, 10, 34, 35; and Greek Orthodox community, 10, 11, 13, 27, 29, 31, 32, 33, 34–35, 37, 38, 175; and Armenians, 10, 13, 26, 27, 29, 30–31, 35–36, 153, 154; and Latin Franciscans, 10, 23, 27, 28, 29, 33–34, 38, 174; interfactional struggle regarding, 10–13, 17, 26–31, 38; status quo agreement regarding, 11–12, 13; door, 12; Muslim entrance tax, 12–13; and earthquake of 1927, 14, 16, 25; and fire of 1808, 14, 16, 25, 39; edicule, 15, 16, 25–30; Muslim gatekeepers, 23, 144; Stone of Unction, 23–25, 34, 117, 224; Chapel of the Angel, 25; ceremony of Holy Fire, 26–29, 153, 175, 229; and Syrian Christians, 27, 28, 30–31; dome of rotunda, 29–30; tomb of Joseph of Arimathea, 30; Chapel of Nicodemus, 30, 31; and Coptic monks, 30, 42, 182; catholicon, 31, 32, 33; as center of world, 31, 32, 33, 108; Chapel of St. Longinus, 35; Chapel of the Division of the Holy Robes/Parting of the Raiments, 35; Chapel of St. Helena, 35–37, 42; Chapel of Varda, 36–37; Chapel of Derision, 37; Chapel of the Invention of the Cross, 37; Chapel of the Nailing of Jesus to the Cross, 37; Chapel of Calvary, 37–38; tomb of Adam, 38; relics in, 40–41; Chapel of St. Abraham, 41; Chapel of St. Michael, 41; Ethiopian Chapel, 41–42; Deir es-Sultan, 42–43, 183; vs. Dome of the Rock, 46–47, 101, 108, 112, 114, 117; in early maps, 56, 57, 60; vs. al-Aqsa mosque, 97, 103; vs. Cathedral of St. James, 154, 157–158; minarets near, 167, 177

Church of the Holy Trinity, 239, 240, 241

Church of the Redeemer, 141–142, 265

Cicero, Marcus Tullius, 211

Citadel of David, 135, 137, 144, 171–174, 210, 221, 263
City of David, 164–165, 199–205, 206, 207–211. *See also* Hezekiah, Tunnel of; Warren's Shaft
Clermont-Ganneau, Charles, 217–218
Cohen, Zvi, 322
Constantine, 152, 178, 179–180; and Church of the Holy Sepulchre, 15, 16, 17–18, 37, 51, 56
Constantinople: church of Hagia Sofia, 53; church of St. Polyeuctos, 53
Convent of the Ascension, 236
Convent of the Olive Tree, 160
Convent of the Sisters of Zion, 182
Cook's Travel company, 273
Coptic Christians, 30, 42, 156, 182
Counter-Reformation, 33
Crimean War, 237–238, 245, 273
Croix, La, 258
Crouch, Nathaniel, 150; on Jerusalem, 136–137
Crusaders, 4, 33, 74–75, 125–126, 146; architecture of, 1, 8, 10, 16, 102, 157–158, 173, 180, 219, 299; and Church of the Holy Sepulchre, 8, 10, 34, 35; capture of Jerusalem by, 26, 34, 39, 53–57; Jews slaughtered by, 38, 39, 54; Muslims slaughtered by, 38, 39–40, 54; Baldric on, 53–54; Bernard of Clairvaux on, 54–55
Curtis, George William, 20; on Jerusalem, 132
Curzon, Robert, 28–29
Cyril, St., 18
Cyril of Scythopolis, 156
Cyrus, King, 71–72

Daily Mirror, 143
Daily Sketch, 143
Dajani, Rafiq, 91
Daniel, Abbot, 26
Darius, King, 72
David, King, 5, 65–66, 101, 108–109, 116, 194, 225; palace of, 202, 209–211. *See also* City of David
David's Tomb, 210, 221–223
David's Tower, 210
David Street, 7
Dawnay, Guy, 144
Dawud, Muhammad, 320

Dayan, Moshe, 243
Dead Sea Scrolls, 50, 203, 327–328
Deir Yassin, 286–288, 317
De Morgan, William, 113
Dhahir, Caliph al-, 102
Diness, 265–266
Dome of the Rock, 3, 21, 55, 56–57, 60, 74, 87, 106–114, 115, 116–120, 150; roof, 5, 112–113, 331; vs. Church of the Holy Sepulchre, 46–47, 101, 108, 112, 114, 117; the rock, 88, 116–118, 224; vs. al-Aqsa mosque, 98, 101–102; *minbar Burhan al-Din,* 107; Dome of the Chain, 107–110, 119; Dome of the Spirits (*Qubbat al-Arwah*), 110; calligraphy in, 111, 114, 116; tiles, 112, 113–114, 300; Cave of the Spirits, 118; *mihrab,* 118; interior decorations, 118–119; and Day of Judgment, 119–120; as image of paradise, 119–120; and Dominus Flevit Chapel, 312, 313
Dominus Flevit Chapel, 312, 313
Dormition Abbey, 141

Easter, 23
East Jerusalem, 140, 267, 281, 285, 295, 307; and Jordan, 162, 168, 169, 212, 236, 279, 281, 318–321
Ebionites, Gospel of the, 49
Ecce Homo arch, 24, 182
Ecclesiasticus, 191
Edward VII, 259
Effendi, Rabbah, 268
Egeria, 309
Egypt, 280, 282; King Farouk, 103; Nasser, 281; treaty with Israel, 281
Eichmann, Adolf, 330
Ein Kerem, 236, 321
Einstein, Albert, 317
Eitan, Rafi, 88
Eliahu, Jacob, 187–190, 191, 269
Elias, Metropolitan, 234–235
Elizabeth, Grand Duchess, 178–179, 235–236
Elon, Amos, 88
Emek Refa'im, 271
Enlightenment, the, 60
Eppinger, Martin, 238–239, 243
Essenes, 50, 327–328

Eudocia, 156
Eusebius, 17–18, 19, 75, 214
Evangelical Christians, 62, 125, 187, 259, 260, 273, 279
Even Yisrael, 272
Exodus, Book of, 66
Ezekiel 11, 22–23, 75

Feinstein, Meir, 242
Ferdinand I de' Medici, 38
Finn, James, 28, 244–245, 263, 265
Fitzgerald, W., 303
Flaubert, Gustave, 146
France, 180, 237, 258–259, 274, 285; Sykes-Picot Agreement, 142–143, 291
Freemasonry, 69, 84, 151
Friedman, Thomas, 88–89
Friedrich Wilhelm IV, 260, 265

Gad, Dora, 323
Garden City movement, 134, 135
Gardens of the King, 196
Garden Tomb, 21, 23, 259, 269
Gate of Mercy, 75
Geddes, Patrick, 298, 304
Gemariah son of Shaphan, 201
Genesis, Book of, 250
George V, 259
Gerer hassidim, 251–252, 255
German Colony, 270–271
Germany, 142, 274. See also Wilhelm I
Gethsemane, 94, 232, 309, 311, 312
Getz, Yehuda Meir, 87–88
Gihon Spring, 190, 191, 192, 193, 195–198, 199, 208, 211
Gill, Eric, 306, 307
Gillitt, Bill, 322
Gladstone, William Ewart, 260–261, 278
Glubb, Sir John Bagot "Glubb Pasha," 318
Gobat, Bishop Samuel, 263, 265–266
Godfrey of Bouillon, 26, 34, 39–40
Golan Heights, 281
Golgotha, 18, 20, 24, 34, 37–39; and Gordon, 21, 22, 45, 46
Good Friday, 26–27
Goodman, Alan Harry, 88
Goodrich-Freer, Ada, 270–271
Good Samaritan, 40, 41, 43

Gordon, Gen. Charles George, 21, 22, 45, 46, 269
Goren, Shlomo, 88
Gothic architecture, 7, 8
Government House, 298–300, 301, 302–304
Grabar, Oleg, 127–128
Graham, Stephen, 227–229; With the Russian Pilgrims to Jerusalem, 228–229
Greece, 283
Greek Orthodox Church: and Church of the Holy Sepulchre, 10, 11, 13, 27, 29, 31, 32, 33, 34–35, 37, 38, 175; Brotherhood of the Church of the Holy Sepulchre, 13; Holy Week, 26; patriarchate, 174, 175–176, 259; and Tomb of the Virgin Mary, 219–220; crosses in, 232; saints of, 235–236, 239; and Church of the Nativity, 237; as landowner, 274
Gregory the Chain Bearer, 157
Gur, Shlomo, 322, 323

Hadassah Hospital, 316, 317, 321
Haddith, 99, 102–103
Hagai, Book of, 72
Hague manuscript map of Jerusalem, 57, 59
Hakarim Street, 170–171
Hakim, Caliph al-, 15–16, 25
Hamas, 293, 329
Haram al-Sharif, 47, 74, 96–97, 120–129, 131, 210; entrance, 62, 93–94; mihrab in, 95, 96; Station of Burâq, 97; Solomon's Stables, 105–106; Cradle of Jesus, 106; the Cup, 107; as center of world, 108; Gate of the Cotton Merchants, 121, 122, 123; during Mameluk period, 121–122; al-Ashrafiyya, 124; Golden Gate, 125–126, 144, 212; Museum of the Haram, 126–127; Fountain of the Qaytbay, 127–128. See also Al-Aqsa mosque; Dome of the Rock; Temple Mount
Harmon, Arthur, 314–315
Harrison, St. Austen Barbe, 298–299, 304, 306–307
Hasmonean aqueduct, 86, 198
Hasmonean wall, 148, 166, 172, 173

Hassidim, 249–256, 294, 319
Heavenly Jerusalem, 51–52, 54
Hebrew University, 316, 317–318, 321
Hebron, 139, 287–288
Helena, St., 18, 37, 51
Helena of Adiabene, Queen, 220–221, 244
Heraclius. *See* Byzantine Empire
Herod Agrippa, 19
Herod the Great, 125, 148, 170, 172, 173, 213; relationship with Mariamne, 72–73; massacre of the innocents, 73; Temple of, 73–74, 78, 82–87, 91, 105–106, 169, 174, 207–208, 209, 282; and David's tomb, 222
Herodian road, 86
Herodotus, 191, 211
Hezbollah, 293, 329
Hezekiah, 68, 165; Tunnel of, 187–191, 192, 194, 198, 207, 208, 269
Hilkiah, 201
Hill of Offence/Hill of Evil Counsel, 198, 298
Hinnom Valley, 212, 218, 308
Hitler, Adolf, 79
Hoffman, Christoff, 270
Holford, George, *The Destruction of Jerusalem,* 52
Holliday, Clifford, 298, 308
Holocaust, the, 222, 256, 280, 286–287, 303, 321, 328–330
Holy Fire ceremony, 26–29, 153, 175, 229
House of Ahi'el, 204–205, 206, 207
House of the Bullae, 200–202, 204, 207
Huizinga, Johan, 252
Hurva Square, 166–170
Hussein, Sharif, 285
Husseini, Adnan, 104–105

Ibn al-Faqih, 118
Ibn Batuta, 112
Ibn Ishaq, 98–99
Ibrahim Pasha, 230, 274
Illes, Stefan, 172
Imperial Hotel, 142
Imperialism, 273–275, 278–279. *See also* British Empire; British Mandate; France
India, 283

Intifada of 2000, 10, 94, 281
Iraq, 143, 280, 283
Ir David complex, 191–192, 199
Irgun, 302, 314
Irineos, 175–176
Isaiah, 217–218, 328
Islam, 4, 24–25, 46–48; importance of Jerusalem to, 5, 100, 115, 119–120; abstinence from alcohol, 99; Mecca, 99, 100, 101, 114, 117, 120; Medina, 99, 100, 114; daily prayer, 99, 101; Shi'ite and Sunni, 99–100; fundamentalism in, 100, 293; Qur'an, 111, 114, 116, 127; pilgrimages, 114; Day of Judgment, 119–120, 212. *See also* Mohammed the Prophet; Muslims
Ismail Bey, 126
Israel, State of, 53, 238, 294, 313, 321; Six Day War, 4, 80–81, 88, 162–163, 168, 223, 249, 279, 281, 295, 296–297, 306, 327, 329; policies regarding Church of the Holy Sepulchre, 12; Office of Religious Affairs, 30–31; creation of, 72, 162, 168, 212, 222, 236, 242, 263, 279, 280–281, 282–283, 286–288, 296, 317, 318, 329; policies regarding Western Wall tunnels, 87–88; policies regarding Haram al-Sharif, 93, 95–97; policies regarding Mount Zion, 222–223; Ministry of Education, 256–257, 258; treaty with Jordan, 281; Yom Kippur War, 281, 329; 1967 borders, 295; Knesset, 321–325, 327; Supreme Court, 325–326, 327; and the Holocaust, 329–330; policies in Gaza/West Bank, 330
Israeli, Raphael, 320
Israel Museum, 203, 327
Italian Hospital, 256–257, 258
Ivanov, Alexander, 234
Izates, King, 220–221

Jaffa Road, 147, 296
Jamâl ad-Din Adhad, 108, 112
Jamal Pasha, 231
James, St., 156
Jebusites, 4, 54, 65, 194, 205, 208, 225
Jehoiakim, King, 201
Jehucal son of Shelemial, 202
Jeremiah, Book of, 200, 201, 202

Jericho, 165
Jerome, St., 51
Jerusalem Syndrome, 287
Jesus: crucifixion of, 5, 14, 18, 21, 23–25, 37–38, 46, 49, 50, 160, 172, 179, 182, 234; arrival in Jerusalem, 11; meeting with Mary Magdalene and Martha, 11; Last Supper, 11, 13–14, 133–134, 221; tomb of, 14, 15, 16, 17–20, 24, 25–30, 46, 60, 140; resurrection of, 26, 49, 234; on the law and the prophets, 48–49; and the Temple, 48–50, 51, 52–53, 74; as Lamb of God, 49; Second Coming, 125, 261; birth of, 158; and Pools of Bethesda, 181–182; in Garden of Gethsemane, 309, 311, 312; temptation of, 315
Jewish immigrants from Russia, 294
Jewish refugees from Arab countries, 282–283
Jewish Revolt, first, 172; destruction of Jerusalem during, 4, 48, 52–53, 67–68, 75, 86, 170–171, 173–174, 327
Jewish settlers, 272, 295
John, Gospel of, 181–182
John the Baptist, 328
John Paul II, 23–24
Jordan: and Haram al-Sharif, 96–97; King Abdullah II, 104; King Hussein, 104, 112–113, 236, 285; King Abdullah I, 104, 231–232, 318; and East Jerusalem, 162, 168, 169, 212, 236, 279, 281, 318–321; as Transjordan, 231, 280, 284; treaty with Israel, 281; and Palestinian Arabs, 285; Amman, 295
Josephus, 64, 73, 74, 78, 89, 171, 176, 221, 222
Joshua, 165
Josiah, King, 68, 200, 201
Joudeh family, 12–13
Judaism, 4, 14, 24–25, 47–49, 152; attitudes of Christians toward, 27–28, 38, 39, 51, 54, 263, 265–266, 273; Passover, 49; the Messiah in, 52, 66, 78, 88, 125; and Western Wall, 62–64, 74–81, 82; Ark of the Covenant, 65–66, 88, 90; Yom Kippur/Day of Atonement, 67, 78–79, 169; the Shehinah, 67–68, 75; Sabbath, 89–90, 254, 328; festival of Succoth, 156; *miqva'ot,* 170; Day of Judgment, 212; Bar Mitzvahs, 222–223; *hassidim,* 249–256, 294, 319. *See also* Ashkenazi Jews; Sephardic Jews; Temple, the

Junius Maximus, Marcus, 176
Justinian, 53, 148–149
Juvelius, Walter, 193
Juvenal, St., 219

Ka'b al-Ahbar, 101
Kabbalah, 67–68
Kahana, Shmuel, 223
Kahn, Louis I., 168
Karaite Jews, 212
Karavan, Danny, 324
Karmi, Dov, 322–323, 325
Karmi, Ram, 322, 323, 325–326
Karmi-Melamede, Ada, 325–326
Keith-Roach, Edward, 79, 80, 290, 291
Kemalettin Bey, 114
Kendall, Henry, 297
Kenyon, Kathleen, 165, 194
Ketef Hinnom, 203, 213
Khalidi, Ruhi, 271–272
Khoury, Nabil, 296
Kidron Valley, 94, 196, 197–198, 211–223
King David Hotel, 313–314
King David's palace, 202, 209–211
King David Street, 313
Kinglake, A. W., 28
Kings, Book of, 64, 66, 68–69, 71, 166, 190, 196, 201
Kiryah Ne'emenhah, 272
Klarwein, Joseph, 322, 323–324
Knesset, 321–325, 327
Knights Templar, 39
Kollek, Teddy, 296, 303
Kommenos, Nikkolaus, 16
Korach, 151
Kotel. See Western Wall
Kutahya tiles. *See* Cathedral of St. James

Lagerlöf, Selma, *Jerusalem,* 45–48, 61, 269
Lawrence, T. E., 144, 146, 231, 269, 289
Lazarus, 11
Lebanon, 254, 280, 281

Lerner, Yoel, 88
Liebeskind, Daniel, Museum of Jewish Life, 330–331
Lubavitch *hassidim,* 319
Luke, Gospel of, 19, 40, 160

MAC (The Hashemite Kingdom of Jordan/Israel Mixed Armistice Committee), 319–320
Macalister, R. A. S., 146
MacMichael, Sir Harold, 302, 303
Madaba map, 56, 57, 126, 148–149, 156, 165, 175, 207
Mahaneh Yisrael, 272
Mahdi, Caliph al-, 102
Mahmud II, 110
Majid I, Abd al-, 11–12
Makarios (bishop of Jerusalem), 17, 18
Mameluks, 121–122, 124–125, 127, 154, 172, 173, 183
Ma'mun, Caliph al-, 120
Mandelbaum Gate, 319
Maps: Church of the Holy Sepulchre, xii; Western Wall, 44; Old City, 44, 130; Madaba map, 56, 57, 126, 148–149, 156, 165, 175, 207; Uppsala map, 56–57, 58; Hague manuscript map, 57, 59; Zuallardo's map, 60, 61; Dome of the Rock, 92; Haram al-Sharif, 92; City of David, 186; Victorian City, 226; Modern City, 276, 277; Rockefeller Museum, 305
Mariamne, 72–73, 172
Martha, 11
Martineau, Harriet, 28, 257–258
Mary, Abbess, 234–235
Mary Magdalene, 11, 40, 234
Masada, 73
Matthew, Gospel of, 49, 73
Maundy Thursday, 13–14
Mausoleum, the, 211
Mazar, Benjamin, 90, 209
Mazar, Eilat, 209–210
Me'a She'arim, 150, 189, 249–256, 258, 271, 272
Meir, Golda, 282, 284, 318
Melisande, Queen, 219
Melville, Herman, 20; on Jerusalem, 132, 224
Menachem Begin Center, 314
Menas, St., 156

Mendelsohn, Erich, 316
Merrill, Selah, 212, 269
Miracles, 40–41
Mishkanot Sha'ananim, 270, 272; windmill in, 132, 245, 247–248, 269; and Montefiore, 244–248, 250
Mishkenot Yisrael, 272
Mishmarot Street, 169
Mohammed the Prophet, 315; Night Journey of, 5, 77, 98–100, 102–103, 220; and al-Burâq, 77, 97, 99; and Dome of the Rock, 88, 116–118, 224; and Day of Judgment, 119–120
Monastery of St. Anthony, 182
Monastery of St. Onophrios, 218
Montanists, 52
Montefiore, Moses, 77, 251, 263; and Mishkanot Sha'ananim, 244–248, 250
Moses, 116, 117, 151, 203
Mount Ararat, 36
Mount of Olives, 75, 94, 106, 119–120, 212, 229–236, 312, 316, 319
Mount Scopus, 229–230, 316–317, 321
Mount Zion, 133, 141, 147, 172, 199, 212, 221–223
Mufti of Jerusalem, 79–80, 96, 167, 287, 303, 304
Mughrabi quarter, 80–81, 95
Mujir al-Din, 112, 124
Muqadisi, Muhammad Ibn Ahmad al-, 111–112, 121, 151
Murphy-O'Connor, Jerome, 181
Museum of Tolerance, 212
Muslims: and Western Wall, 75–76, 77, 79–80, 82, 87, 88; Mufti of Jerusalem, 79–80, 96, 167, 287, 303, 304; Umayyad period, 87, 90, 95–96, 120; Muslim quarter, 138, 152, 180–185. *See also* Islam; Ottoman Empire
Mussolini, Benito, 103
Myth-making, 77–78, 108, 128

Nahalt Shivah, 272
Nasir-i-Khusro, 116–117
Nasser, Gamal Abdel, 281
Nathan, 66
Nea Church, 148–149, 163
Nebuchadnezzar, 55, 69, 166, 202

Netanyahu, Benjamin, 87, 314
New Jerusalem, 52
Newman, John Henry, 262
Newton, Isaac, 69
Nissim, Rabbi Yitzhak, 90–91
Nistarot Rabbi Shimon ben Yochai, 52
Noah's Ark, 36
Notre Dame de France, 258–259
Numbers, Book of, 203–204
Nusseibeh, Sari, 147, 267, 293, 296, 318
Nusseibeh family, 12–13, 303

Occupied Territories, 272, 330. *See also* Palestinian Arabs
Ohanessian, David, 113–114, 300, 307
O'Hare, Patrick, 113
Old City, 247, 319; the cardo, 56, 148, 163–164, 165, 166; Muslim quarter, 138, 152, 180–185; Armenian quarter, 138, 152–158, 160, 162; French hospice, 139; Italian hospital, 139; Russian Compound, 139, 178, 236–239, 240, 241–244, 258, 303; Jewish quarter, 147–148, 162–171, 295, 296, 298; Broad Wall, 165–166, 194, 199; minaret of Jami Sidi Umar, 167; Christian quarter, 171–180. *See also* Walls of Old City
Olga, St., 239
Omar, Caliph, 15, 85, 100–102, 144
Origen, 38, 51
Osman Hamdi Bey, 126
Ottoman Empire, 4, 184, 230, 296; Suleiman the Magnificent, 112, 121, 133–134, 139, 148, 172–173, 180, 222; and Armenians, 113–114, 152, 157; collapse of, 138, 142–143, 231, 273, 274, 278–280, 285, 291; relations with Germany, 142; and Sykes-Picot Agreement, 142–143, 291; policies toward Jews, 167–168; relations with France, 237; relations with Russia, 237–238; policies regarding land ownership, 245–246
Owen, Robert, 247
Ownership of property: *waqf* property, 2, 3–4, 80, 96, 104–105, 113–114, 126–127, 293; as multidimensional, 3–4
Oxford Movement, 262

Pakistan, 283
Palatial Mansion, 169
Palestine Exploration Fund, 56, 82–83, 126, 146, 165, 189, 279
Palestine Liberation Organization (PLO), 293
Palestinian Arabs, 208–209, 241, 279, 282–288; Christians among, 175, 266, 293, 296; as refugees, 280–281, 282, 283, 284, 286–287, 293; cultural/national identity among, 292–294; elite class, 293; as residents of Jerusalem, 295–296
Palombo, David, 323
Parker, Montague, 192–193
Paul, St.: 1 Corinthians, 50; on Christian community, 50; on sexual immorality, 50; on the Temple, 50
Pausanias, 221
Perowne, Stewart, 284, 290
Persians, 15, 40, 71–72, 100, 149
Philip, Prince, 232
Philistines, 65
Pilate, Pontius, 24, 160, 172, 182
Pizzamano, Joseph, 265, 266
Plato, 160, 162
Plumer, Lord Herbert, 304
Polomer, John, 154
Pool of Bethesda, 180, 181–182
Pool of Hezekiah/Pool of the Patriarch's Bath, 176–177, 182
Porter, J. L., 216
Procopius, 148
Pro-Jerusalem Council, 136, 146, 173
Prophet Elijah Synagogue, 169
Protestantism, 18, 19–21, 26, 48, 140–141, 177, 259–261
Prussia, 260, 263, 265
Psalms, 65; Psalm 122, 36
Punch, 141, 143–144
Putin, Vladimir, 244

Qaytbay, al-Ashraf, 97, 124, 126, 127
Queen Helena Street, 7
Qumran, 327

Radulph of Caen, 54
Ramban, the/Nachmanides, 75, 167
Ramban Synagogue, 167
Raphael's *Betrothal of the Virgin,* 60
Rashi, 151

Ratner, Yohanan, 323
Raymond of Aguilers, 54
Reformation, 33
Reich, Ronnie, 191, 195–197
Relics: of True Cross, 15, 18, 37, 40,
    125; of Good Samaritan, 40, 41, 43;
    in Church of the Holy Sepulchre,
    40–41
Restoration of the Jews movement,
    261, 279, 280, 289–290
Revelation, Book of, 52
Richardson, Robert, 131
Richmond, E. T., 289–290, 306
Riots of 1929, 80
Riots of 1936, 183, 280, 287, 302–303
Riots of 1996, 87
Ritmeyer, Leen, 85
Robert the Bruce, 308–309
Robinson, Edward: on pious fraud,
    19–20, 56; *Researches in Palestine and
    the Adjacent Regions*, 20
Robinson's Arch, 19, 83, 85, 191
Rockefeller Museum, 10–11, 113, 126–
    127, 298, 304, 305, 306–308
Rohan, Dennis, 105
Roman Empire: Jerusalem/Temple
    destroyed by, 4, 48, 52–53, 67–68,
    75, 86, 170–171, 173–174, 327;
    Constantine, 15, 16, 17–18, 37, 51,
    56, 152, 178, 179–180; Hadrian,
    17–18, 19, 149–150, 178, 179–180;
    Christians martyred in, 49, 156;
    Pompey, 66–67; Antony, 72; Augus-
    tus, 72; Diocletian, 156; Tiberius,
    234; Syria-Palestina, 283–284
Romanesque architecture, 8, 180, 299
Rostropovich, Mstislav, 239, 241
Rotunda of the Anastasis, 15–16
Ruppin, Arthur, 271
Rushdi Bey Ahmad, 114
Ruskin, John, 134
Russell, Lord John, 273
Russian Compound, 139, 178, 236–
    239, 240, 241–244, 258, 303
Russian Empire, 237–238, 265, 274,
    291
Russian Orthodox Church, 179–180
Russian pilgrims, 228–229
Russian Revolution, 179, 228, 235–
    236
Russian tower, 229–230, 232, 236, 316

Sabbah, Michel, 175
Safdie, Moshe, 297, 329, 330–331
Saladin, 2, 5–6, 10, 102, 103, 121, 174,
    180, 219
Salzman, Auguste, 216
Samuel, Book of, 65–66, 194, 213–214
Samuel, Sir Herbert, 290–291, 302, 317
Satmer *hassidim,* 252, 253–254, 294
Saudi Arabia, 280
Saulcy, Louis Félicien Joseph Caignart
    de, 216, 220–221
Schick, Conrad, 150, 188–189, 251
Schmidt's College, 150
Scholem, Gershom, 255
Scott, Walter, 39
Scroll of Achima'az, 53
Sebeos (bishop of Bagratunik), 76
Sefer Zerubbavel, 52
Sennacherib, 190–191
Sephardic Jews, 90–91, 169, 294
Sergei Hostel, 243–244
Shaphan, 201
Sharon, Ariel, 94
Shaw, Sir John, 314
Shebna, 217–218
Shefatiah ben Amittai, 53
Shekhunat Khap, 248
Shelly, Percy Bysshe, 211
Shepherd, Rezim, 245
Shevet Ahim, 272
Shevet Tzedek, 272
Shiloh, Yigal, 191, 254
Shrine of the Book, 327–328
Siloam Channel, 192, 196, 198
Siloam Pool, 190, 191, 194, 207–208
Silwan Village, 204–205, 215–218
Solomon, King, 109, 116, 216, 298;
    Temple of, 53, 55, 64–66, 68–69, 70,
    71, 76, 117, 164, 199, 200
Solomon ha-Kohen ben Yehosef, 75
Soloveichick, Rabbi Joseph Ber, 237
Sophronios, 101
Souk el-Dabargha, 7
Spafford, Anna, 21, 45, 48, 132, 142,
    187, 190, 268–269
Spafford, Bertha, 230, 269, 270
Spafford, Horatio, 187, 190, 268–269
St. Andrew's Scottish Church, 113,
    308
Starkey, G., 304
Stations of the Cross, 23–25

Stephens, John Lloyd, 224
Stern gang, 302
St. George's Cathedral, 259, 266–267, 284, 308
St. George's School, 259, 267, 284
St. George's Street, 176
Storrs, Ronald, 79, 269, 290; and Dome of the Rock, 113; relationship with Ashbee, 134, 136, 298, 300; and Pro-Jerusalem Council, 136; on restoration of the Jews, 289, 291
Strouthion pool, 86, 87
Suk al-Qatanin, 121, 122, 123, 135–136, 137, 183, 207, 267
Suleiman the Magnificent, 121, 172–173, 180, 222; and walls of Old City, 112, 133–134, 139, 148
Supreme Court building, 325–326, 327
Swedish Bible Study Center, 147
Sykes, Sir Mark, 146
Sykes-Picot Agreement, 142–143, 291
Syria, 143, 280, 282, 285

Tacitus, 67
Talmud, 204, 323; Middoth, 85–86
Teitelbaum, Rabbi Moshe, 253–254
Templars, 270, 271
Temple, Sir Richard, 176
Temple, the: Holy of Holies, 26, 66–68, 69, 85, 86–87, 93, 108, 110, 118; and Jesus, 48–50, 51, 52–53, 74; animal sacrifice in, 49; Paul on, 50; of Solomon, 53, 55, 64–66, 68–69, 70, 71, 76, 117, 164, 199, 200; future restoration of, 63, 78; and Ark of the Covenant, 65–66; statues of cherubim in, 66; as "House for the Name of God," 66–67; uniqueness of, 68, 72; dimensions of, 68–69, 70; of Zerubabbel, 72, 73, 74, 78; of Herod the Great, 73–74, 78, 82–87, 91, 105–106, 169, 174, 207–208, 209, 282; ritual of the Red Heiffer, 125; and book of the Law, 201; priestly blessing, 203–204
Temple Mount: as hamakom/"the place," 5; Jewish attitudes toward, 5, 62; Christian attitudes toward, 46–48, 49–57, 60–62; entrances into, 62; Muslim attitudes toward, 62; secu-

rity checks, 62, 93, 105; Eastern Wall, 75; Royal Portico, 83, 89, 105; Court of the Gentiles, 89; Hulda Gate, 89, 207; Moroccans' Gate, 95–97. See also Dome of the Rock; Haram al-Sharif; Temple, the; Western Wall
Terrorism, 284, 290, 295, 302, 313–314, 317–318
Tertullian, 52
Thompson, William, 279
Thucydides, 288
Ticho, Albert, 257
Times of London, 141, 142, 279
Toldos Aharon sect, 251, 255
Tomb of Absalom, 213–214, 325
Tomb of Bene Hezir, 214–215
Tomb of St. James, 214
Tomb of the Kings, 220–221, 259
Tomb of the Pharaoh's Daughter, 216
Tomb of the Virgin, 218–219
Tomb of Zechariah, 214–215
Torat Hayim synagogue, 183
Tourism, 273
Touro, Judah, 245, 246
Tower of Phasael, 172, 173
Transitus Mariae, 218–219
Trollope, Anthony, The Bertrams, 228–229
Truman, Harry S., 72
Turkey, 283. See also Ottoman Empire
Twain, Mark, The Innocents Abroad, 38, 39
Twal, Fouad, 175

Umayyad period, 87, 90, 95–96, 120
UNESCO, 96
United Nations, 284, 298, 301, 304, 319, 320, 321; and creation of Israel, 280–281, 318
Unterman, Rabbi Isser Yehuda, 90
Updike, John, 25
Uppsala map, 56–57, 58
Urban planning in Jerusalem, 134–136, 238, 295, 297–299
Ustinov, Count Jona von, 268

Van Geldern, Simon, 168
Van Passen, Pierre, 79
Veronica, St., 24
Via Dolorosa, 24, 87, 180, 182–183

Vincent, Fr. L. H., 172, 187–188, 193, 195
Vladimir, St., 239

Wailing Wall. *See* Western Wall
Walid, Caliph al-, 100, 102
Wallace, Rev. Edwin, 212–213
Walls of Old City, 132–139, 331; rampart walk, 5, 135, 136–139; Jaffa Gate, 7, 133, 137, 138, 139–144, 145, 146–147, 148, 171, 175, 176, 263, 297; and crucifixion of Jesus, 18–19, 60; Damascus Gate, 21, 137, 138, 139, 149–150, 160, 163, 297; and Suleiman the Magnificent, 112, 133–134, 139, 148; St. Stephen's Gate, 126, 137, 180; and British Mandate, 133, 134–139, 146–147; Zion Gate, 137, 147–148; Dung Gate, 137, 148; Herod's Gate, 137, 149; New Gate, 137, 149
Waqf property, 2, 3–4, 80, 96, 104–105, 113–114, 126–127, 293
Warren, Charles, 21, 93–94, 146, 215–216, 263, 265, 278–279; and Western Wall tunnels, 82–83
Warren's Gate, 84–85, 88
Warren's Shaft, 187–188, 191–195, 197, 198
Wauchope, Sir Arthur, 284, 302
Weitzman, Chaim, 317
West Bank, 281, 285, 330
Western Wall, 5, 74–87, 97, 105, 117, 204, 222, 223, 224, 295; plaza, 24–

25, 62–64, 77, 80–82, 91, 93, 128–129, 196; tunnels, 69, 81–89, 128, 198; Commission on the, 302
Wilberforce, Samuel, 260
Wilhelm I, 140–142, 143, 147, 177, 230–231, 265, 269
Williams, George, 262
Wilson, Sir Charles, 20, 82, 85
Wilson's Arch, 20, 83–84, 85
Wohl Archaeological Museum, 169
World War I, 275, 279–280, 304, 308; Allenby's entrance into Jerusalem, 101, 140, 142–144, 145, 146, 174, 279
World War II, 303
Wright, Frank Lloyd, 134

Yad Vashem, 327, 328–332
Yehuda ha-Chasid, 167
Yemen, 283
Yemin Moshe, 248–249
YMCA, 313, 314–316
Yofe, Hava (Israeli artist), 36

Zechariah, 214
Zelatimo's sweetshop, 179
Zerubbabel, 72, 73
Zionism, 208–209, 222, 261, 274, 316, 329–330; and British Mandate, 241–242, 248, 280, 289–292, 302, 303, 313–314; and red-tiled roofs, 271–272; and Deir Yassin, 286–288
Zohar, 67–68
Zuallardo's map of Jerusalem, 60, 61